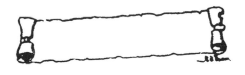

Music Analysis in Theory and Practice

JONATHAN DUNSBY
AND ARNOLD WHITTALL

YALE UNIVERSITY PRESS

New Haven

First published in Great Britain in 1988 by Faber Music Ltd.
First published in the United States in 1988 by Yale University Press

Copyright © 1988 by Jonathan Dunsby and Arnold Whittall.

Printed in Great Britain.

Library of Congress catalog card number: 86–51282
International standard book number: 0–300–03713–9

10 9 8 7 6 5 4 3 2 1

CONTENTS

PREFACE

The primary purpose of this book is to stimulate interest in music theory and analysis, not so much among those already committed and informed, but among sceptics and those who have so far read little or nothing on the subject. In particular, we hope the book may be of use to those musicians who do not expect to specialize in theory and analysis, but who are prepared to explore the possibility that some general knowledge of the subject might nevertheless do them more good than harm. As we say several times in the pages that follow, this is not a textbook: it is an attempt to provide a background to the study of theory and analysis rather than to lay down the structure of a particular course. What we offer is our view of the current state of a rapidly changing subject; and so, while we give clear pointers to how the systematic study of particular techniques can be pursued, our principal intention is to provoke the curiosity without which that study may well fail to prosper.

Even though we have not written a textbook, *Music Analysis in Theory and Practice* would have been inconceivable without our teaching experience. We are therefore grateful to all those colleagues and students, and especially those associated with King's College London, whose interest in and aptitude for the subject has led us to believe that a book like this one may actually be of some use. We owe a special debt to those whose support has taken an active form, whether of help in producing a final typescript or of advice about presentation and content: for such assistance, far beyond the call of duty, we thank Craig Ayrey, Esther Cavett-Dunsby and Allen Forte.

Throughout the book we have chosen to follow British usage for note values and other terms (except in quotations from American sources), and we are confident that these will be readily understood by readers more familiar with American usage.

London, 1986

JONATHAN DUNSBY
ARNOLD WHITTALL

ACKNOWLEDGEMENTS

For permission to reproduce copyright material, grateful thanks are due to the following:
Arnold Schoenberg Institute, California (transcription of extract from Arnold Schoenberg, *Chamber Symphony, op. 9*); Belmont Music Publishers, California (Schoenberg, *Six Little Piano Pieces, op. 19, nos. 2 & 6*); Chicago University Press (Leonard Meyer, *Explaining Music*, 1973, p. 250, Ex. 141); Dover Publications, New York (Felix Salzer, 1962, Vol. II, p. 30, Ex. 118, and p. 123, Ex. 331. Heinrich Schenker, *Five Graphic Music Analyses*, 1969, ed. Felix Salzer, pp. 32–33); Faber and Faber, London, and W. W. Norton & Co., New York (Rudolph Réti, *The Thematic Process in Music*, 1961, pp. 53–54, Ex. 83, p. 228, Ex. 365, and *Thematic Patterns in the Sonatas of Beethoven*, 1967, pp. 48–49, Ex. 56, p. 103, Ex. 140, p. 112, Ex. 157. Arnold Schoenberg, *Structural Functions of Harmony*, 1954, p. 112, Ex. 122); Princeton University Press (Arnold Schoenberg, 'Analysis of the Four Orchestral Songs Opus 22', *Perspectives of New Music* 4/2, music extract on p. 5. Roy Travis, 'Directed Motion in Schoenberg and Webern', *PNM* 3/2, analytical graph on p.13); Schott & Co., London (Paul Hindemith, *The Craft of Musical Composition*, 1945, trans. A. Mendel and O. Ortman, Vol. I, pp. 210–211, Ex. 4, bars 1–13); Universal Edition, London (Alban Berg, *Violin Concerto*, piano transcription of 3½ bars from Finale. Pierre Boulez, *Domaines*. Anton Webern, *Violin Piece, op. 7, no. 3; Cello Piece, op. 11, no. 3; Variations for Piano, op. 27, no. 2*); Yale University Press (James Baker, 'Schenkerian Analysis and Post-Tonal Music', in *Aspects of Schenkerian Theory*, 1983, ed. David Beach, analytical graph on p.185. Allen Forte, *The Structure of Atonal Music*, 1973, p. 97, Ex. 100, p. 127, Ex. 116. Robert Morgan, 'Dissonant Prolongations: Theoretical and Compositional Precedents', *Journal of Music Theory* 20/1, p. 80, extract from Ex. 13).

PART I

1

Introduction

Pierre Boulez has defined what he calls

the indispensable constituents of an 'active' analytical method: it must begin with the most minute and exact observation possible of the musical facts confronting us; it is then a question of finding a plan, a law of internal organization which takes account of these facts with the maximum coherence; finally comes the interpretation of the compositional laws deduced from this special application. All these stages are necessary; one's studies are of merely technical interest if they are not followed through to the highest point – the *interpretation* of the structure; only at this stage can one be sure that the work has been assimilated and understood. [Boulez, 1975: 18]

The Boulez 'method' is a stimulus and a challenge, especially in view of the fact that he is scathing about

those would-be 'historical' surveys of the present situation which resemble both journalism and the distribution of prizes . . . the 'tactical gossip' on which such accounts depend can neither cover up nor compensate for their weakness of thought and total lack of serious study of the scores themselves. [: 16]

Although this invective is aimed specifically at commentators on contemporary music, it is undeniable that analysis, which Boulez calls 'the serious study of the scores themselves', is vulnerable to superficiality and incompetence, whatever the period of the music in question. For too long it has been assumed that analysis needs only to be applied, as a direct outgrowth of the analyst's innate musical sensitivity and understanding, rather than studied, as a discipline in its own right.

Boulez is less concerned with providing detailed models for analytical activity than with stating the necessary qualifications for the analyst. Analysts must be able to undertake 'the most minute and exact observation possible' of the 'facts' presented – presumably by a score – with the aim of establishing 'a plan, a law of internal organization'. Boulez does not speculate on the likelihood of this plan resembling that of other collections of musical facts, but since the plan is to be 'a law of internal organization which takes account of these facts with the maximum coherence', it will probably display certain fundamental features of musical organization that tend to occur whatever the period, or style, of a work: repetition, variation, contrast, connection, juxtaposition – bearing in mind always that 'the maximum coherence' implies a unity that embraces diversity, an emphasis on musical similarity rather than on musical contrast. It follows that, in order to begin to discover such a plan, the analyst will need to be familiar with plans, with analytical models, that have been proposed already – and accepted – for music of different periods, and familiar too with how they work.

Boulez believes that the 'highest point' of his active analytical method is a demonstration that 'the work has been assimilated and understood'. Of course, there is a widely held belief that, just as education can only 'bring out' something already there, so analysis can only strengthen innate understanding: that is, it can encourage us to make more of our innate understanding through the exercise of the intellect, rather than actually create understanding from scratch. Nevertheless, the specific goal of analytical activity as defined by Boulez is clear, and there can be no denying that the main aim of the analyst is, through study, the enhanced under-standing and enjoyment of particular compositions – even if the feeling that, literally, 'I fully understand this work' is likely to be experienced by few musicians, analysts or not. Nor should Boulez's emphasis on 'the work' be taken to mean that the study of analysis must of necessity begin with complete compositions, any more than does the study of composition or performance. Indeed, if Boulez had been writing about the study of analysis rather than, essentially, the application of analysis, he might well have proposed the study of analytical techniques and models, rather than compositions, as a preliminary to analysis itself.

It is this latter kind of study which we propose. Although the reader will find a significant difference of emphasis between the approaches to the study of tonal and post-tonal music, in neither case is 'analysis' presented as a sequence of case studies, moving from small pieces to large across as wide a range of genres and styles as possible. The 'scores themselves' remain subordinate to the demonstration and discussion of analytical techniques (primarily those associated with writers other than ourselves): in other words, this book is an introduction to the study of analysis as a subject with its own history, and only a prelude to the kind of wide-ranging, sophisticated, analytical practice to which most students (and specialists) aspire. It is not a textbook or workbook, or a course programme complete with exercises and answers, as normally understood. It is a guide to ideas and methods. Its object is not to lay down programmes, but to encourage students to press for them, and teachers to provide them.

Analysis is not universally accepted as a necessary part of all curricula. Yet a slow but distinct change in academic attitudes has been taking place in recent years, perhaps reflecting a significant shift of opinion in the wider musical world. Boulez, for one, does not regard analysis as arid or intrusive: 'I am convinced that however perceptive the composer, he cannot imagine the consequences, immediate or ultimate, of what he has written, and that his perception is not necessarily more acute than that of the analyst (as I see him).' [: 18] Others are less tolerant, more ready to dismiss the activity of analysis as destructive dissection: assertions, like the literary critic Denis Donoghue's, that analysts are 'zealots of explanation' who 'want to deny the arts their mystery' may still be heard today (see Whittall, 1982). It will come as no surprise that this book takes issue with the argument that 'mystery' is a necessary part of all pleasure. Indeed, our account is founded on the belief that analysis can and should enhance appreciation, or aesthetic enjoyment, and intensify rather than inhibit instinctive responses to music. In any case, we do not believe many would subscribe to the idea that a piece of music can be said to be fully understood (and Boulez is not, surely, using the word in an absolute sense) or fully explained: perhaps the greatest analytical zealot of explanation to date, Heinrich Schenker, himself regarded the effect of musical organization as essentially mysterious: 'The power of will and imagination which lives through the transformations of a master-work reaches us in our spirit as a power of imagination.' [Schenker, 1979: 6]

It may still be claimed in some quarters that it is wrong to bring to expression or consciousness, through analysis, precisely those factors which composers wish to suppress. And it is true that many composers find most kinds of analysis irrelevant, even improper, in their probings and exposings; so the analyst can offer only the evidence of experience – that knowledge leaves the experience of music richer, not poorer.

This book emphasizes 'analysis' rather than 'theory', the practical application of particular techniques rather than the theoretical preliminaries which deal generally with technical matters in ways not restricted to a few simple compositional instances. We do not wish to press for a hard-and-fast distinction between the two terms – not least because, in America at any rate, the latter implies and subsumes the former. But, for the most part, the 'theory equals general, analysis equals specific' emphasis obtains in the following pages.

It follows that we indicate what the basics for the study of analysis might be rather than offering a history of analytical theory and practice or a comprehensive demonstration of analysis *in* practice. Thus another preliminary issue arises, for even if it is accepted that analysis is far from counterproductive, some may object that it depends, like both composition and criticism, too crucially on the inventiveness and imagination of individual minds to be taught and studied systematically. Difficult though it always is to recognize the difference between what can and cannot be taught – to whom and by whom – some suggestions can be offered.

To consider first the obvious analogy, it is sometimes stated that 'composition cannot be taught'. This implies that there is a clear division between the study of, say, strict counterpoint or figured bass, as relatively 'concrete and explicit "musical disciplines" whose rules can be stated simply and without restriction in terms of tangible musical entities' [Rothgeb, 1981: 144], and free composition in a contemporary style. In free composition, an experienced teacher can still be of great help to a relative beginner, but any 'rules' proposed are just as important as stimuli for contradiction as they are for literal guidance. Many teachers argue that composers are most likely to thrive if they have first worked through the relatively concrete and explicit musical disciplines. Similarly, students of analysis can only benefit from a course of study that concentrates on fundamentals, that detaches technical matters, provisionally, from the more general historical and stylistic contexts to which they belong. Indeed, as the next chapter will argue, the need for a distinct discipline known as 'music analysis' is itself the result of the increasingly urgent need to complement – not to replace – the evidently technical and theoretical aspects of all historical, music-ological studies. If analysis prospers as a discipline concerned with the 'serious study of the scores themselves', then the general musical histories of later generations may come to differ greatly from many of the histories, the 'lives and works', admired today.

It is not our intention in adopting this technical, and fundamentally preparatory, approach to aim also at the kind of comprehensiveness that discusses and demonstrates the application of analytical techniques to music of all periods, in all styles and forms. Anyone who regards as 'fundamental issues' the analysis of music from before 1700, opera and music drama, large-scale twentieth-century works (including indeterminate or minimalist compositions), or the whole field of non-Western music, will be disappointed to find these topics ignored or barely considered. Our attention is confined to the particularly significant developments in analysis that have taken place in connection with the study of non-operatic music from the eighteenth and nineteenth centuries, and of relatively small-scale atonal and twelve-note compositions. One of the factors that has so far prevented analysis from becoming a more useful servant of music history is the long-standing yet never substantiated assumption that such relatively restricted fundamental studies are unnecessary. In fact, engagement with what Schenker called 'masterpieces' and with the most compelling examples of early post-tonal music is an education that any modern musician should feel privileged to undergo. Many students aspire to it, and few regret it.

Nevertheless, any publication that concerns itself exclusively with such matters must inevitably be intended to accompany and stimulate close study, rather than to be read casually. One runs the risk of exhausting a reader's patience in demonstrating, verbally and graphically, the inexhaustibility (and mystery!) of even the shortest composition. But patience here means taking the time to study all the issues raised and their implications. Too much would-be analysis jumps to conclusions; while the inspired leap of imagination may be invaluable to the analyst as much as to the composer, it cannot be a substitute for thoroughness and clarity. Relatively general, selective technical accounts of a work may well be analytical in intention, but only if they reflect the rigorous analytical discipline that emerges from rigorous study *of* the discipline.

One further introductory point needs to be made, concerning the contrasts of approach between the two central parts of this book, 'Aspects of Tonal Analysis' and 'The Elements of Atonality'. Schenker has become the recognized point of reference for theories of tonal structure, and we begin with the main issues in Schenkerian method – its theoretical origins, the most pressing questions to arise in its practice, and its development to a state where its application to post-tonal music seemed one viable option for bringing 'Schenkerism' up to date. All subsequent discussion in Part II – of Tovey, Schoenberg, Meyer and others – is therefore conducted against this Schenkerian backdrop (though, admittedly, there is competition from a Schoenbergian backdrop, which is as unavoidable as it is welcome). Such emphasis could well lead to the brusque dismissal of all 'non-Schenkerian' ideas, or to an unproductive focus on conflict and polemic. It is all too easy to place the great analysts of the past in apparently terminal conflict; to show how Schoenberg, taken literally and fully, could make nonsense of Schenker, just as Tovey could make nonsense of both. We have aimed to cull what is most instructive from various analysts considered by a measure of common consent to have put forward valuable thoughts that a student may not only find inspiring, but may also use in practice.

In 'Aspects of Tonal Analysis', therefore, we have chosen to present and comment on a relatively wide variety of music, which the student can follow up in recommended literature. The implication here is that (as was indicated earlier) it is possible and desirable to acquire experience of particular analytical techniques without seeking at the earliest opportunity to explore them in complete compositions, whether small- or large-scale. (An experienced teacher could well decide to supplement such a scheme of study with model analyses of entire pieces, even if students themselves cannot immediately be expected to undertake similar analyses.) It is with some confidence, with respect to tonal music, that we separate specific technical elements from complete context, given that the significance of various techniques for the analysis of this repertoire is not in much doubt. There is more doubt about techniques for the analysis of post-tonal music; and so the fundamental contrast between tonality and atonality is reflected in the way these topics are approached. Other writers, for other purposes, might find it perfectly credible to present an account of all-important 'Aspects of Tonal Analysis' by means of a discussion of a few complete, small-scale works by seminal composers: chorales, minuets, mazurkas, intermezzos. Equally, they might be able to devise a study of the 'Elements of Atonality' that instances certain essential analytical consequences of particular theories or of acknowledged compositional procedures without restricting the materials of that study to a few complete miniatures. It is for readers to decide, as always, whether particular ends are justified by particular means.

Such is the diversity and richness of twentieth-century composition that considerable dissent may be aroused by the implication of Part III that, of all its aspects, atonality as practised by Schoenberg and Webern between *c*. 1910 and 1940 is the most important. Of course, atonality is not in itself all-pervading in twentieth-century music. But we believe that more purposeful progress through that diversity and richness is likely after an exploration of the issues and compositions emphasized in Parts III and IV of this book. Historical and critical awareness will probably exceed analytical experience to begin with, and the process of putting the latter at the service of the former (to such effect that the student's awareness may eventually be transformed) should never be rushed. Simply because so many major composers of this century have made pronouncements, often quite elaborate, about technique and style, and so many books and articles have given prominence to the discussion of repertoire, the possibility and desirability of an approach that involves what are in some respects very elementary preliminaries should, for once, be argued and demonstrated at length.

It may seem that by not only separating 'Aspects of Tonal Analysis' from 'The Elements of Atonality', but also adopting different approaches to them, we are inviting the reader to work through Parts II and III in tandem or, indeed, through one to the exclusion of the other. It is certainly hoped that in analysis courses, or in courses on tonal or post-tonal music, either part will be found useful on its own. Nevertheless, we recommend that the book be read sequentially from beginning to end. It attempts to provoke thought about analysis, a constant attention to premiss and goal, a continual musical and intellectual self-awareness. Just as our contemporary musical culture cannot be adequately comprehended if all reference to events before 1908 is rigorously excluded, so a musician who fails to study the eventual response or reaction to tonality – in the subsequent period when, after all, most of the highly valued theories of tonality were written – will be missing a vital ingredient in developing a sensitivity to the art of music over the last few centuries. It will be evident that we feel it is premature to attempt a consistent overview of analytical issues from Bach to Webern, or from Aristoxenus to Forte, and intend instead to show the discipline as turning prospectively and retrospectively around the axis of the early years of this century. Nevertheless, it is much more likely that the student will be able to think clearly and confidently about the hard issues of atonality if he or she has explored how the hard issues of tonality have been discussed by theorists.

One final, immense topic should be touched on here, if only then to be evaded: the question, not of why, or of how we analyse, but of *what* we analyse. Much energy continues to be channelled into attempts to develop theories centering on the simple fact that music is a phenomenon we perceive: it is not just marks on a page, but sounds experienced in performance or in the mind and 'inner ear'. Analysts who try to exclude from their accounts the impact of how the score sounds are rightly ridiculed (though there may be some ultimate purpose in trying to distinguish theoretically between 'sense' and 'sound'). Yet the 'reception' of music can be represented in one particularly compelling way through analytical techniques primarily concerned with the score as an actual structure. A score is as potentially expressive in performance as it is inherently good, bad or indifferent in quality – judged by those who choose to become familiar with it. An analytical technique that can account definitively for all the elements in a piece of music would be almost unimaginably sophisticated compared with present-day methods; and, for the moment, we must be content with what we have, not using the imaginary as a stick with which to beat the actual. Analysis is a young discipline, and even today its main weakness is not that its fruits are immature, in the sense of unformed, but that they are sketchy. The analyst who reaches the stage of working with complete compositions must be exhaustive without – when it comes to communicating the results – also being exhausting. An ability to achieve such balance can, like outstanding success in composition, be encouraged, but probably not taught.

The History of Theory and Analysis: A Short Survey

Music analysis is not just a discipline in its own right, but part of that larger whole called musicology, the serious study of music, and because 'study' is an intellectual activity there is always a sense in which it is at odds with certain aspects of music as a creative and performing art, at odds with the inspiration of the composer, with the intuitive, aesthetic, critical responses of the listener, and with the instinctive interpretative reactions of the performer. Most people involved in teaching music will agree that the relatively intellectual and relatively non-intellectual aspects of their discipline are creatively, positively complementary. There need be no irreconcilable conflict, but rather a fruitful interaction. It is important, then, that one's understanding of the nature of the various branches of musicology, and therefore one's definition of basic terms of reference, should not actually serve to confuse elements that are necessarily distinct: 'musicology' is not just 'historical musicology', and the importance of technical commentary to histories of music and biographies of composers suggests that analysis is entitled to an independent existence – and to a degree of separate development.

Musicology has developed in such a way that a distinction is both possible and necessary between 'history' and 'analysis', in the sense that, while analysis is most centrally concerned with the technical exploration of compositional technique and the structures of finished compositions (and also with theories of music which provide those concerns with their technical content), music history can nevertheless range widely over such issues as the lives of composers, the musical institutions and attitudes of particular societies, the 'quality' of 'periods' (Baroque, Romantic) and, increasingly, the tracing of the process of composition through notation and manuscript sources. More often than not analysis means the attempt to explain the processes at work in particular compositions, chosen less for their historical context or significance than because they are held to represent certain specific technical features – of genre, form, style or structure. As such, analysis may well attach less importance to how the composer may have conceived and executed the work – to the 'compositional process' – and concentrate primarily on the compositional 'product', the definitive, publicly 'owned' representation (as far as can be ascertained) of the composer's actual work.

In Britain, certainly, analysis courses at colleges and universities may still be called 'Form', reflecting a concern with frameworks that need not lead to thorough study of pitch and rhythmic structures, and with categories that relate to broad notions of period and style. Such courses are often used as supplements to history courses, and their 'products' are likely to be rather fuller verbal or tabular examinations of works that might also be dealt with more generally in history essays. Indeed, the somewhat hybrid nature of analysis in this context is reflected in the fact that an analysis course may well avoid any discussion of 'theory' and any use of techniques other than those involving thematic manipulation or formal segmentation. It is only when analysis is seen more in relation to the study of particular techniques or to the study of harmony and counterpoint than to history that it seems appropriate to require technical exercises rather than essays as course work; and it is to this kind of analytical study that our book is most relevant.

Clearly, there is a great deal of writing about music that contains some element of technical commentary, from programme notes and concert reviews to histories, biographies and technical textbooks. To encourage the independence of theory and analysis within academic curricula is not to propose the pointless ideal of excluding 'superficial' technical comment from all historical or more general writing, but to aim at a better quality of such technical comment. The study of theory and analysis can help to make good theorists and analysts: it can also help to make better historians, composers, editors and critics. Equally, therefore, the analyst needs to study history and composition, at least at undergraduate level. And an awareness of the relationship between current concerns in the practice of analysis and the long history of music theory is a particularly vital part of the analyst's general education.

The practice of analysis as discussed and demonstrated in Parts II, III and IV below is a matter of the testing and application of techniques established or refined in this century. Even when those techniques do have a history, therefore, it is by no means self-evident that their history needs to be studied in depth. A look at pre-twentieth-century analysis may well leave the student with the impression of little but superficiality and primitivism – and the advanced study of music theory (if only as the prehistory of modern analysis) is certainly a specialized activity, not least because the necessary knowledge of languages, including Latin and Greek, and the grasp of philosophical and acoustical principles, comes easily to very few. Yet it is precisely because so much theoretical writing from the earliest times does contain a technical, practical element that it can be seen as potentially, if not always actually, analytical. The history of analysis is, therefore, present in the history of music theory: even when theory is studied only as a 'background' to modern techniques (and introduced only in postgraduate courses), it provides invaluable perspective. Moreover, in institutions where it is possible to work at undergraduate level at strict counterpoint and figured bass alongside simple voice-leading analysis, the 'modern' analytical technique is itself provided with a supportive historical and theoretical perspective.

The analytical potential of early theoretical writing is evident in the work of the Greek theorist Aristoxenus, who offered an exhaustive description of musical materials, reducing the diverse phenomena of Greek music to 'a coherent and orderly system' [*New Grove*, 'Aristoxenus', vol. 1: 592], thereby anticipating that 'classificatory work carried out by the Carolingian clergy in compiling tonaries' which Ian Bent sees as an early instance of analytical activity [*New Grove*, 'Analysis', vol. 1: 343]. Such 'classificatory work' leads on to the discussions by Renaissance theorists of modality in actual compositions – for example, Glarean's study of Josquin – and, in due course, to those innumerable modern commentaries on the musical language of specific composers: ultimately, indeed, to more general accounts of particular 'languages', such as are to be found in the work of Schenker, Schoenberg, Hindemith and Piston – among many others – on tonality and harmony. The kind of classification and system-building most commonly found in both modern and not-so-modern textbooks on harmony and counterpoint involves the use of extracts from existing compositions, and analytical observations on those extracts, to demonstrate particular small-scale procedures to students.

Yet it is perfectly possible for a theory text to avoid examples from 'real' music – Schoenberg's *Theory of Harmony* is probably the most significant modern example of a study that for the most part deals with specially devised examples that are in no sense miniature compositions. And although it is possible to use complete pieces to demonstrate particular harmonic progressions or contrapuntal procedures in context from the outset, such comprehensiveness does not necessarily lead to an efficient and orderly learning process. The typical theory text employs analysis, but only in so far as analysis can illuminate the particular technique in question. Even Schenker's *Free Composition*, which will be central to the discussion in Part II, is more a theory text using analysis to demonstrate and exemplify the elements of the theory than it is a demonstration of analytical technique or a collection of analyses. The theorist will often use analysis in this specifically selective sense, as a means to an end. But in the higher reaches, where the model is more that of philosophical investigation than pedagogical system, music theory need not depend for its development on the analysis of highly valued music at all. The theorist may wish to reach out far beyond the mundane matters of compositional technique.

The student of the history of music theory can refer to useful surveys of the subject, for instance Palisca's 'Theory' article in the *New Grove*, and to an increasing library of translated texts and specialized articles, many of which draw attention to the connections between theory and analysis. What is lacking at the moment is a substantial one-volume account of the whole subject. Since the main danger of any short survey is over-simplification (closely followed by over-selectiveness), what follows in this chapter can do no more than announce themes and sketch developments in this area (with references mostly to the *New Grove* so that readers can consult one accessible source). With the emergence of analysis out of theory in mind, we pay particular attention to theorists who, like Aristoxenus, were concerned with specific musical materials and therefore with the relevance of theory to composition.

The emergence of analysis, like the various other musicological disciplines, is closely bound up with the gradual development of the 'composition', not just as something written down, but as something created by a particular individual, and in some respects expressing the personality of that individual. The term 'composition' has been traced back to Guido d'Arezzo's *Micrologus* (*c.*1030), which includes the chapter 'De commoda vel componenda modulatione' [Concerning the appropriate composition of a melody]. Two chapters on organum in the *Micrologus* 'come closer to describing and illustrating real music than any previous account' [*New Grove*,

'Theory', vol. 18: 747]. Nearly a millennium ago, therefore, relatively practical concerns inevitably required the kind of treatment
that we would now term analytical. Towards the end of the
fifteenth century, Tinctoris used *componere* and *compositor* to
reinforce the distinction between improvised and notated music.
Yet another century passed before developments in music theory
promoted a significantly analytical dimension, and they came from
outside music itself.

Renaissance music theory achieved its most lucid and comprehensive account of available musical materials in Zarlino's *Istitu-
tioni harmoniche* of 1558. But a complete composition came to be
described and interpreted only with the application of rhetorical
terminology to music as the basis for analytical demonstration.
Hence the particular significance of Burmeister's study, first published in 1606, of Lassus's motet 'In me transierunt', in which the
analyst 'succeeded in defining the structure of the work and explaining the compositional methods' [*New Grove*, 'Burmeister',
vol. 3: 486]. Such 'definitions' were inevitably circumscribed by
their literary priorities, but from the early seventeenth century
onwards actual composition featured with increasing prominence
in the writing of theorists who were becoming more and more
concerned with the practicalities of composition and performance
and the need to offer comprehensive instruction to students. Given
those concerns, theorists were still not primarily concerned to
provide detailed accounts of particular pieces solely because those
pieces were so admired. Instruction demanded altogether simpler,
shorter examples. And so even when seventeenth- and eighteenth-
century theorists such as Bernhard, Mattheson, C. P. E. Bach and
Kirnberger seem closest to the truly seminal modern figures of tonal
analysis in their consideration of such issues as the use of ornamentation to 'prolong' an essential tone, or (in figured bass) dist-
inguishing between structural harmonies and contrapuntal motions,
they were still not normally concerned with the analysis of existing
pieces as an end in itself. Both Fux and C. P. E. Bach, to whom
Schenkerians attach particular importance, were principally concerned with issues of theory and practice that could be illustrated
through relatively small-scale, specially devised examples.

It has undoubtedly given particular impetus to analysis since
Schenker to discover the importance that Haydn, Mozart and
Beethoven attached to Fuxian counterpoint (as opposed to Rameau's
Fundamental Bass); but such analyses can scarcely be imagined in

the time of those composers themselves. The history of analysis between Fux and Schenker, and between Rameau and Schoenberg – that is, the story of the gradual emergence of analysis as a pursuit 'in its own right' – can of course be linked with developments in the whole field of theory and aesthetics (see *New Grove*, 'Analysis', vol. 1: 344). Most crucially of all, however, the gradual emergence of analysis as a distinct area of music study during and after the nineteenth century was the result of separating the study of compositions from the study of composition itself: it resulted, in fact, from a more intense awareness of the past and of the value of masterpieces as durable objects to be revered, enjoyed and studied, even when the relevance of such study to the study of composition remained unclear.

There was therefore an increasing tendency in theoretical writing after the later eighteenth century to use the music of the 'greatest' composers to illustrate particular points of harmonic organization, phrase structure and formal design – a development foreshadowed by Rameau's discussion of one of his own motets in the *Traité de l'harmonie* (1722) and Mattheson's of an aria by Marcello in *Der vollkommene Kapellmeister* (1739). After J. A. P. Schulz's 'fundamental bass' analysis of the B minor Fugue from Book 1 of the *Forty-eight* and the A minor Prelude from Book 2 in Kirnberger's *Die wahren Grundsätze zum Gebrauch der Harmonie* (1773; see Beach, 1974, Beach and Thym, 1979) came Koch's examples from Haydn, C. P. E. Bach, Graun and others in his study of melodic phrase structure (*Introductory Essay on Composition*, 1787; see N. K. Baker, 1983). Momigny examined the phrase structure of the first movement of Mozart's D minor Quartet (K. 421) (*Cours complet d'harmonie et de composition* 1803–6), and Reicha similarly studied the 'Hunt' Quartet finale, as well as other music by composers including Mozart, Haydn and Cimarosa (*Traité de mélodie*, 1814; see Bent, 1980). By the middle of the century, with A. B. Marx, Lobe and Czerny, examples from Mozart, Beethoven and Chopin were being used (see Bent, 1980 and 1984), and the growth of music journals made possible such technical commentaries on contemporary works as Schumann's article on Berlioz's *Symphonie fantastique* (1835: see Cone, 1971). As far as the nineteenth century is concerned, then, the crucial question is not whether there was any extended technical discussion of actual compositions, but rather whether those discussions entail analytical processes of sufficient interest to remain valid as models in the late twentieth century.

It was one of the orthodoxies of early twentieth-century Schenkerian theory that the nineteenth century failed to develop adequately sophisticated analytical methods for the truly tonal music of the eighteenth and nineteenth centuries because of the baneful but persistent influence of Rameau's Fundamental Bass, and the ensuing notion of 'functional' harmony. The view of music as a succession of 'vertical' states that informed the theory of Fundamental Bass misrepresented, in Schenker's view, the linear, contrapuntally controlled strands that actually express those states or 'harmonies' and which, being essentially diatonic, could support, that is, explain the tonal meaning of, incidental dissonant or non-harmonic notes. This failure was fuelled by Gottfried Weber's development (after G. J. Vogler) of the Roman Numeral system of chord identification (*Versuch einer geordneten Theorie der Tonsetzkunst*, 1817–21; see Beach, 1974), and culminated in Schoenberg's typically intransigent claim that, not only could tonality be enriched and extended – even suspended – without loss of coherence, but also that 'there is no such thing as non-harmonic tones' [Schoenberg, 1978: 309]. Even though it might be claimed that the most worthwhile analytical activity during the nineteenth century was not in the sphere of tonality or harmony, but in that of 'phrase structure and formal model', the Schenkerian would counter that the entire development of so-called *Formenlehre* was a consequence of a false separation of 'form' from the living tonal language. (This issue will be discussed more fully in Part II in respect of its history and its consequences in Schenkerian analysis.) And although the emerging notion of tonality as a coherent and all-embracing system in the work of Choron, Castil-Blaze and Fétis was certainly not negligible, helping as it did to adumbrate the organic essence of tonal structures (see Simms, 1975), the apparent divorce of harmony from counterpoint prevented insights about tonal organicism achieving adequate realization in analyses of music until Schenker himself began his great work, the *Neue Theorien und Fantasien* [New Theories and Fantasies], after 1900.

However, the authors of nineteenth-century theory texts were by no means as fixated on vertical, rather than linear factors as various Schenkerian apologists have implied. Schenker's theory of 'structural' levels, for instance, was clearly anticipated by Sechter and Hauptmann (see Bent, 1980, and Wason, 1985), and aspects of such a theory have been discerned even in the work of the theorist usually regarded as Schenker's opposite, Hugo Riemann (see Christensen, 1982). A rather more positive picture of pre-Schenkerian development therefore becomes possible, and this serves to underline the fact that theorists and analysts whose concerns seem quite remote from Schenker's did share his sense of the organic coherence and essential unity of a work of art. Even Alfred Lorenz, at first sight the analyst at the furthest remove from Schenker, with his concern for certain types of form in Wagner's music dramas, emphasized the unity and coherence of those works [Lorenz, 1966, first published 1924–33].

To build bridges between Schenker and other earlier or contemporary theorists, and to regard the work of those theorists as, historically, of interest, is not to argue that the analytical techniques they proposed should be revived. Even if there is a case for considering certain notions from Riemann, Kurth, Schoenberg or Tovey in the analysis of tonal music, these should be presented alongside Schenker's rather than instead of them. It is a measure of Schenker's achievement that, retrospective though his work has been in the sense that it was not designed to be relevant to most twentieth-century music, he was able to do convincing justice to the essential organicism of tonality in its purest form at precisely the time when the organicist aesthetic notions most directly associated with that tonality were coming into question. Schenker may well have sensed that the very different issues absorbing composers after 1908 freed him from the need to believe that he was aiming his own theories at composers, or at least at those composers who did not share his belief in the essential role of tonality and whom he despaired of being able to 'enlighten'. Though he could not influence the creation of the new music that was generally held to be most important, he could guide, and even transform, the understanding of old music. And he could best do so by establishing analysis as an activity in its own right, a branch of musicology whose influence on other branches could only increase as its own character and qualities were refined.

As Part III of this book maintains, the deeply ambivalent status of organicism in many varieties of twentieth-century composition poses an exceptional and severe challenge for analysts, dedicated as they are to discovering 'the coherence of music'. When a tonal structure can no longer be demonstrated, it may indeed be necessary to change one's notion of what the 'whole' comprises. As

T. W. Adorno put it in a remarkable lecture:

It is particularly in new music . . . that analysis is concerned just as much with dissociated moments [*Dissoziationsmomente*], with the works' 'death-wish' — that is to say, with the fact that there are works which contain within themselves the tendency to strive *from* unity back into their constituent elements — as it is concerned with the opposite process. [Adorno, 1982: 182]

The value of this idea in relation to the 'new' music commonly called 'atonal' will be considered in Part III. Whether certain important types of 'old music' — cantatas, operas, music dramas, nineteenth-century collections of short piano pieces — would also benefit from more concern with 'dissociated moments' is another large question which cannot be answered in this volume. But as far as the analysis of tonal music is concerned, we should reinforce the point that, however un-Schenkerian nineteenth- and early twentieth-century techniques may have been — especially with their increasing emphasis on matters of form and motivic procedures — they sought to do justice to organic processes and to the aesthetic principle that unity, the creation and resolution of tension, was the most vital concern of creative artists and their interpreters, both executants and analysts. It may well be that significant developments in the practice of analysis will occur in the future only if there is a thorough understanding of how the discipline developed as it did during the long history of music theory. That possibility is sufficient justification for taking the history of analysis seriously. But it is time for this book to proceed to its own principal concern, the nature — in theory and practice — of those analytical techniques most likely to illuminate music for us today.

PART II

Aspects of Tonal Analysis

3

Schenker the Theorist

Schenker's exposition of the laws of organic coherence inevitably involved a critique of current theory; he was not inventing a new discipline, but trying to replace a time-honoured accumulation of pedagogical habits and assumptions which he held to be largely 'false'. Wrong theory had alienated the majority of musicians to the extent that studying music theory as such had come to be seen as an irrelevant, self-gratifying activity. Schenker's insight into this historical development must have strengthened his resolve to promote his own new theories in the face both of ridicule and – perhaps worse – of being ignored. He realized that disreputable theories had brought into disrepute the very practice of intellectual speculation about musical works of art, as is noted in *Harmony* (1906):

It is unbelievable, alas! what hecatombs of young people, full of talent and industry, fell victims to that confusion between harmony and counterpoint! I do not mean here those professional musicians, whether they blow the oboe or stroke the fiddle, whether they sing or play the piano, conducted or conducting themselves, who finally put themselves beyond all theory (I am the last one to grudge them such an attitude under the circumstances). Still closer to my heart are those numerous amateurs – good fellows, really good fellows – who, moved by sheer enthusiasm, would sacrifice to art their scarce leisure hours, to gain insight, if possible, into the inner workings of a composition. Shortly, alas! such people will take leave of textbook or teacher, driven off by a disillusion which is as bitter as it is incurable.

Owing to these people's favorable social position, their specific musical talent, their intellectual power (the importance of which is not to be underrated in art), they should have become the best possible media for the transmission of artistic achievement. Yet the disillusion they had to undergo in some cases so disgruntled and disoriented them that all too often they turned their backs on art and artists when, under other circumstances, they would have embraced their ideal joyfully. [Schenker, 1973: 178]

Not only did the average student and the amateur experience this alienation – a conflict between the art they cared about so much and the teachings they believed so little: it is well known that composers too throughout the nineteenth century (and beyond) recorded for posterity how the progress of their creative life accelerated in proportion to their disregard for music-theoretical prescriptions.

In Schenker's view, dissociation of theory and practice was a natural consequence of the obvious poverty of current theory. So ineffective was, for instance, harmonic theory, that it had to be taught from examples specially written for the purpose of harmonic analysis. What the student is 'yearning to see, the confirmation of theoretical propositions in examples from the works of the great masters', was not to be found in textbooks, and 'in other disciplines such books would be unthinkable!' [Schenker, 1973: 176] As he pointed out, Rameau's theories, disseminated in German by Marpurg after 1757, were not taken seriously by the Bachs, Haydn, Mozart or Beethoven, composers who remained faithful to the teachings of Fux. Oswald Jonas, who in 1934 published the first codification of Schenkerian theory (see Jonas, 1982), even goes so far as to suggest that C. M. von Weber's relative lack of distinction is no surprise, considering that Weber was the first acclaimed German composer to fall under the influence of French theory (as transmitted by his teacher Vogler, whom Mozart regarded as a charlatan!). Further, although Schenker does not seem to have specifically berated Simon Sechter for his influential development of Rameauism (*Die Grundsätze der musikalischen Komposition*, Leipzig, 1853), it seems that Schenker perceived a connection between the continuation of an inferior theoretical tradition and the supposed fall in standards of German music in the hands of Wagner and Bruckner. (For a full account of these developments, see Wason, 1984.)

What did Schenker mean by his ideal of a 'confirmation of theoretical propositions'? As an example, in *Harmony* he compares an exercise from Franz Xaver Richter's *Lehrbuch der Harmonie* (23rd ed.; Leipzig, 1902) with one from J. S. Bach's *Generalbassbüchlein*. Richter's is a four-part progression typical of harmony books. Schenker observes that its bass is too unbalanced to be a *cantus firmus* and must therefore represent the bass of a 'free' composition. Yet the upper parts could not conceivably appear in a piece of real music, nor do they illustrate any fundamental types of voice leading (and are in fact simple neighbouring-note prolongations in all three parts). Because of these contradictions, the exercise is a 'logical misfit, which does not belong either in the theory of harmony or in the theory of counterpoint' [Schenker, 1973: 176]. The Bach exercise, with a relatively elaborate bass line and upper parts that are 'fillers' realizing the figuring, seems to Schenker a proper kind of theoretical example since it 'may well be considered a compositional possibility' [: 180]. It has a practical purpose, since it could be an example of real song accompaniment – though Schenker does note that it 'would not serve any purpose today', long after the age of practical thoroughbass.

This case illustrates the flavour of Schenker's view both of the history of theory and of its contemporaneous purpose. He was not, of course, trying to replace Rameauism by reviving the practical tradition of improvised accompaniment – his own compositions, after all, are in a late-Romantic style exhibiting the habit 'formed . . . long since of executing . . . compositions thoroughly and completely, taking care even to cross the *t*'s and dot the *i*'s' [: 181]. But he observed that, even at the time when eighteenth-century masterpieces were written, it had been without reference to Rameau's harmonic theories – just as, by and large, the best nineteenth-century music was written without reference to Riemann's functional theory of harmony or indeed any theories then current about musical structure. What was needed, therefore, was a twentieth-century equivalent of eighteenth-century German theory, a theory of free composition, but one developed from Fuxian contrapuntal theory and the kind of practice represented in C. P. E. Bach's guide to accompaniment and improvisation. Since Schenker was convinced that tonal masterpieces after the age of thoroughbass had, nevertheless, been a development of German Baroque and Classical precedents, this was no quixotic project.

Whereas Schenker's view of recent music history showed much insight and passion, his relationship to contemporaneous musical life was an awkward one. His new contributions to the theory of tonal harmony in Austro-German music coincided with the widespread abandonment by leading composers of the tonal tradition. With such a striking impact as came from Debussy and Stravinsky, German musical culture was in any case less obviously the mainstream of European composition. More specifically, it is easy to see, almost a century after the fact, how Schenker came up against a revolution even within the Austro-German musical tradition, a factor that would put the purpose of his work seriously in question. A series of new Viennese masterpieces was emerging, from a composer who took an equally passionate (and rather learned) interest in theory and analysis. To Schoenberg, in the early twentieth century, it was nonsense to suppose that tonal music represented an absolute value – just as much nonsense as it would have been in the early nineteenth century to claim that Beethoven's music was meaningless because the style was no longer so familiar, so embedded in a widespread practice, as to allow it to be notated and performed in the thoroughbass tradition. The first opposition we discussed, that between theory and practice, is supplemented by a second, found in Schoenbergian thinking, the opposition between defunct and living compositional concerns (not that Schoenberg excluded the possibility of new tonal masterpieces). In this light, a new level of conflict appears in Schenker's position. Not only was he intent on reunifying theory and practice, thus challenging conventional ideas on the role of theory, but the practice he valued was rapidly dying out. A composer and theorist of the stature of Schoenberg could challenge Schenker on two counts: first, that Schenker was seeking the reanimation of a practice that could no longer be taken seriously as a measure of creative progress; second, that the theory appropriate to Schenker's aim was actually inappropriate to musical life, since one had to find out what a Mozart and a Schoenberg had in common, not what a Mozart had in common with that ghost born of nostalgia and creative impotence, the early twentieth-century tonal (in its eighteenth-century sense) composer. And this was no abstract conflict: Schenker placed his credibility in the view that Brahms had been the last great composer.

Concerning Schenker's position as a theorist of harmony, it is worth considering finally, beyond the sources of opposition, the weight of complacency in the reception of his work. By the early twentieth century, tonal harmony was regarded as a pedagogical and historical field that had been ploughed rigorously a century and half a century before, by Gottfried Weber and by Riemann. The 1906 *Grove's Dictionary* provides a typical view of 'Analysis of Harmony', describing the former's Roman-numeral notation and the latter's functional system. Weber's is considered 'the first comprehensive system for the purpose of indicating definite facts about the nature and function of chords'; and in Riemann 'the harmonization of any part may be indicated with very considerable detail' [*Grove*, 1906, vol. 2: 321–3]. From at least as early as Weber's *Versuch einer geordneten Theorie der Tonsetzkunst* of 1817–21 (translated into English in 1846), an inversion theory of harmony was central to technical analysis in whatever form – it was with the subject of harmony that Schenker himself began his series of comprehensive theory books, and harmonic theory was a source of pride rather than despair to the increasingly historically conscious musicologist (the *Musikwissenschaftler*). However and wherever Schenker's contribution was assessed, therefore, its reception was coloured by the fact that he alone – or virtually so – could see any need for new theories. A century after Momigny had been greeted with resounding complacency by the French musical establishment with his limited theory of tonal prolongation, Schenker faced a similar problem. The extreme conservatism of German music theory continued long after his death, ensuring that the absorption of a new way of considering the very role of harmony in general theory, and in the theory of analysis, would arise in America rather than Europe.

Schenker's role in music theory cannot be considered only through his treatment of harmony. The tradition of harmonic theory that he abhorred had been promoted at large in the first place in response to the weakness of thoroughbass and contrapuntal theory. The frustration with thoroughbass was expressed by Gottfried Weber himself, establishing a critique that took a profound hold over theory and analysis in the German- and English-speaking world. Thus his complaint against composition books:

. . . instead of attending to the essential and fundamental *properties* of the different harmonic combinations and of each of their elements, they give us rather a troublesome set of mere casuistic prescriptions upon the treatment of the intervals of the bass tone. [Weber, 1846: 222]

As far as contrapuntal theory is concerned, Riemann noted how it was an anachronism even at the time of its most seminal formulation in Fux (1725), and it was current well into the next century in Heinrich Bellermann's influential *Der Kontrapunkt* (1862), a tome owned by Schoenberg, who recycled this august tradition for American students in *Preliminary Exercises in Counterpoint* (published posthumously in 1963; see Schoenberg, 1970a). Through Fux, Riemann says, 'all of the archaisms made ridiculous by Mattheson almost two hundred years earlier are seriously being taught again, and the salvation of musical art is sought in the hollow imitation of a past age . . .' Riemann measured Fuxian theory against Bach's contemporaneous 'harmonic art', and found that 'the application of Fux's rules to Bach's work leads to a completely distorted judgement of them. Only the harmonic theory developed from the figured bass [that is, thoroughbass], embraced by Fux with little affection, gradually reveals that complete mastery which is the essence of Bach's art'. [Riemann, 1977: 121]

What offended Schenker was the trust that Weber and Riemann, as representatives of German theory, placed in 'harmonic theory'. What was needed in the early twentieth century, and indeed had been needed a hundred years before, was an approach that, rightly recognizing the archaism of traditional thoroughbass and counterpoint, would rewrite them to suit the 'modern' music of the late eighteenth and early nineteenth centuries (and Brahms's). This would be a theory, not only of *Generalbass* and *strenger Satz* (composition using strict counterpoint), but including the further development of the laws of *freier Satz* (free composition).

Whether we consider Schenker as a worthy German idealist, or as distastefully chauvinist, it is certainly a conspicuous truth in the history of German theory and analysis that, whereas its compositional models were indigenous (the Viennese tradition), its conceptual model was imported. It was to Rameau that early nineteenth-century thinkers turned for a way out of the impasse left by the death of thoroughbass practice. For Schenker, this not only seemed to be a dangerous capitulation to second-rate foreign influence, but it showed a poverty of musical spirit: Brahms had been 'the last master of German music' (to whom Schenker's *Beethoven's Ninth Symphony* book is dedicated), but C. P. E. Bach had been the last master of true theory (and such was Schenker's view even though he does not appear to have been an expert on eighteenth-century theory). Schenker's antipathy to Reger and Schoenberg was strong indeed, perhaps even stronger than his antipathy to 'foreign' music – as might be expected of alienation turned, culturally, inwards; but there was an equal antipathy to the German theorists who had for so long betrayed their 'art' by failing to develop new, indigenous concepts that would explain the linear aspects (and their contrapuntal origin) of free composition.

4

Schenkerian Analysis

Introduction

Although no one has so far written a full-scale biography of Heinrich Schenker (1868–1935), his career as far as it is known indicates relentless activity as composer, pianist, writer and teacher, editor and archivist. As a young man, he knew Brahms, who recommended his compositions to the publisher Simrock, and by the time of his death he had laid the basis for a theory of tonal music that was to become a major concern of American analysis in the 1970s, after having been introduced to that country in the early 1930s. Schenker wrote fifty years ago that 'for more than a century, a theory has been taught which claims to provide access to the art of music, but in fact does quite the opposite' [Schenker, 1979: xvi], and such old theory is still to be found in much discussion of music. But this is a function of the great disparity in musical life between a professional and an amateur knowledge and taste, and between the history of musicians, of documents and instruments, institutions and markets, and the history of musical composition. Schenker was primarily concerned with theory for those with a knowledge of and taste for tonal music, theory that can arise only from years of intimate preoccupation with a large repertory. It excludes any 'student or the serious music-lover' who suffers from 'ignorance of the true nature of strict counterpoint and thoroughbass' [: xxii], and it is indeed remarkable how close Schenker's notion of musical education was – noting the best example conceivable – to Mozart's, who systematically integrated Thomas Attwood's study of counterpoint and thoroughbass into free composition [Heartz, 1965]. In an age when eighteenth- and nineteenth-century musical skills are by and large unknown, even disliked to the extent that their nature is understood, it is ironic that Schenkerian theory has nevertheless firmly taken hold of tonal analysis and makes increasing inroads into music history, especially in autograph study, of which Schenker was a pioneer.

A distinction must be made between Schenker's work and its subsequent interpretation. It was not until the late 1920s that he devised methods which have subsequently caught the imagination of analysts and have been discussed, exemplified and modified widely in the English-language literature. Two factors support the view that it is the techniques of his final years, and their development in the half-century since his death, that should be the basis of analytical method now.

First, as far as theory is concerned, it was only after his discovery of the concept 'fundamental structure' (*Ursatz*) that Schenker was able to codify its types and its means of presentation, a process that seems to have taken him a decade or so in the 1920s. The theories put forward in *Free Composition* (published posthumously) make a richer and more coherent explanation of tonal structure than is to be found in *Harmony, Kontrapunkt, Der Tonwille* or *Das Meisterwerk*. Secondly, Schenker refined his graphic technique in harness with his more comprehensive theorizing. In the Introduction to *Five Graphic Music Analyses* he went so far as to claim that verbal commentary was, at last, unnecessary. If it is accepted, then, that theory and analytical practice developed hand in hand over Schenker's career, these two factors combine into the same argument – that what is most useful in Schenker is to be found in his two last publications, *Five Graphic Music Analyses* and *Free Composition*. For the analyst, the disadvantage of being familiar with those two sources alone would be ignorance of Schenker's extensive writings on interpretation and autograph study, aspects of musical understanding that he considered integral to realistic analysis, if less integral to theoretical codification.

Schenker's urge towards graphic self-sufficiency has often alienated casual observers. On the one hand, in its partiality, with its concentration on notated pitch relationships, on tonality viewed as contrapuntal pitch-structure, a Schenker-graph is aesthetically displeasing to critics dedicated to comprehensive description – who represent a common idealistic impulse, to say all there is to be said about a piece of music. On the other hand, the more successful a graphic analysis seems to be, the more it can raise suspicion that one set of symbols (musical notation and all it implies to a musician) has merely been translated into another (a voice-leading graph and all it implies to those who understand its 'language'). Nevertheless, the graphic techniques Schenker both invented and adopted to express his theory of tonality shared a common motivation with other theory, while establishing, he believed, a reanimation of the long-defunct, eighteenth-century unity of music-making and musical understanding. Symbolic analysis – though nothing to compare with Schenker's unique graphics – is to be found everywhere in music theory, from the diagrammatic phrase-analysis of Koch to the melodic and harmonic notations of Hindemith's *Craft of Musical Composition*: even Schenker's contemporary Alfred Lorenz, with his comprehensive schemata for the diagrammatic summaries of Wagner's music dramas, was following the urge to combat the ineffectiveness of purely verbal music analysis. But the more substantial vindication of Schenker's graphics, in a general sense, is their kinship with composition and with composition teaching. Reductive notation in the form of seventeenth- and eighteenth-century thoroughbass, and generative practice from the same period, the art of elaboration or 'diminution', which he studied in the virtually inseparable fields of composition teaching (Bernhard and Fux), ornamentation and improvisation (C. P. E. Bach), were to Schenker the historical antecedents that he drew together in a symbolic concordance of remarkable clarity and scope. 'The graphic representation', he came to believe, 'is part of the actual composition, not merely an educational means' [Schenker, 1979: xxiii].

The threads trailing backwards and forwards from the early 1930s are important to a full appreciation of the place of voice-leading analysis in general musical practice and in the history of analysis. The understanding of Schenker's analytical evolution is incomplete if studied only at the level of theory. Only when we begin to sense his creative development, especially as a performer, do we sense also his motivation for extensive 'theories and fantasies' (as he dubbed his major books) about tonal music, just as it is necessary to give thought to his rejection of contemporaneous composition. Not only his own creative work needs to be considered, but also his musicological approach to the legacy of the Viennese 'masters', or of Bach and Chopin, Scarlatti and Paganini. His activity as music editor contributed as much to his search for what is musically 'true' (in German, *wahr*, which connotes 'genuine' and 'authentic' as in C. P. E. Bach's title *Die wahre Art das Clavier zu spielen*) as any purely conceptual constructs – which included not only music theory, but also a measure of social philosophy (Schenker's so-called 'political' writings). In the second half of the century, Schenker's final theory and practice were preserved through the teachings of his pupils Oswald Jonas and Ernst Oster, and more recently through Allen Forte's authoritative writings. Felix Salzer, however, Schenker's most influential advocate in the English-speaking world of the 1950s and 1960s, disseminated a revised form of analysis that has come to be known as neo-Schenkerian (though it must be recorded that Salzer's English edition of *Five Graphic Music Analyses* was the first milestone in publication of Schenker's own work). Salzer's *Structural Hearing* (1952) launched a brilliant exposition of Schenkerian voice-leading techniques into the field of analysis in general. As far as Schenker's original theory is concerned, it is derivative rather than strictly representative. There are new chord classifications in Salzer, new, more systematic formal typologies and graphic symbols, and – perhaps most conspicuously – Salzer is less concerned with linear connection in a pitch-graph (see Chapter 5). Perhaps most notably of all, Salzer applied voice-leading methods to both pre- and post-tonal music – these epithets being convenient over-simplifications, of course, in cases like Monteverdi or Debussy. Schenker's vision of 'masterpieces' as tonal – triadically based – and, let it be said, as German, was quietly abandoned: neo-Schenkerism imported into the New World a new way to analyse Western music from Leoninus to Hindemith in reductive structural levels.

In this respect, we can see how 'Schenkerism' has followed the trend in analytical technique – indeed, in the history of ideas in general – for dissemination to amount to diffusion, even corruption, if the origin of a theory is the benchmark against which subsequent applications and adaptations are compared. It is implicit in what follows that no post-Schenkerian discussion can detract from the explanatory impact and artistic vision of Schenker's own writings; and the discoveries of neo-Schenkerian analysis, however sharply at odds with Schenker's own viewpoint, are a necessary further study. The tension in the development of Schenkerian theory over the best part of a century reflects the march of history, with its changes in attitude and need, in the same way that Schenker's own work was a transformation of seventeenth- and eighteenth-century teachings, designed to assimilate for analysis the masterpieces of eighteenth- and nineteenth-century composers.

Rudiments

Few analysts have sought to formulate the Schenkerian method, to show how every stage of a 'correct' analysis is to be executed. And Schenker himself never did so in print: in *Free Composition* he formulated a theoretical, to some extent even pedagogical, exposition, not an analytical guidebook. Nevertheless, several generations of analysts have provided a fund of understanding of tonal voice-leading technique through discussions of Schenker, translations and editions of his work, pedagogical formulations and countless new analyses (see Beach, 1969 and 1979). It is clear by now what models an introductory account should argue towards – the incisive if fragmentary examples in *Free Composition*, the handful of complete examples in *Five Graphic Music Analyses*, the compendium of examples and explanation in *Introduction to Schenkerian Analysis* (Forte and Gilbert, 1982). It is less clear just how it should do so, whether through analytical theory dedicated to Schenkerism (Jonas, 1983), through technical commentary on *Free Composition* (Schachter, 1981; Laufer, 1981), even through a critical history of Schenkerian theory (Federhofer, 1981) or a concatenation of Schenkerian analytical theory (Plum, 1979). Certainly any modern approach must not only concentrate on Schenker's method but must also assume its codifiable existence and, in the main, its validity. Here, we will indulge immediately in some technical exposition of Schenkerian analysis based on the opening of a Bach chorale, then consider the wider aspects of form, tonality and background, and specific analytical techniques.

Example 1(a) shows the first two phrases of the Bach chorale setting of Hassler's 'Ich bin's, ich sollte büssen', from the *St Matthew Passion*, No. 16. This is written in two parts with figured bass, so that the harmonic progression is certain, if not the configuration of inner parts. Note that this is itself a kind of 'reductive' analysis where essentials are represented without all the details of the musical surface. A virtually infinite variety of inner-part elaboration is conceivable, with a wide choice of dissonance treatment, but it would be acceptable only if it expressed the harmonic progression in crotchets (thus example 1(f) is right, assuming chords 1 and 3 are heard as root and $^6_3$ respectively, whereas example 1(g) is wrong at *, if pleasing); yet any musician will accept example 1(a) as a true representation of Bach's work – that is, it represents Bach's four-part setting correctly but not literally.

Ex.1 Hassler arr. J.S. Bach: chorale, 'Ich bin's, ich sollte büssen'

Since we are interested in how the music unfolds in time, we can now use Bach's articulatory notation (pause marks) to identify phrases and examine where each begins and ends. As example 1(b) shows, in both parts the first ends where it began in terms of pitch; the second does not: the first actually *prolongs* (broken slurs); the second prolongs by means of *progression* (slurs), and the reduction makes good note-against-note (first-species) counterpoint (marked 3–5–3). There seems to be an underlying consonant progression. Without doubt something is wrong about the analysis of the second phrase, but that of the first makes intuitive sense. This intuitive sense is clarified in example 1(c) (still far from Schenker's own analysis or analytical style) where the metrical stress is taken into account: the stressed first and third beats reveal, first, a double prolongation (C over A flat comes three times articulating two prolongations) and, second, contrary motion between the parts, which move between different intervals (3rd against 4th, 2nd against 3rd). But two musical features are missing – the melodic apex at E flat, and the (implied) dominant harmony at bars 1^2 and 2^2, which seems to direct the harmony of this phrase, however 'plagal' it sounds. Example 1(d) analyses these features, revealing motivic correspondences (marked with horizontal brackets) and implying a 'structural' hierarchy by the use of stemmed white notes, stemmed black notes, black notes and quavers. 'N' means 'neighbouring note', and in the bass here it indicates how the (figured) dominant harmony in bar 1^2 attaches to – or gives rise to – the most coherent melodic relationship.

Already some basics of Schenkerian analysis have to be grasped here. Note how in example 1(d) a structural hierarchy is expressed by the scale of (non-rhythmic) values ♩/♪/•/♪ . The analysis is portraying a pitch-structure 'grounded' on a sustained or prolonged C over A flat (a 'background' on a small scale): there are two phases of prolongation with the parts in contrary motion (see example 1(c), which sketches the 'middleground' shown in white notes in example 1(d)). The foreground shows so-called 'diminutions', and it is here that the explanatory force of Schenkerian analysis may be easiest to appreciate. Assuming that example 1(c) is a fair reduction with which most listeners would or could agree, the analyst's job has been to answer, graphically, rather obvious questions. For example, does the melody express C – D flat of example 1(c) (bars 1^3–2^1) in the same way as D flat – C (bar 2^{1-3})? It is implicit in all this that the individual structural levels are musically meaningless: in themselves, examples 1(b) and 1(c) make no sense of any importance, but they do when read in relation to example 1(a), as does example 1(d), which collects all the analytical information into what Schenker called a 'foreground graph' (*Urlinietafel*).

The problem with the second phrase in example 1(b) is now evident. It was not, at that stage, analysed in context. Certainly

Ex.2 Hassler arr. J.S. Bach: 'Ich bin's, ich sollte büssen'

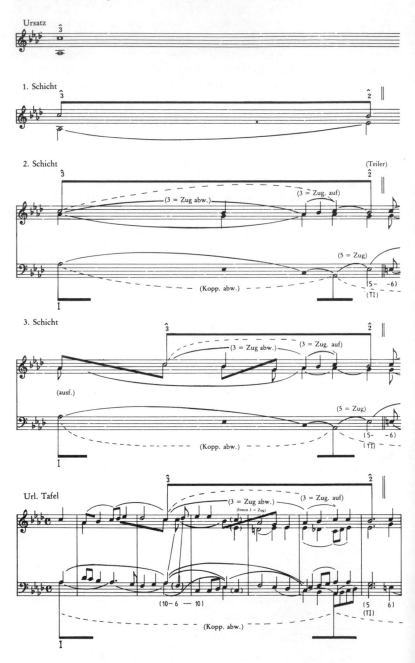

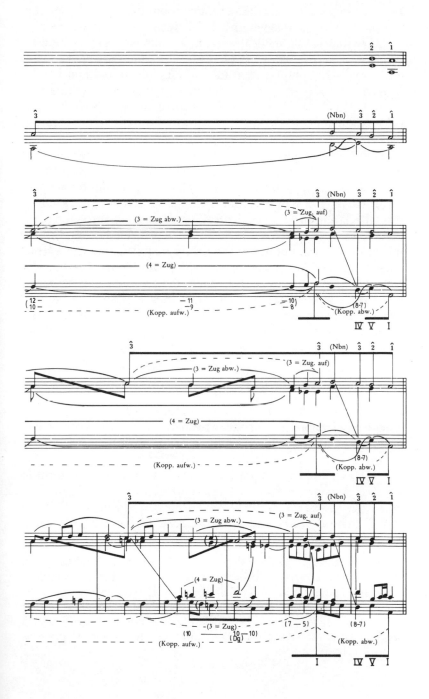

there is progression rather than prolongation. Example 1(e) sketches this (and it is debatable whether bar 3^3 is so hierarchically strong – a matter that would be dealt with in a complete analysis showing connections to the following phrases). The continuity of the voice-leading structure, however, rules out a middleground F at bar 2^4: conventional formal analysis tells us that there are two phrases, separated at bar 2^{3-4}, but the voice-leading analysis shows how the phrases are connected, in so far as contrapuntal pitch-structure is concerned.

This observation represents a theory crucial in Schenker, one that distinguishes his work sharply from formal/stylistic and thematic approaches. For Schenker, form is not a basic quality of tonal music (or, if so, only of bad tonal music). In a masterpiece, the kinds of formal relationship that had preoccupied analysis throughout the nineteenth century are not, Schenker claimed, fundamental to the musical structure, but are expressed by that structure. An extract from Schenker's complete graph of this chorale in *Five Graphic Music Analyses* illustrates this convincingly (example 2) by showing bass 'couplings' that cross the pauses marking the ends of phrases. His simplest reduction, the fundamental structure, crosses all articulations and embraces the whole piece in one formal unit.

The Principle of Form

Formal typology is a complex topic in *Free Composition*; so diverse are the implications of Schenker's theory of form that Oster needed to supplement his treatment of sonata form with a suggestive, but all too brief note on Beethoven and Brahms (Schenker, 1979: 139–41). Of course, a chorale does not have a traditional form in any case, beyond the stylistic constraints of phrase length, number of phrases and so on. But in fact all form is, in Schenker's theory, a surface feature not necessarily coincident in time with the background structure:

All forms appear in the ultimate foreground; but all of them have their origin in, and derive from, the background. This is the innovational aspect of my explanation of forms ... I have repeatedly referred to form as the ultimate manifestation of that structural coherence which grows out of background, middleground, and foreground ... but I here reiterate in order to stress the difference between this new theory and all previous theories of form. [: 130]

The fourth song from Schumann's *Dichterliebe* is a case of the basic Schenkerian form, 'undivided form'. His graph (which is not a full analysis, and which may be regarded as a controversial reading) indicates how 'all the rhythmic, prosodic events brought about by the setting of the text, as well as the characteristic features of the piano part, fall within the undivided progression $\hat{3}$–$\hat{1}$ [: 130 and figure 152[1]]. The foreground articulation suggests three sections, bars 1–8, 9–16 and 16–21, and in this case it is coincident with the fundamental structure. Thus a formal analysis that identified a binary form with coda or a ternary form would be confirmed in the contrapuntal pitch-structure. In contrast, Schenker's much-discussed analysis of *Dichterliebe* No. 2 throws into relief the old and new principles of form (see Schenker, 1979, Figure 22[6]; Forte, 1977; Kerman, 1980; Komar, 1971): a two-section, divided structure ($\hat{3}$–$\hat{2}$ ǁ $\hat{3}$–$\hat{2}$–$\hat{1}$) is the background of a ternary foreground.

This aspect of Schenker's theory is a radical challenge to other views, which nonetheless continued to cling to what Schenker condemned. In Schoenberg's posthumous *Fundamentals of Musical Composition* ternary form is described thus:

An overwhelming proportion of musical forms is structurally composed of three parts. The third part is sometimes a true repetition (recapitulation) of the first, but oftener it is a more or less modified repetition. The second part is organized as a contrast . . . Sections producing contrasts of various types and degrees are to be found in a great many forms: e.g. Small Ternary Form (formerly called Three-Part Song Form) . . . Contrasting sections . . . must utilize the same processes by which motive-forms are connected in simpler formulations. [Schoenberg, 1970b: 119]

These sentiments, and the kind of analysis and pedagogical examples Schoenberg derives from them, are theoretically defunct according to Schenker:

I reject those definitions of song form which take the motive as their starting point and emphasize manipulations of the motive by means of repetition, variation, extension, fragmentation, or dissolution. I also reject those explanations which are based upon phrases, phrase-groups, periods, double-periods, themes, antecedents and consequents. My theory replaces all of these with specific concepts of form, which, from the outset, are based upon the content of the whole and of the individual parts; that is, the differences in prolongations lead to differences in form.

These prolongations in no way determine the actual length of compositions; consequently, the customary distinction between large and small song forms must be discarded. [Schenker, 1979: 131–2]

In general, Schenker did not reject out of hand familiar formal categories, but simply characterized them as aspects of contrast rather than unity and was anxious to explain how true form (in the sense of structural articulation) lies in the presence of either an undivided or divided fundamental structure (see Jonas, 1982: 129–48).

Tonality and Background

Two analytical assumptions have been implied by the discussion so far and have become increasingly vital to accepting the theory that – as we have seen – asks us to abandon two centuries' worth of collected wisdom (for Schenker: 'false theory') about the nature of musical form. First, Schenker is concerned with music that expresses major–minor tonality. In example 1, the criterion of progression versus prolongation, which could be applied in principle to all kinds of pitched music, revealed little compared with the fruits of specifically tonal perceptions (for instance, the perception that, in A flat major, A flat – F in bar 2^{3-4} in the bass is not the step progression that G sharp – F could be in A minor; or the very perception of 'consonance' in example 1(b)). This specificity in Schenker is, in a general way, what characterizes his work as analytical theory, by which 'is meant a theoretical system that has been induced from a body of existing compositions', according to one historian who notes that Schenker's theory 'operates most successfully' within the chronological limits 1720 to around 1900 [Palisca in Harrison, 1963: 114]. In particular, Schenker's stylistic corpus is determined not only chronologically but also qualitatively. Not only did he assume the value of tonal expression in master-pieces, but he went so far as to use the analytical theory based on them to attempt to discredit more recent music, specifically Reger and Stravinsky [Kalib, 1973: II, pp. 451–90 and 212–16]. He dealt with relatively few works from a vast chronological corpus (though few musicians may know intimately as much music as Schenker did). Indeed, such are the demands of Schenkerian analysis for detailed study that it can seem to be at odds with the normal requirement for a musician to be familiar, if vaguely familiar, with a large repertory.

Secondly, it is implied by the more technical points in this discussion that a Schenkerian knows well enough what the structural foundation of tonal masterpieces is: in this respect, one is using a technique for demonstrating rather than discovering; or it is not for discovering a structural foundation but for discovering the function of that foundation in a particular piece. Schenker's decades of research on masterpieces, trying to formulate in a concrete musical form the 'very secret and source of their being: the concept of organic coherence' [Schenker, 1979: xxi] did succeed. This is what he concluded:

The *background* in music is represented by a contrapuntal structure which I have designated the *fundamental structure* . . . :

Fundamental line is the name which I have given to the upper voice of the fundamental structure. It unfolds a chord horizontally while the counter-pointing lower voice effects an *arpeggiation* of this chord through the upper fifth.

Since it is a melodic succession of definite steps of a second, the fundamental line signifies motion, striving toward a goal, and ultimately the completion of this course . . . Similarly, the arpeggiation of the bass signifies movement toward a specific goal, the upper fifth, and the completion of the course with the return to the fundamental tone. [: 4]

The descent from 3, and descents from 5 $\left(\begin{smallmatrix}\hat{5}&\hat{4}&\hat{3}&\hat{2}&\hat{1}\\ I&&&V&I\end{smallmatrix}\right)$ and 8 $\left(\begin{smallmatrix}\hat{8}&\hat{7}&\hat{6}&\hat{5}&\hat{4}&\hat{3}&\hat{2}&\hat{1}\\ I&&&&&&V&I\end{smallmatrix}\right)$, Schenker's structural norms, present in virtually all organically coherent tonal music. (He finds exceptions, e.g. Brahms's Intermezzo, Op. 118, No. 1; see Figure 110[d3].) Only a ramified theoretical codification can begin to show how this is so.

Analytical Techniques

While the discussion of the theory of fundamental structure in *Free Composition* is rich and wide-ranging, it does not amount to a clear analytical programme. A survey of the technical skeleton of the book suggests that categorization of analytical techniques according to the requirements of analytical practice would differ from the theoretical presentation Schenker provides, an account of background, middleground and foreground musical features (see Dunsby, 1980). But certain recurrent criteria in a Schenkerian analysis form a basic guide for the student.

Ex.3 Brahms: Variations and Fugue on a Theme by Handel, Op.24
Handel: *Aria con Variazioni*

(a)

(b)

(c) Var.1

Var.2
(d)

Ascent, Structure and Peroration

The structural unit of the fundamental line and bass arpeggiation is often prepared, and prolonged at its completion. There are diverse forms of 'introduction' in a tonal piece (that is, an introduction in the voice-leading which rarely coincides with formal introduction, as should be expected in the light of a theory that shows how foreground contrast is underpinned by background continuity). While the music leading to the primary melodic note (the 'Kopfton' that begins the fundamental line) is structurally preparatory, it may often present the main melodic material of a piece. In example 3(a), a stepwise initial ascent expresses what any musician will recognize in Handel's *Aria*, that the melody as a whole turns around D (with the fundamental line falling through C to B flat in the closing bars), but the motive of an ascending third shapes the thematic flow in the foreground. Handel's first variation (example 3(b)) provides an emphatic registral interpretation: while the upper line shows a rhythmic diminution further stressing the foreground motive, the bass highlights the arrival of the structural D.

It is evident that in some pieces much of the dramatic weight of the music will be expressed in the initial ascent. Schenker's analysis of the 'Emperor Hymn' (from Haydn's String Quartet, Op. 76, No. 3), for instance, shows the fundamental structure, a descent from $\hat{5}$, beginning only in the second half of the theme [Schenker, 1979: figure 39[3]]. In his early analysis of the Brahms *Handel Variations*, Schenker analysed ascents that are theoretically indistinguishable from the descents (thus $\hat{3} - \hat{4} - \hat{5} - \hat{4} - \hat{3} - \hat{2} - \hat{1}$ and similar formulations), which in his final theory makes structural nonsense [Schenker, 1924]. In a piece like Brahms's *Variations*, the need for a coherent theory is especially acute, if the aim of analysis is to understand and express the diversity of ways in which the opening is treated (so that, for example, Variation 2 already shows a prolongation of the ascent, that is, a delay of the primary melodic note: d^1 in bars 1^3 and 2^1 is ornamental to the underlying c^1 of bars 1^4–2^2; compare examples 3(c) and 3(d)).

Once the fundamental structure has reached $\hat{1}$ it has reached its structural goal. The rest is peroration. Schenker offered no theory to explain types of peroration (which would concern only the middleground and foreground levels), even though he may analyse the ends of pieces with care graphically. And it must be remembered that the capacity of a composer to prolong structure can be the mark of extraordinary creative vision. Schubert's song 'Der Tod und das Mädchen' may be analysed as approximately half fundamental structure, half structural 'stasis' following completion of the fundamental line and bass arpeggiation. This makes for a strong musico-dramatic image: the character of Death in the text sings, with the piano, a prolongation of the 'dead' structure after the 'live' $\hat{3} - \hat{2} - \hat{1}$ descent of the first half.* This illustrates more concretely Schenker's view, already noted, that structural features 'in no way determine the actual length of compositions' (see above, p. 39). It may be objected that he undervalued, critically, how pieces end in a structural peroration; analytical procedure must in this case be inferred from Schenker's work, and it is often a cause of disquiet to students who reasonably expect, in the light of his extreme claims, that all aspects of analytical practice are covered in *Free Composition*.

Middleground Arpeggiation

During the course of the fundamental structure, at the middleground level the bass arpeggiation often provides a clue to the overall musical gesture of a piece. Perhaps the most significant distinction in Schenker's description of the middleground is between arpeggiations that fall within the 'obligatory' register (established by the primary note of the fundamental line and the first bass note of the background) of the bass (from tonic up to dominant) and the diminution that does not (via the submediant, which lies 'above' the dominant). In example 4, a colourful progression sustains the second phrase (see example 4(a)). But the submediant (bar 164) cannot form the underlying prolongation of the fundamental structure: being 'above' the dominant, it is always, in this specific sense, more decorative. Thus the energy carries through to the focal third phrase (example 4(b)) with its subdominant arpeggiation. Such is the structural force of the subdominant arpeggiation compared with the submediant that, when in the reprise of this passage Chopin substitutes IV for VI in the second phrase (bars 295–98), the redundancy of the third phrase (bars 303–6) guarantees a more extended phrasing with new continuation: example 4(d) is not expected; example 4(c) is the actual continuation. As the horizontal bracket indicates in example 4(c), the continuity across bars

---

*In Carl Schachter's motivic analysis in 'Motive and Text in Four Schubert Songs', another possibility is suggested by the idea that the second half is a 'recomposition' of the first [Beach, 1983: 67–70].

Ex.4 Chopin: Scherzo in C♯ minor, Op.39

295–310 makes for a kind of hemiola, breaking down the regular phrasing of this chorale-like section as it leads into a retransition.

This suggests the strength of Schenker's theory of middleground arpeggiation only in an applied, small-scale way. As a theory of entire pieces it provided a release from the functional concept of Riemann. The idea of extended composition founded on a I–V–I arpeggiation is at least as old in music theory as C. P. E. Bach. Riemann's refinement – claiming that V and IV are counterpoles around I and other harmonic degrees relate always to one of these three functions – appeared to Schenker merely to coarsen the picture of a middleground: it denied the linear control of two-voice counterpoint on harmonic progression. Schenker proposed that, on the contrary, the subdominant degree (or the subdominant 'key' in a piece) is one of the diatonic 'scale-steps' which may be prolonged, and these have no privileged status outside the system schematized (and therefore to be read only informally, since it represents the most varied musical practice) in example 5. The hierarchical classification of any structural feature is vital here: just as Schoenberg claimed that plagal cadences cannot establish or annul a tonality [Schoenberg, 1978: 136], so Schenker claimed that, following a structural V, only middleground descent through III is normal tonal practice, so that any expression of '*' in example 5 must be a foreground diminution.

Ex.5

Finally on this topic, it may seem that to speak of the relationship of embedding or reduplication between hierarchical levels is theoretically insensitive to compositional practice. Since Schenker's guiding principle was that of hierarchical reduplication, it may be thought that the same contrapuntal, melodic or harmonic form can appear on any level of structure, as a foreground detail or shaping a symphonic movement. But hierarchic levels are specific and, indeed, to be distinguished referentially by virtue of their specific features. Underlying Schenker's reduplicative exposition in *Free Composition* (where similar features are discussed in relation to different structural levels) is a non-reduplicative theory in four categories (see Dunsby, 1980). And, clearly, the valid middleground progressions we have been discussing here are relatively specific. They carry the empirical imprint of a style; they are more susceptible to criticism, if such it is, not for being wrong about the music they explain, but for being stylistically narrow, barely transferrable outside their period without radical redrafting of the whole theory of organic coherence.

Voice-leading, Part-writing and Texture

The concept of a two-voice representation of tonal music, be it a solo song or a Beethoven *tutti*, is the most familiar theoretical premise of Schenkerian analysis:

> The combination of fundamental line and bass arpeggiation constitutes a *unity*. This unity alone makes it possible for voice-leading transformations to take place in the middleground and enables the form of the fundamental structure to be transferred to individual harmonies . . . Neither the fundamental line nor the bass arpeggiation can stand alone. Only when acting together, when unified in a contrapuntal structure, do they produce art. [Schenker, 1979: 11]

In the acquisition of Schenker's techniques, students of analysis stumble as often over this premiss as over the actual unfolding of the two-voice counterpoint it implies. With example 6 we shall attempt to convey the meaning of Schenker's voice-leading concept in relation to part-writing and texture. The chorale analysed in example 2 was not given the fullest possible explanation by Schenker in the sense that the role of the inner parts was assumed, not expressed graphically. Example 6(b) does attempt to express graphically the nature and role of all the parts – the whole musical texture – in a chorale excerpt, example 6(a). In the passage from example 6(d) through 6(c) and (b) to (a) we can see a passage (if we choose to read it in this direction) from voice-leading frame in two parts, through voice-leading of the whole texture to the actual part-

Ex.6 Hassler arr. J.S. Bach: 'Vater unser im Himmelreich'

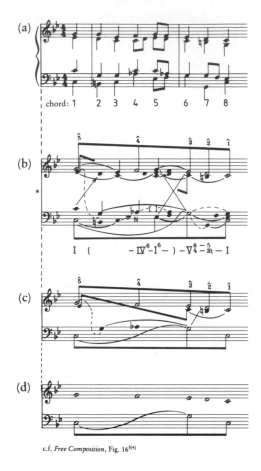

c.f. *Free Composition*, Fig. 16[5][4]

writing in which this voice-leading structure is presented. At chord
4, Bach has written parts that cross (bass and tenor), and between
chords 4 and 5 there is the unusual progression of $\frac{6}{3}$ chords over
disjunct motion in the bass. With reference only to the part-writing
and to conventional harmonic analysis, it is not possible to explain
the structural effect of these features. But the voice-leading analysis
does make it possible: the A flat and E flat supporting chords 4 and
5 are not in fact connected by one voice-leading strand – one part,
the bass, takes the note of an inner voice between two outer-voice
notes (C–*A flat*–E flat), the note of a middleground counterpoint

shown in example 6(c). The part-crossing apparent in the music is, then, an audible signal that the apparent real bass line is moving between different hierarchical levels: there is a double approach to the structural dominant in the lower part (chord 6), from above via an upper neighbouring note, and from below via the ascending arpeggio C–E flat–G, with one part singing the effective notes of both progressions. It was noted that, in a figured-bass reduction, there are many potential realizations of harmony and voice-leading in the texture between top and bottom lines. Here, there could be many potential realizations of examples 6(d) and (c). In the actual realization, there is an underlying ambiguity in the way $\hat{4}$ is made consonant (thus: in example 6(c), how are we to understand the 'suspension' of the bass C if $\hat{4}$ is to be expressed as the top of a $\substack{6 \\ 3}$, not a $\substack{6 \\ 4}$?): this ambiguity cannot be understood solely in terms of the melodic progression of the bass or that of the tenor in example 6(a). Note too that the voice-leading implies sometimes more, sometimes fewer than the four lines of singing. For instance, between chords 1 and 2 there are at least five voice-leading connections, though only four part-writing connections.*

This example illustrates an indispensable distinction and a technique for expressing it, but it also illustrates why in practice Schenker rarely tried to analyse, explicitly, all details of the musical texture. In more complex music, as often as not there is little chance of being able to determine the so-called part-writing in any case. (As an example: note how the first six chords of Beethoven's *Pathétique* Sonata, Op. 13, chorale-like though they are in Beethoven's style, are literally 7-, 3-, 4-, 4-, 4- and 3-note respectively.) Voice-leading must therefore be the focus of analytical attention and must be understood both in relation to the actual texture through which it is expressed and the two-part contrapuntal frame (itself, of course, a voice-leading structure) of which it is the diminution. In the analysis of more elaborate music, Schenker did in fact approach a theory of part-writing, but only in the sense of seeing voice-leading as controlled by register. The concept of 'obligatory register' is really a parallel, in theory, for the harmonic concept of traditional German theory, the 'law of the shortest way', described by, among others, Schoenberg [Schoenberg, 1978: 39]. In the kind of structural 'part-writing' examined by Schenker, in

---

*Example 6 should be compared with Salzer's different analysis in *Structural Hearing* [Salzer, 1962: example 179(b)].

which the points where a single line is picked up in the texture may be separated by many bars of music occupied with diminutions at a different level, registral continuity replaces the function of contiguity in a single voice – a function central to strict counterpoint: in free composition, when the notes of a structural line will rarely be contiguous, registral continuity is often the central criterion for analytical practice (see, for example, Oster, 1977).

Summary and Prospects

Evidently, one cannot expect on the basis of this discussion, if it is a first contact with Schenker, to be able to produce an analysis in his manner. What may have emerged, however, is confidence in the effectiveness of Schenkerian analysis, the kind of confidence that arises from study of how deeply Schenker was able to penetrate certain issues about tonal music, and, most of all, issues about how to express an understanding of aspects of tonal structure. Key points in this direction are:
• to distinguish between form and contrapuntal–harmonic structure and to examine their interaction;
• to recognize that tonal structure formulated in the abstract is necessarily a simple concept – hence the limited number of backgrounds in Schenker's theory – but that the very point of analysis is to explain the complex expression of the background in any particular piece;
• that most pieces reveal, structurally, three phases ('ascent, structure and peroration');
• that the way the bass moves from tonic to structural dominant will reveal the most important harmonic character of the music;
• that the workings of the outer structural voices are central to a full picture of the voice-leading.
In general, we have emphasized the urge towards completeness in Schenkerian thinking: hierarchical levels in themselves mean little (and mean literally nothing musically), and must be drawn, read, heard and understood in conjunction with all other levels; similarly, bass lines in themselves cannot be presented as analyses – despite the temptation fuelled by the thoroughbass tradition – however elaborately they are figured, however suggestive, or 'implicative', they may be in relation to the music in question; nor should we, in principle, discard any further aspect of analysis that may not sit comfortably in a graphic representation (for instance, the relation of

musical structure to textual imagery or poetic structure) – if these aspects cannot be understood in relation to a graph, the graph itself must be questioned.*

The discussion of various analytical approaches presented in this volume involves evaluation along with exposition, and it is already a strong comment on Schenker to say that the significance of his work cannot be criticized tersely and in relation to the general analytical field. Schenkerian analysis will be superseded, inevitably, as attitudes and needs change (to reiterate a point made earlier), but meanwhile the student will be well aware that there is no serious alternative to this approach at present in the fields of explanation on which it focuses – though there are, as this book hopes to indicate, many other fields to consider. The path to learning the method is clear but, as various commentators have observed, daunting:

It seems perfectly clear what we must study to understand Schenker's work: (1) strict (species) counterpoint, (2) harmony (including traditional thoroughbass), and finally (3) the music of the masters . . . but there is an important distinction between learning about Schenker – treating him as an historical figure – and learning his theories . . . the latter, which includes developing a skill for graphic notation of musical structure, requires years of diligent study and practice. The conflict, as I have called it, results from the difference between the time needed to develop these skills and the time pressures at institutions of higher education . . . [Beach, 1983: 3]

Yet there are encouraging factors to bear in mind. For instance, although few people may have had the chance to study strict counterpoint, the misunderstandings to which ignorance of it can lead have been well aired in recent Schenkerian literature. One of the achievements of the last two decades is a record of informed discussion about Schenkerian theory to which student and teacher can, and should, refer. Further, the pedagogical codification of his theories, especially in the *Introduction to Schenkerian Analysis* by Forte and Gilbert, means that even a limited familiarity with voice-leading analysis – which no student should be denied – may be partial but secure rather than superficial and confused. The reward, of a firm point of reference in thinking about tonal music, and a

---

*In *Der Tonwille* and *Das Meisterwerk* Schenker provides remarkably comprehensive narrative accounts to supplement, and often reinforce, his voice-leading graphs, accounts that include commentary on text–music relationships, considerations of previous analysis by others, and almost always points about performance and interpretation.

point of reference for comparing other approaches and making constructive use of them, is found by most to be worth the patient study involved.

5

Developments of Schenker: Katz and Salzer

Schenker's own compositions are evidence enough that he was not, as a musician, quite the radical conservative he appeared to be as a theorist and historian. Yet his theory of tonality set sharp limits on which music could and which could not be shown to be of artistic value. The idea of value proved by the existence of tonality, and especially by the particular concept of consonance and dissonance implied by tonality as the expression of the triadic chord of nature, must seem progressively weaker if Schenker's theory is tested on later nineteenth-century and early twentieth-century music. Since so many composers no longer felt bound to the 'language' of major–minor tonality, it would seem simply inappropriate to apply Schenkerian techniques in the analysis of their music. Yet the history of analysis of twentieth-century music shows that Schenker has been interpreted in a way of which he could not have approved. He has been considered, by and large, right about tonal music, but wrong about most of the music of his own time. His own analysis has been taken very seriously, but in this sense his wider theory has not, and it must be acknowledged that this calls into question what might be termed the Schenkerian 'aesthetic'. Schoenberg took a more profound view of what the concern of music theory should be – to explain the continuity of compositional practice between first and second Viennese periods (and, in a wider sense, between tonal and post-tonal music), not to explain any so-called death of German culture.

Schoenberg's definition of tonality (1922) is a double-edged sword that implicitly cuts down any claim of Schenker to have been theorizing in a way that could be thought relevant to contemporaneous music:

The word 'tonal' is incorrectly used if it is intended in an exclusive rather than an inclusive sense. It can be valid only in the following sense: everything implied by a series of tones (*Tonreihe*) constitutes tonality, whether it be brought together by means of direct reference to a single fundamental or by more complicated connections. [Schoenberg, 1978: 432]

Thus, Schenker's is too limited a theory in that it is certainly 'exclusive', applying as it does exclusively to tonal masterpieces. And, in any case, the notion of tonality constituted by anything but direct reference to a single fundamental – tonality constituted 'by more complicated connections' – was inconceivable to Schenker. Least conceivable of all would be what Schoenberg, in the same passage, supposes might be 'the tonality of a twelve-tone series'. Such is the irrelevance of the authentic Schenkerian theory of tonality to late-tonal and post-tonal music that its shortcomings in this respect are barely worth discussion. It was neither designed to apply to, nor foreseen as adaptable to, the most seminal music of the early twentieth century. Admittedly, Schenker himself considered the very inapplicability of his theory of musical coherence to be an indication of musical nonsense in the unfortunate targets of his negative analyses (see p. 40 above), but this has little bearing on the history of analysis (and, as far as analytical practice is concerned, this is a pointed warning about the danger of taking the past as a basis for evaluating the present and future). As a result of Schenker's creative myopia and Schoenberg's distinctly biased theoretical scrutiny of Viennese Classical music (the bias being towards the reading of Classical music heavily conditioned by his compositional preoccupations), the potential great debate between Schenker and Schoenberg never took place, though historians and theorists have tried to discern it (see Dahlhaus, 1974; Dunsby, 1977; Simms, 1977).

Nevertheless, both the subsequent history of Schenkerian analysis and the actual self-awareness of Schoenberg have proved that there was a common ground, a unity of aesthetic response to the legacy of tonal masterpieces. This is evident even in the two men's slogans, their encapsulations of position and purpose, which are not to be underestimated. Schenker inscribed *Free Composition* with the aphorism: 'always the same, but not in the same way' (*semper idem, sed non eodem modo*). Thus, the laws of organic coherence are recognizable in the most heterogeneous presentations. Schoenberg believed that: one uses the row; otherwise, one composes as before. Schenker recognized continuity of tonal coherence, and Schoenberg recognized continuity of 'musical logic' (see below, pp. 76–7). For Schoenberg, musical logic meant the 'laws' of how musical ideas are connected, by repetition, variation and contrast. In post-Schenkerian analysis of late- and post-tonal music, the focus is similarly on musical connectedness: on structural prolongation regardless of whether a consonant contrapuntal fundamental structure is prolonged, or some more complicated background, and on progression at distinct hierarchical levels regardless of whether an underlying progression is more 'consonant' than its diminution. In this sense, post-Schenkerians have united with Schoenberg's desire to interpret post-tonal music as a development of tonal music. And they have therefore, like analysts of thematic unity, closed down many options on what seems to be effectively analysable: the more features a piece of twentieth-century music appears to have in common with the traditional repertoire, the more amenable it seems to analysis from this point of view.

The ground for post-tonal voice-leading analysis was prepared by Adele Katz's *Challenge to Musical Tradition* (1945) and Felix Salzer's *Structural Hearing* (1952), both major contributions to the development of analytical awareness in a century when the kind of music Schenker valued was barely being written.

Because Katz's work has a consistent critical orientation that is ultimately pessimistic about the relevance of old analytical precepts to new music, it was swept aside by enthusiasm for Salzer's more liberal and optimistic approach. Salzer's neo-Schenkerian method seemed to claim freedom, the freedom to contemplate backgrounds without descent or arpeggiation and with prolonged dissonant sonorities, but in truth it may have sought licence, the licence to analyse 'dissonant' music without showing whether it is good or bad. Katz was far from this. Through detailed study of typical passages from Debussy, Stravinsky and Schoenberg, she tried to assess how far the tonal tradition, represented through Schenker's theory in J. S. Bach, C. P. E. Bach, Haydn, Beethoven and even Wagner, was being challenged in the early twentieth century. Specifically, her purpose was:

(1) to interpret that law [of unity represented by tonality] and show how it has functioned for over two hundred years; (2) to clarify the difference between its practical application and the theoretical explanation of its function; (3) to point out the various factors, both in the music and in the method of analysis, that have led to its decline; (4) to demonstrate various instances of mistaken identity, which contemporary composers cite as containing the germ plasms of the atonal and polytonal systems; and (5) to investigate these systems, to find the new concept of unity they express. [Katz, 1945: xxvii–xxviii]

Her achievement in the first four of these intentions was far from negligible. Penetrating technical analysis is tempered continuously by critical response – and responsibility. It is the preserve of few to be able to mould analysis into such comprehensive musical discourse, and it was never likely that such work, with no easily reproducible method, would become fashionable. Her last intention, however, was not fulfilled. As far as actually identifying a 'new concept of unity' for atonal and polytonal compositions is concerned, she made no significant progress beyond Schoenberg's simple faith that their harmonic coherence would, some day, be fully understood. Indeed, Katz continually comes up against the boundaries of 'stretched' Schenkerism and refers to the need for a new 'system' of analysis (see, for example, p. 293). She was to be proved right in principle, though in a way that would have seemed alien to her. Fortean set-structural theory, which is considered in Part III, was to place at the centre of many analysts' understanding of post-tonal composition, not just a new system, but a mode of analysis that is systematically distinct from hierarchical, voice-leading approaches, while retaining a distinction between 'explicit' motives and fundamental harmonic elements.

In *Structural Hearing*, Salzer concentrated mainly on tonal structure, interpreting Schenkerian teachings (Salzer was a pupil of Schenker and of another emigré Schenker pupil in America, Hans Weisse) both more fully and more systematically – as he regarded the result – in a way that offered the chance of extension to post-tonal music and to the pre-eighteenth-century repertoire. His harmonic classifications, with clearly defined chord-types such as embellishing, voice-leading and double-function chords, give a more ramified picture of harmonic function than is to be found in Schenker. But what is crucial in Salzer is the classification of structure itself in a new light, not through Schenker's unitary view of the contrapuntal–harmonic framework, but through balancing the elements of Schenker's view in a trio of structural types, harmonic, contrapuntal, and contrapuntal–harmonic. What is not only new but also radically distinct from Schenkerian theory is the second type, contrapuntal structure. By tracing the concept and application of the contrapuntal–structural chord (CS) we can lay bare the essence of Salzer's understanding of what structural hearing must mean for the mid-to-late twentieth-century musician.

Salzer unveils the idea of contrapuntal prolongation with simple, telling examples (7(a)–(c)). The arrows in all three cases in example 7 show passing motions, and the chords above them (VI in (a) and (b), V^6–IV^6–III^6 in (c)) are passing chords which serve to prolong

Ex.7

Ex.8

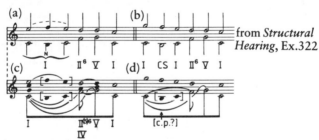

from *Structural Hearing*, Ex.322

from *Free Composition*, Fig.15^{5b}

from *Free Composition*, Fig.16^{5c}

the harmonic structure (I–II–V–I); 'passing' as they do from one structural chord to another in forms that are readily explicable in terms of tonal counterpoint, they are reckoned to be of 'contrapuntal origin'. For instance, Salzer notes that the dominant in bar 1 of (c) is different in status from the dominant in bar 3, the latter being a structural chord, the former being contrapuntal–prolonging [: 99]. Contrapuntal chords do not only prolong, however: 'Chords whose status is clearly contrapuntal may assume structural significance. If a contrapuntal chord is used to support a structural tone in the melody, it has the significance of a structural chord.' [: 161] As an abstract case, Salzer provides example 8(a) and (b). B in the bass supports a diminution, the upper neighbouring note F (example 8(a)), and the chord is therefore a prolonging neighbouring chord (marked N). In example 8(b), however, the bass B supports a note of the fundamental-line descent from $\hat{5}$. It is a contrapuntal prolongation of the bass (a lower neighbouring note to the C) but supports structural progression in the upper part – so it is a CS chord. (Examples 8(c) and (d) show how Schenker might have analysed these two examples without making the distinction Salzer identifies between the second chords in either case.) Example 9 is a real, more elaborate, and self-explanatory example of CS chords connecting tonic and dominant: note that Salzer interprets the second CS scale-degree IV as supporting a $^6_4$ rather than the inessential $^5_3$ (E and C over A), which another analyst might hear as lending a subdominant function to the last downbeat.

Ex.9 Vaughan Williams: Symphony No.5

From this firm basis in tonal theory, Salzer takes the first momentous step in a new definition of what can constitute tonal structure:

Just as harmonic progressions may serve in a prolonging or structural capacity, so also have contrapuntal progressions the inherent possibility of fulfilling either function . . . the literature, especially of the last decades, proves conclusively that contrapuntal progressions in regard to larger organisms can be key-defining and capable of assuming structural significance . . . It will hardly surprise us that contrapuntal structures mostly make use of motions around a chord to define a tonality. Whereas a harmonic structure permits the motion within a framework-making I–V–I progression with its space-outlining and -filling possibilities, the elimination of the harmonic principle quite naturally brought about the increased use of neighbour and embellishing chords as chords of structure. [: 204]

Example 10 is extracted from Salzer's analysis of the opening of Prokofiev's Piano Sonata No. 8. Chord 'X', though a mediant that could proceed in a harmonic-structural progression (III$^\#$–V), in fact moves down in octaves with the structural, stepwise descent to the tonic in the upper part. The sense in which 'X' can be said to be of 'contrapuntal origin' is dependent on three factors: (1) it is not part of a regular underlying harmonic progression via bass arpeggiation; (2) it does however support a note of the fundamental line; and (3) it supports it consonantly and proceeds to consonant support of the next fundamental-line note. Significantly, Salzer has analysed here a passage of tonal prolongation in which there is no structural dominant at level (b). Chord 'Y', also a CS chord, is not interpreted as a second-inversion dominant ninth as, technically, it might have been; Salzer considers that the structural framework is entirely contrapuntal [: 204–5].

The final step in Salzer's development of a theory of contrapuntal structure is the abandonment of fundamental-line descent as a criterion of tonal coherence. This is exemplified in his analysis of Debussy's *Bruyères* [: example 478], the background of which is formed by triads on A flat, B flat and A flat. The second triad is marked CS in the bass, but the structural upper-line note it supports is a neighbouring note (E flat–F–E flat) and not part of a descent. Salzer gives two other full hierarchical analyses to confirm the new interpretation of the concept of structural background: Gesualdo's madrigal *Io pur respiro*, with the background of a 'Phrygian' descent (G–F–E) over a bass E prolonged by the lower neighbouring-note CS chord (E–D–E = I–CS–I); and the first

Ex.10 Prokofiev: Piano Sonata in Bb major, Op.84

movement of Bartók's Piano Concerto No. 3, with a more complex background where the upper part is a fifth above the base E-G-F sharp–E–D sharp–E=I–CS–CS–I–CS–I), which supports major triads only. It must be remembered that Salzer's aim is not to impose a theoretical or analytical concept, but to interpret the music. He stresses continually that relatively new music of high quality simply demands an explanation of this kind.

Towards the end of his inquiry, Salzer writes an important section on the 'significance and range of tonality' [: 226–32]. He concludes that, since an entire piece may express a harmonic progression, or a purely contrapuntal progression (which may prolong sonorities other than the triad), or a fusion of the two, then the 'ultimate definition of tonality' is that it is 'synonymous with chord prolongation' [: 232]. What is required for tonality to be discerned is that the pitch-structure of a piece be demonstrably coherent: 'To speak about colourful progressions without being able to explain their musical meaning seems tantamount to an admission of complete failure to understand the music's structure and significance.' [: 262] Salzer has certainly retained the Schenkerian process, the musical logic of prolongation understood (and explained) hierarchically. But the basic empirical element in Schenker's thought, the 'diatony' of the chord of nature, has been thrown to the winds of history. Salzer's conviction that 'on the basis of these principles, musical expression, modern in every sense, appears entirely possible' [: 282] renders his theory strictly non-Schenkerian, though the analytical practice rests crucially on Schenker's discoveries about linear and contrapuntal relationships. The issues raised by this initiative are followed further in Chapter 10. Ironically, Salzer's view of tonality was nowhere more clearly anticipated than in Schoenberg's *Theory of Harmony*. Salzer was the pioneer of analysis of the 'more complicated connections' by which a series of tones could be brought together.

6

The British Context: Tovey

The kind of analysis we would nowadays recognize as 'technical' has been in practice for more than two centuries. Yet it came to be regarded as a discipline apart from compositional theory only at the turn of this century. Around this time, the relationship between traditional analysis and compositional theory ceased to be significantly reflexive. Analysis became the technical or systematic study, either of the kind of familiar tonal style few composers felt to be current any longer, or of new music that the wider public found profoundly hard to understand, and the challenges of which seemed to focus on the question of whether tonal comprehensibility was present at all. As in the early seventeenth and mid-eighteenth centuries, a radical change in musical taste, leading to a divided musical culture that supported the tension of different 'languages', spawned a climate favourable to intense theoretical activity.

The sense of urgency was impelled by very different motives in the minds of the leading thinkers in musical commentary. Both Donald Tovey (1875–1940) and his approximate contemporary, Schenker, were intent on explanation of what Tovey called the 'main stream' in music, which had ended with Brahms. They were not addressing the same interest groups: Tovey wrote for the ordinary listener; Schenker for the gifted, expert musician. Schoenberg's motivation was hardly to be compared with that of either contemporary, and he was living if largely unacknowledged proof that the mainstream of Viennese music continued far beyond the vision of the tonalists. Not surprisingly, Schoenberg understood and analysed the tonal repertoire differently. Yet all these viewpoints were rooted in tradition. Schoenberg had more to explain, and his theories could not logically be as specific about tonal music as are theories devoted only to that repertoire. (This is discussed in relation to Schoenberg's work on 'The Musical Idea', see pp. 74–6). In aiming to be relevant to the musical present, however, Schoenberg could claim to make worthwhile use of the common German tradition.

Such trends, of consolidation and synthesis, were in contrast to another strand of musical thought. Inevitably, there were musicians who were intent on the theoretical exploration, if not explanation, of new music with little reference to the past. Ironically, one can regard these less seminal figures as the most direct heirs of the eighteenth- and nineteenth-century analysts who formed the discipline as a reflection of compositional theory (a role for analysis with which Schoenberg and Schenker were also much preoccupied). They were the forebears – notably Bernhard Ziehn (1845–1912) and Josef Hauer (1883–1959) – of later composer–theorists; in Europe, for instance, Messiaen, Xenakis and Boulez; in America, Carter and Babbitt.

By the early twentieth century, Classical and Romantic music seemed to have been thoroughly assimilated in theory, as had the very mechanisms of common-practice major–minor tonality. English readers had available, for example, the late nineteenth-century writings of Ebenezer Prout, reflections – though not strictly derivative, and effective as simple teaching manuals – of the relatively comprehensive coverage of tonal music and tonal musical materials to be found in Hugo Riemann's half-century of publishing from 1873. The high point of codification, however, coincided with the revolution in compositional style. Studies of form by Macpherson (1908; see Macpherson, 1930) and Leichtentritt (1911; see Leichtentritt, 1951) were, indeed, repositories of knowledge so standard that they are still used as textbooks, as is Schoenberg's *Theory of Harmony* (1911).

Allen Forte describes this period as follows:

At the onset of the century there was little new musical theory in the sense of systematic approaches to general problems of musical structure. Instead theory was generally only a classroom discipline, and theory textbooks were usually pastiches of nineteenth-century writings by A. B. Marx, Bellermann, Sechter, Reicha, Cherubini and others. The subjects included harmony stemming from Rameau, species counterpoint stemming from Fux, fugue, and eighteenth- and nineteenth-century forms. [Forte, 1974: 754]

Although it would be hard to overestimate the implicit dependence of Tovey and Schoenberg on inherited theoretical concepts and practices, they both made a virtue of conservatism, tacitly exploiting received wisdom in the service of fresh critical perception. In

Schoenberg's case, the wake of his restless creative involvement with German music has washed the banks of musical onlookers only pedagogically and vicariously (excepting *Style and Idea* of 1950, which began to represent the true scope of Schoenberg's writings only in the 1975 revision). Tovey, however, made a direct assault on the musical public through a 'populist critical dogma' [Kerman, 1977: 175], in programme notes, lectures, dictionary entries, essays, articles and books. In Britain, his *Companion to 'The Art of Fugue'* (1931), *Essays in Musical Analysis* (1935–9) and *Companion to Beethoven's Pianoforte Sonatas* (1948) became standards of what the business of technical criticism should be – while Schoenberg's teachings were practically unknown outside continental Europe (though his influence spread erratically through America from the late 1930s) and Schenker's were known only to a small circle in Germany and Austria. The lack of interaction between German and English thinking was not, in essence, a linguistic, geographical or political matter. It was a question of temperament. Tovey came from *das Land ohne Musik*, where, as he complained, 'a person of general culture is a person who knows nothing about music and cannot abide musical jargon' [Tovey, 1949: 134]. In context, it was a radical option for him to bring a modest technical element to criticism, lending it relatively more professional and intellectual credibility. But what could thus seem to merit the name 'analysis' was a far cry from that activity as understood within the German discipline of *Musikwissenschaft*. Such few contemporaneous pioneers of rigorous analysis in Britain as Edwin Evans senior and C. F. Abdy Williams had no chance of popular appeal, and their professional market was miniscule in times when the concept of musical pedagogy and research had little place in tertiary education.

Both, in different ways, pursued extremes well beyond the boundaries of Tovey's area of activity, and both produced the kind of work that is, from the Toveyan viewpoint, a hindrance rather than a help to general musical understanding. Williams was primarily concerned with the theory of composition, especially rhythm:

Harmony and Counterpoint have long been recognized as branches of the science of composition, and students are familiar with their technical terms, and with rules which are the result of generations of observation and experience. Rhythm, an equally important element in modern music, has not yet taken its place as a theoretical study . . . A few rules have been deduced from observation of the works of the best composers, and it is hoped that this little introduction may be useful to those wishing to commence the study of the art of composing songs. [Williams, 1925: preface]

In *The Rhythm of Modern Music* (1909) he did indeed anticipate many of Schoenberg's analytical observations in 'Brahms the Progressive' [Schoenberg, 1975: 398–441]; this was technical study for the specialist. Similarly, Evans took what he considered to be a scientific approach – though analytical, with no claims in respect to compositional theory – in response to the impressionistic criticism he deplored:

Such excursions have . . . been made at the fancy of authors and have consequently little value for the student who, being thoroughly determined to possess an accurate knowledge of these creations, requires an account of them so exhaustive as to comprise everything he can reasonably desire to know. To supply this nothing can be effective but analysis reaching to the rhythmical significance of every bar; accounting for all material, whether subjects or intermediate motives; laying bare all formal proportions and developments; and fully describing all contrasts and characteristic features. [Evans, 1935: ix]

His exhaustive account of nearly all of Brahms's music follows a consistent plan. Each work is treated to a concise description through preliminary notes ('The object of this is to exclude from the articles under movement headings . . . everything which is not strictly technical comment' [: p. x]); a complete rhythmic chart listing 'portion' (the overall formal functions), 'material' (thematic and motivic classification), number of bars of each phrase and their articulation ($8 = 2 \times 4$, $19 = 2 \times 8 + 3$, etc.); quotation of the 'subjects' or themes corresponding with the rhythmic chart; and finally an 'epitome' or outline of each movement, which shows the main formal divisions and numbers of bars. As one reviewer noted, 'There is a reaction today against detailed analysis of music: it is called "dissection" (the word being used in a disparaging sense)' [Evans, 1936: 803]; and Tovey was seen as the musician who held out some hope of giving a meaning and use, a sense of explanation, to technical description.

Tovey's character as a musician was decidedly reactionary. Even in the British musical establishment he was criticized for his deafness to new music. Intellectually, he indulged in the typical philosophical promiscuity of the Victorian man of letters, which did not, however, extend to post-Kantian European ideas: he was untouched by the fever of literary and philosophical radicalism that gripped late nineteenth- and early twentieth-century Europe – of which no continental musician could be unaware, and few wanted to be. But his knowledge of European music up to Wagner and Brahms was profound, as was his desire to see it valued and understood. Like many fine musicians with only minor creative talent but a restless intellect, he was impatient with academic musical writings excepting his own: he indulged often in shadow-boxing with the generation before, whose unmusical approach he deplored (as is noted in Keller, 1956: 49). The most telling legacies of his critical essays are summaries of form and style, which have, in many cases, become everyday assumptions in tonal analysis. In Britain, it was Tovey who shifted attention away from a doggedly thematic view of sonata form. He often wrote of first and second 'groups' rather than 'subjects' or themes. A Toveyan analysis was integrally, at its best, an analysis of tonal relationships.

The essay 'Tonality in Schubert' represents this aspect of his work at its most concentrated. 'Tonality, or the harmonic perspective of music,' he begins, 'is a subject which most writers avoid', and 'it is high time that the facts of classical tonality were properly tabulated' [Tovey, 1949: 134]. We must note the ignorance of which Tovey was certainly guilty. Even when he confesses to being 'not a great reader of textbooks' which 'have enormously improved since 1890' [: 136], it is probably a reference only to the literature in English, not to Schenker's or Schoenberg's books on harmony. Of tonal 'facts', the most significant for placing Tovey in the history of analysis is his equation of tonality and form, which merits some scrutiny.

The notion that form is inherently tonal (that without tonality music must be amorphous) is, of course, valid only as a personal statement of non-interest in pre- and post-tonal music. Tovey held this notion implicitly, but did not theorize about it. As an educated specialist, he could be frank about what he did and did not value without needing to prove that the latter was of no absolute value at all. The notion that tonality is inherently formal, however, is a theoretical premise of great consequence for analytical theory, and Tovey adopted this premise consistently:

Probably the most fundamental rule for operations in large-scale tonality is that key-relation is a function of form. It is no use citing passages from the course of a wandering development to prove that a composer regards a key as related to his tonic: the function of development is contrast, not tonic relation. The choice of a key for the slow movement of a sonata, or for the trio of a scherzo, or for the second group (miscalled 'second subject') of a first movement, implies key-relation; but episodes and purple patches in these divisions must be referred to the key of the division, not to that of the whole. [: 145]

Now, the problem with formal, sectional analysis independent of any hierarchical considerations is easy to identify. One cannot account by means of formal analysis for how sections are joined, for when and how in music formal divisions come to be understood as special boundaries. We must ask of any claim that certain stretches of music make 'episodes', 'patches' or 'divisions', when? from their first notes? and throughout? and consistently to the end? In directly equating tonal with formal relationships, Tovey is simply attaching these problems of analytical theory to a wider field of musical structure. And for all his apparent concern with the flow of musical time, he offers in fact no theory substantial enough even to begin to address such problems. Significantly, it does not strike him as strange that the articulation of form and of keys should of necessity coincide, in an art so fundamentally based on the inter-play within simultaneous but non-coincident domains (in texture, in counterpoint, etc.).

Tovey was not unaware of the puzzles to be explained. In 'Musical Form and Matter' he observes that explaining tonality to the non-musician is not like the problem of explaining red to the colour-blind, but like that of describing any sensation to anyone [: 167]. And there are imaginative strokes in his technical descriptions of tonal structure – example 11 for instance, where rhythmic notation is used to give hierarchical meaning to a tonal reduction (which is, however, meaningless from a Schenkerian point of view in its arbitrary voice-leading). Yet his theoretical stance is so strongly maintained, usually showing an awareness in principle of the alternatives, that it would probably have withstood any amount of challenge in any case: in other words, it is probably more

Ex.11 Key relations in Schubert's String Quintet [first movement]

(adapted from Tovey: 'Tonality in Schubert', Ex.15)

important to remember how adamant than how narrow-minded Tovey was. He believed optimistically in this 'best of all possible worlds, since it is the only one that exists' [: 352]. The Victorian analyst was not given to speculation on a world that could be changed, least of all to doubting the existence and meaning of the facts he observed in it.

Yet doubt may well be cast on the meaning of his typical analytical exposition, a subject worth illustration because it illuminates why there was such interest, then as now, in thematic analysis (especially Schoenbergian) as an antidote to the Toveyan style of informal description. Tovey's essay on the finale of Brahms's Piano Quartet in C minor, Op. 60, provides telling examples:

The first theme is a long plaintive cantabile, with a flowing accompaniment that contains a very important figure:

A

I need not quote the transition, which is in a triplet rhythm that becomes a hail-storm accompaniment to the second subject [*sic*] which, itself completely new in character, foreshadows in its opening notes the extraordinary developments that are soon to be made from (*a*) by augmentation:

B

This subsides into a quiet cadence-theme in equal notes –

C

which dies away in two notes –

D

... (*a*) dies away in a chromatic scale and the violoncello introduces a new figure:

E   

[Tovey, 1944 : 212–13]

Ex.12   Brahms: Piano Quartet in C minor, Op.60

Example 12 suggests how deeply questionable is this analysis. In (b), both the dominant-to-mediant incipit, *x*, and the rhythmic motive *y* show Tovey's example B to be misleading: the 'second subject' cannot be analysed in terms of a single function (*a* having been augmented already in *y*). It is evident from (c) that the equality of notes of the cadence-theme is not their most pertinent characteristic. The mere progression from quavers, example A, to crotchets, example B (actually set as quavers in the music), to minims here

suggests a quadruple augmentation ($\downarrow = 4 \times \downarrow$): the very rhythmic inequality of the melodic pattern in these equal notes, expressing
a syncopation ($\circ$ | $\circ$ | $\circ$ | $\circ$), makes the rhythmic progression
musically pertinent as a derivation from z in (a) ($\downarrow \downarrow$ $\downarrow$). System (d)
shows how Tovey's simple initial reading of a theme, *b*, over a
motive, *a*, fails to express why *a* is 'a very important figure'. He
intends to show that *a* will indeed become important, but such
retrospective analysis flouts the reasonable demand for attention to
musical time, and is quite unnecessary. The crucial analytical
question in such a case is: *when* is *a* 'very important'? Later, Tovey
implies, thus failing to observe the nature of its significance in the
first place. Finally, (e) shows the quadruple augmentation of *w*: for
Tovey to write that example E is a 'new figure' is, by any normal
standards, wrong.

While not all of Tovey's detailed analysis suffers from this degree
of inaccuracy, such a passage is not untypical. Indeed, the degree to
which apologists for Tovey will accept such analytical standards
suggests that they are applying non-analytical criteria. Kerman, for
example, explains away analytical deficiencies thus:

> To object that he was insufficiently sensitive to thematic relationships, to
> phraseology on larger levels, to the force of register and tone colour
> is . . . beside the main point. It is the constant link with musical effect that
> distinguishes Tovey's analytical method, not the details of the analysis
> itself. [Kerman, 1977: 181]

True, no historian of analytical theory would envy Kerman his
chosen task of accounting for Tovey's influence and prestige; it
leads all too easily to a condemnation of the audience that approves
of such material – hardly conceivable in the scholarly literature in
other arts and humanities subjects. Yet Kerman also notes that
many of the unfortunately titled *Essays in Musical Analysis* 'do not
carry forward analysis with any kind of rigour' [: 179] and he is
evidently familiar with appropriate criteria. That Tovey 'deals with
the foreground of music – and deals with it very well' [: 181], if
'well' means with reasonably consistent accuracy of observation
about simple musical relationships, could be disproved only by
detailed review of the *Essays* and similar writings along the lines
given in the above sample.

None of this is to deny Tovey's influence as a critic and historian
of tonal music in the British mould. He established much of the
protocol for discussion of form and style. When Charles Rosen

observes how, in twentieth-century musical thought, 'the primacy of the tonal over the thematic structure is accepted, along with the importance of periodic phrasing in eighteenth-century form' [Rosen, 1972: 32], he is registering Tovey's influence as much as Schenker's and Schoenberg's. Indeed, in *The Classical Style* Rosen refers to observations by Tovey, often sweeping generalities about the style, more than twenty times. Kerman, himself a critic of wide influence, claims that Tovey 'must still be the most widely read music critic in English-speaking countries' [Kerman, 1977: 171]. Bent considers that Tovey has been 'the strongest influence on British analytical and critical thinking', through the method of bar-by-bar analysis that was 'a blend of the hermeneutic and the formalistic which implicitly stated that there are things in music beyond explanation' [*New Grove*, 'Analysis', vol. 1: 364].

It would be futile too to challenge the significance of Tovey principally on the grounds of inaccuracy (as the kind of detailed review mentioned above might well do). What is of most interest to the student of analysis is the cause of such inaccuracy, which may well lead us to sympathize with Kerman's view that it is a trivial symptom. How justified are we, after all, in speaking of 'accuracy' with such an interpretative and controversial area of inquiry as music analysis? How useful is it to be able to claim, as above, that Tovey is plainly wrong, when what is plain is a failure to observe, rather than a systematic error in whatever has in fact been observed? In face of such questions, it becomes clear that Tovey, in his intellectual and musical isolation, and with his lack of coherent method (of a method that the student can use with some confidence that the result would be recognized as a Toveyan analysis) provides a good lesson in the nature of analytical theory if not a good model for analytical practice. Analysis has often been called a comparative discipline, but let us use a less sweet, a more clinical term in calling it relativistic. It is purely by appeal to relativism that the above sample criticizing Tovey's technique can seem purposeful: the critique rests on agreement that further information about a particular analytical point is actually an *addition* to that point. And even where it is said that Tovey is 'wrong', relativism is in play, through the assumption that one point can effectively contradict another. Yet for Tovey to observe that an idea is 'new' and another analyst to show that it is 'derived' merely reflects the rich implication of any musical idea. What is really misleading, then, in Tovey's critical vocabulary, and what is the cause of his symptomatic inaccuracy, is his use of absolute terms. Without a systematic set of relations constantly held in play (such as, to take a simple case, Schoenberg's continuum of repetition–variation–development–contrast) virtually any description takes on a critical quality. It is taken to be absolute, and inevitably misrepresentative of whatever aspect of the music has not, at that moment, been brought into consideration. While Schoenberg and Schenker both laboured to find comprehensive theories where the relative meaning of any analytical observation would be implied in the observation (thus making it not so much 'true' as evidently and comprehensibly meaningful), Tovey attended instead, in comparison with his greatest contemporaries in Europe, to matters of critical decorum.

The student of analysis will consider these matters deeply. They are, of course, central issues in approaching the study of music with the intellectual responsibility that is proper to it, as to any other serious inquiry. But, more pragmatically, they also colour the trends of analysis in this century, trends that can be seen as quite incompatible, and that have been pursued in a large literature on which it is understandably hard for any student of analysis in general to be a general specialist. If the trends in analysis are seen as incompatible, there is a natural tendency to argue strongly in favour of a 'correct' approach (though, as we shall see in Part IV, one may try to avoid a normative position of that kind). Certainly Schenkerians have done so, but this form of argument is equally evident in the work of the post-Toveyan analysts of form and style. Since the tonal musical style has come to have adopted a sense of ending as well as of having emerged from earlier musical 'language', there is all the more temptation to regard it as an historical 'fact' of which there should be a 'best' explanation. Tovey, Schenker, Hindemith (though without believing in the 'end' of tonal music) and, most recently, Meyer, have all offered such 'best' explanations, but Tovey alone offered no allegedly systematic analytical theory to support the contention. This is why British research was for so long starved – it starved itself – of analytical confidence. It had a favoured model in Tovey, but not the means to develop that model since there was no system on which to build. An account of a tonal piece that describes 'modulations' can never amount to more than self-evident description – unless there is a theory of modulation, the German *Modulationslehre*, which is only one step away from the truly effective Schoenbergian and Schenkerian concepts of monotonality, and of which Tovey's work of the 'Tonality in Schubert' kind is but a small, unreliable part. Similarly, an account of thematic relationships in terms of unity and contrast can describe only a perceived 'tension' of varying degrees: without a theory of what varieties of tension are the result of what kinds of thematic variation, there is a constant, logical flaw at work; contrast may be asserted when in fact there has been a failure to observe unity (as in the Brahms example above), but an observed unity is unlikely to be proved 'wrong' because some overriding contrast has been missed.

Tovey, like later analysts determined to explain how music is perceived, placed as much emphasis on the non-perceived pattern (contrast) as on the pattern (unity). Yet neither non-hierarchical unity nor the complete absence of unity can be particularly interesting for the music analyst, since music (atonal no less than tonal) simply does not ever seem to connote absolute unity or its logical opposite. Ironically, the school of thought (from Tovey to Rosen) that accuses the other of a failing in so-called 'musicality itself' takes a purely logical premiss.

In summary, we can thematize analytical theory on two axes that swing between on the one hand what is systematic and what is wilful and on the other hand what takes a logical premiss and what takes a metaphorical premiss. Tovey, the grand old man of British analytical history, cannot be accused of aiming for a systematic theory of tonal music, but he did pursue with some tenacity logical concepts to try to explain music to the masses. What of the analyst who decries the notion of 'system' in any aspect of music theory, but who tries to explain a specifically 'musical logic'? This was Schoenberg's role in the early twentieth century. It began, superficially understood, as a contentious example of avant-garde propaganda:

When I say: tonality is no natural law of music, eternally valid – then it is plain for everyone to see how the theorists spring up in indignation to cast their veto against my integrity . . . To hell with all these theories, if they always serve only to block the evolution of art and if their positive achievement consists in nothing more than helping those who will compose badly anyway to learn it quickly. [Schoenberg, 1978: 9]

But the depth of Schoenberg's thinking has gradually come to be realized, still not fully perhaps, though the analyst should bear in mind that, whereas the creative musician and the historian can choose how fully or distantly to take cognizance of Schenker, the imprint of Schoenberg is wellnigh unavoidable.

7

Schoenberg and Musical Logic

Considering Schoenberg's ascendant position in theory and analysis in the twentieth century, and considering the emphasis in his aesthetic legacy on continuity in the Viennese tradition, it may seem misrepresentative to discuss his contribution under the general rubric of 'tonal analysis'. We must weigh against these misgivings the fact that the modern understanding of tonal music is, almost without fail, coloured by Schoenberg's understanding of Viennese Classical music, transmitted in texts and through teachings that may be interpreted as vicarious Schoenbergian analytical texts (see, for example, Frisch, 1984; Leibowitz, 1975; Rufer, 1961). Further, the Nazification of Germany happened to throw up an important effect in analytical theory. Whereas Tovey lived in a comfortable and victorious world where the opportunity presented itself to enlighten the general musical public, Schoenberg, driven out of Europe to the friendly but alien American culture, turned a potentially humilating necessity, of teaching the 'naive student', into the humble exercise of a great musician explaining tonal music to the un-initiated (or explaining all they could hope to understand in the early stages of tuition). This resulted in various pedagogical works, of which two, *Structural Functions of Harmony* and *Fundamentals of Musical Composition*, are of significance to analytical theory.

Schoenberg was able to meet this necessity so effectively partly because he had been assembling a theory of music, characterized by the simplest possible explanations of the most general questions to be answered, since the 1920s. His working title for this study was 'The Musical Idea and the Logic, Technique and Art of its Present-ation', which has remained unpublished, partly because Schoenberg used it as a source for concepts and examples to be found scattered throughout his American pedagogical books and the essays in *Style and Idea*. His thinking centres on the desire to explain all the types and gradations of musically logical relationship that are the signs of 'continuity' (*Zusammenhang*). The techniques to which he refers, compositional techniques in principle, but in practice also the procedures that are the proper concern of the analyst, come under the general rubric of 'presentation' (*Darstellung*), the manipulation of the idea, or the musical figure or basic shape (*Gedanke, Gestalt, Grundgestalt*). The art of presentation is measured in terms of 'comprehensibility' (*Fasslichkeit*). It is, indeed, the concern with explaining how music is comprehended that marks out Schoenberg's work as an outstanding fusion of compositional and analytical discipline. No other musician of such genius has left a record of this kind, a detailed consideration of the reflexive relationship between the process of musical construction and response to the product. To see the flavour of this approach, we can usefully absorb some extracts from the section of Schoenberg's notes entitled 'Laws of Comprehensibility', dated 11 June 1934:

As a consequence of the difficulties music offers, the laws of comprehensibility must be grasped especially strictly and narrowly. Since music is (in the first place) a matter of hearing (and of reading only in the second place), and since its tempo determines the course of ideas and problems so that it is impossible to dally over an idea that has not been understood (as can, for example, the reader of a novel or the observer of a picture or sculpture), every idea must be presented so that the listener's capacity to grasp it is met. The following laws correspond to these difficulties:

I.   What is said once cannot be taken to be important.
II.   Main and subsidiary material must be very clearly distinguished by presentation.
III.   Main material must include a number of expositions of the idea to be developed.
IV.   Subsidiary ideas must be characterized as such in several ways . . .
VIII. The presentation of ideas rests on the laws of musical coherence. As a consequence of these everything in a rounded piece of music must be explicable as having its origin in, as being inferred from, or as being the development of a basic motive or at the least of a basic shape.
IX.   A piece as a whole will seem most comprehensible to the listener if, at every moment, or at many points, he has the feeling that a question is at issue to which he always knows the answer: 'How does that come to be here?' In older music this demand was met by many repetitions of smaller and larger sections (making every digression legitimate), mostly little altered . . .
XXI.   Among the most comprehensible forms is the 'Period'. For it repeats in the consequent almost the whole antecedent. The so-called 'Sentence'

is already a higher form of art, because it repeats in general the first figure, but then develops relatively new figures until it is over.*

Although this gives only a taste of Schoenberg's approach, certain strong trends emerge. First and foremost – at least for the student of analysis – Schoenberg conducts his inquiry without explicit reference to tonality. This does not mean that some arbitrary theoretical aspect of music is in play: it is not, for instance, a strictly thematic inquiry, since the forms of connection between ideas are a function of all musical variables – a 'basic motive' may be developed rhythmically, harmonically, in tempo or texture, and so on. Rarely is Schoenberg explicit about the tonal materials in question, but when he is, there is no doubt about the generalized level at which he is trying to construct his theory. For example, in a passage on 'The Form-building Capacities of the Scale and of Broken Chords' we read that:

If a composition is built from a series of simple repetitions or, better, of sequences, there will always be a rising or falling scale which regulates the progression of the main tones (or whatever conspicuous points).

It is obvious why such a progression has a convincing and logical effect: because the succession of tones works according to a clear, comprehensible rule. Accordingly, other such rules may be tried. For example, a series of thirds (minor or major, or alternating); a series of fourths or fifths; a series which controls the whole piece, that is, a twelve-note basic shape and its three permutations – or also, though, the main theme; the main shape, or its intervals, etc. [24 June 1934]

On the other hand, we can see how far Schoenberg is prepared to go in specific inquiries in examining the most minute aspects of musical logic, on the assumption of what might be called extended tonal hearing. He uses themes from the First Chamber Symphony to illustrate specific mechanisms of contrast and unity – the obligatory transpositional relationships of tonal forms, compensation for displaced transposition by means of pitch repetition, and the interplay of competing harmonic regions:

The discussions of music theorists designate certain formal elements as contrasts, e.g. the second subject, and explain them in terms of the Kapellmeister music [they analyse]: as unconnected, in so far as that is ever possible in music.

*This quotation and the following two are translated from a body of texts by Schoenberg customarily grouped under the title 'Der musikalische Gedanke', which is unpublished and the originals of which are held in the Archives of the Arnold Schoenberg Institute in Los Angeles. For further information see Goehr, 1977.

[*] indecipherable annotation, which may indicate 'transposition' or 'C♯ major'

This example shows convincingly that a logical brain simply cannot write something independent, even when quite unaware of its sense, and follows only instinct . . . I already discovered some time ago the connection, of which I was unaware when composing, by which this theme is joined to the main theme. But now the second subject is in A major. But if figure A1 expresses E major, A2 expresses G sharp major. So the second subject should begin like B1. Here natural logic is shown in that this C sharp, which is not achieved here by the upbeat figure [first bar of second subject], appears in the course of the theme no less than 5 times [N.B. Schoenberg's crosses on the above example], but [natural logic is also shown in that] the C in the next three notes, like the three upbeat notes to C sharp, fell into G minor , just as figure B is G-minorish, though really it must

represent A major. This is the way continuity can appear in contrasts. [24 August 1934]*

We could wish for no clearer or more authoritative indication (Schoenberg's scrappy, unrevised prose aside) of the Schoenbergian notion of musical logic.

Just as, in his generalized theory, Schoenberg avoided factors to

*It should be noted what an important document this analysis is for an appraisal of Schoenberg's concept of tonicity. Theorists have been extremely reluctant to take seriously the idea that pitch-repetition should be understood as a structural process, even though Schoenberg's explanations of his sense of twelve-note harmony suggest time and again that this process should be taken literally. The reluctance derives from our lack of understanding about how pitch-repetition – the mere statistical aggregate of pitch-class presence in a tonal piece – may be relevant to pre-twelve-note music. See Dunsby, 1982.

do with specific tonal usage, so in his specific explanation of major–minor tonality he devised an elaborate general picture of harmonic relation, a rich source of analytical guidance on the relativities of tonal flux. This explanation, set out in *Structural Functions of Harmony*, hinges on the concept of regions, which 'is a logical consequence of the principle ōf *monotonality*. According to this principle, every digression from the tonic is considered to be still within the tonality, whether directly or indirectly, closely or remotely related. In order words, there is only *one tonality* in a piece, and every segment formerly considered as another tonality is only a region, a harmonic contrast within that tonality.' [: 19] Here, then, we see a bridge – one that had been anticipated in Weber's attempt to establish a scheme of relationships between keys (see Weber, 1846) – between Toveyan multi-tonality, as it may be called, and Schenkerian structural tonality. Schoenberg's desire for systematic explanation (or a 'system of presentation') made the traditional theory of modulation quite unacceptable, analytically ineffective, and, in his view, unrepresentative of the composer's principles of construction. He did not, however, go so far as to share Schenker's view that the expression of diatonic tonality is the actual source of all meaning in music, the coherence on which every aspect of musical structure depends.

The Chart of Regions Schoenberg produces shows the forces of attraction between harmonies classified, not fundamentally in terms of the circle of fifths, but on a common-note principle. There are five categories of connectedness, direct and close, indirect but close, indirect, indirect and remote, and distant. The justification for direct and close relationships (subdominant, dominant, submediant minor and tonic minor, in the major mode) is that the regions have either five or six notes in common with the tonic. (Schoenberg is concerned with tonal regions, rather than common-note relationships between triads, which select only three notes from the scale of a region.) Indirect relationships (the third category) have a negligible number of notes in common with the tonic (in major, six regions come into this category: the flat mediant minor, flat submediant minor, mediant major's mediant major – in C, G sharp – mediant major's mediant minor, submediant major's flat submediant minor, and submediant minor's flat submediant minor). And here Schoenberg makes the important point that 'structurally' the rather distant regions can arise either through flat- *or* sharp-side movement away from the tonic. This would seem to be opposed to the

Schenkerian view of harmonic relatedness as a function of tonic–dominant attraction. But here we have to bear in mind Schoenberg's distinction between a system of relationships and the system of their presentation. Presentationally (and structurally), progressions are not all of equal effect: there are three categories, ascending (by a fourth or a sixth), descending (by a fourth or a sixth) and super-strong (stepwise root progressions up or down).

Without going into the kinds of discussion that would be more appropriate to a study of harmonic theory, it can at least be said that Schoenberg provides (in a detailed account of tonal harmony of which this summary presents only the bare starting points) a sensitive interpretation of the kind of harmonic reasoning familiar in German theory since Gottfried Weber. The many clear readings of excerpts from a wide repertory in *Structural Functions of Harmony* repay close study. There is, nevertheless, a conspicuous weakness, or at least under-emphasis, in the analytical results. It is the inevitable consequence of Schoenberg's unsophisticated approach to voice-leading (though, as we have learned in the discussion of Schenker, this makes *Structural Functions of Harmony* a genuine part of the theory of harmony in the Schenkerian sense, appropriately restricted to an abstracted and consistent aspect of musical structure). Not only is his analytical classification designed to examine, in the true Rameauist tradition so scorned, though well used, by Schenker, the flow of root progressions – a succession of vertical slices through the music – but it takes a blunt symbolic approach to the presence of 'substitute' notes, which 'can be introduced either quasi-diatonically or chromatically' [: 18]. Example 13, Schoenberg's harmonic analysis of an extract from Schubert's 'Der Wegweiser' (example 98 in *Structural Functions of Harmony*; cf. Aldwell, 1979: 220–1), illustrates this in brief.

Out of ten root chords identified between the first tonic and the first dominant, no less than seven are cancelled, that is, qualified, by means of substitute notes. But evidently the substitutes neither arise nor function structurally in similar ways, especially in the sense that some cancellations represent substituted roots (and implied roots), some only substituted third and fifth degrees. This produces a rough picture indeed of the linear connections. For example, whereas the first $\mathrm{I\!I}$ is a neighbouring chord prolonging the tonic, the next $\mathrm{I\!I}$ is without doubt a passing chord and the third $\mathrm{I\!I}$ a structural chord. Even if we accept that these three points in the music carry a supertonic harmonic implication, there is, from a Schenkerian point

Ex.13 Schubert: 'Der Wegweiser', D.911/20 (*Winterreise*)

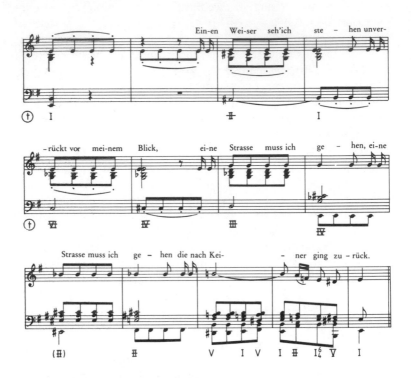

of view, only one effective supertonic chord functioning as part of an ascending or 'strong' progression. The virtue, however, of this blunt approach is that Schoenberg can consider, under the same system, both the most rudimentary kinds of harmonic relation and manifestations of 'extended tonality', in the chapter in which this Schubert example appears. Ultimately, he can begin to explain genuine 'suspended tonality' in this way. His account of his own song 'Lockung', Op. 6, No. 7, begins with a telling analytical extension of his principle of monotonality. He first referred to this music in the *Theory of Harmony* noting how it 'expresses an E flat major tonality without once in the course of the piece giving an E flat major triad in such a way that one could regard it as a pure tonic' [Schoenberg, 1978: 383]. By the time of *Structural Functions of Harmony* Schoenberg seems to have come to a more radical view, or to have assimilated the style of suspended tonality more easily in an analytical concept, implying that monotonality could

not adequately capture the full implication: even though there is a
key signature, the music must be explained in terms of the fusion of
keys a third apart, tonic and submediant minor. Example 14 is
extracted from example 122 in *Structural Functions of Harmony*.

Ex.14 Schoenberg: 'Lockung', Op.6/7

Fundamentals of Musical Composition treats of much wider
aspects of musical construction than *Structural Functions of
Harmony* and can rightly be considered a textbook of thematic and
formal analysis. It deals with the construction of themes, and with
small and large forms (a concept Schenker considered quite mis-
guided, see p. 39). Perhaps its most significant contribution to
analytical technique is in its classifications of motivic manipulation
and of the internal structure of phrases. It is never entirely clear
how exhaustive Schoenberg considers this classification to be. For
instance, is the list of treatment and utilization of motives in
selected examples [Schoenberg, 1970b: 10], with its six types of
rhythmic change, six types of intervallic change, four types of
harmonic change and three types of melodic adaption, to be taken
as a thorough compositional and analytical guide? Schoenberg's
answer is revealing: 'Some of the methods which can be applied are
shown as systematiclly as is practicable' [: 9]. This may seem a
casual pedagogical comment, but we should take its implication as
literally as possible. Schoenberg is doubtful whether a 'thorough
guide' is conceivable (and offers, with characteristic expertise, just as
much as the student needs). There is no hint here of the Schenkerian

ideal of a complete key to the understanding of all aspects of musical structure. We have already seen how central to Schoenberg's thinking is the distinction between phrases based mainly on repetition and phrases based on development and contrast, yet once again his exposition of period-types and sentence-types is rich rather than exhaustive. As a repository of analytical method, it must be used to give the student a fund of experience based on observation, and a flexible analytical vocabulary – antecedent and consequent, melodic contour, liquidation and so on – as well as the stimulus to consider its relevance to post-tonal processes. Among many illustrations from the literature, Schoenberg intersperses specially composed pieces and extracts to provide models of construction and analysis, of which example 15 (an extract from example 122 in *Fundamentals of Musical Composition*) is a typical example. It is, incidentally, typical too of the very awkward, not to say unpleasant music Schoenberg often produces for this purpose, a kind of exercise that, as he confessed, he found extremely difficult to carry out divorced from the white heat of 'real' composition. The analysis of motive and of functional relationships attached in letters and brackets is a fair picture of the kinds of structural explanation Schoenberg thought were of use and demonstrably true of the music.

What is not present in this or any other writing by Schoenberg is a commensurably full account of the concepts 'basic shape' and 'developing variation': he used these terms extensively in (oral) teaching, but wrote relatively little about them. 'Basic shape' (*Grundgestalt*) is a source of much excitement to analysts and theorists who find it difficult to accept the sceptical, empirical approach that Schoenberg forced on to the theoretical and even philosophical pretensions of his generations of pupils. Many writers have misguidedly tried to find a Schenker-style 'key' to tonal structure and second Viennese post-tonal structure in these general ideas of Schoenberg. These have mostly been attempts, however, in a reactionary spirit, to try to trace the origin of Schoenberg's analytical inclinations in tonal music, often in Brahms – ironically enough in view of Schoenberg's compositional indebtedness above all to Mozart and Beethoven, and in view of the fact that in his 1933 essay 'Brahms the Progressive' (see Schoenberg, 1975) 'developing variation' is not an explicit concept.

One follower of this lead from Schoenberg does, however, merit attention because of his attempt to take the best, analytically, from Schoenberg and Schenker. In *Beyond Orpheus* (1979), David

Ex.15

c) Elaboration 3

Epstein set out to examine the consequences of a synthesis of what are, after they have been watered down, simple premisses. From Schoenberg, Epstein takes the assumption (which Schoenberg never fully demonstrated) that some underlying thematic or at least pitch-determinate entity lies behind the variety of a tonal piece. Despite speculation on just what Schoenberg meant by an 'idea' or a 'shape', it is clear from 'The Musical Idea' that Epstein's reading of Schoenberg's intentions is justifiable. The question for the analyst is not really to discover what was Schoenberg's concrete experience of these concepts, but to see how they can now be used in sensitive analytical practice; whether that practice is authentic is not the issue. The application of Schoenbergian guidance in such considerations by Epstein as that of Brahms's Second Symphony seems to confirm the value of the approach.* Epstein's use of Schenker is essentially limited to an informal adoption of the concept of prolongation.†

*However, the degree to which the results enlighten us only about the musical surface should not be underestimated. See, on the one hand, Schachter's deeper approach to some of the same music (Schachter, 1983), and, on the other, the essentially superficial investigation of Brahms in Frisch, 1984.

†Despite the evident virtues of Epstein's work, it has been criticized for its preliminary nature, where extensive concentrated analysis might have better justified his analytical claims. See, respectively, Dunsby, 1979, and Whittall, 1981a. See also Carpenter, 1983.

8

Revision and Reversion

Hindemith

Few analysts, or few of any influence, have aimed at the systematic
scope to be found in Schenker and Schoenberg. One such was
Hindemith, who may yet come to be regarded as a minor hero
of analytical theory, but a knowledge of whose work has been
restricted in America, where his music is relatively highly valued,
and even more restricted in Europe. His *The Craft of Musical
Composition* is as much an analytical work as any volume so
called. The theoretical part (Book 1) deals with the 'The Medium',
the overtone series, 'The Nature of the Building Stones', about
harmonic constituents, 'Harmony' (progression) and 'Melody'.
Hindemith aimed at a truly universal set of analytical principles (or,
at least, universal for Western music), and it is in this sense that he
may be thought to have revised the German theoretical tradition.
For instance, 'all chords that may be used in music must be covered
by our new system in a clear and easily understandable order'
[Hindemith, 1945: 95]; and he notes that there has never been a
definite melodic theory, even though there is no reason why one
should 'not be able to analyse melody, when it is possible to reduce
the incomparably more numerous and more ambiguous phenomena
of harmony to a comparatively small body of rules' [: 176]. Towards
the end, in his sample of analyses, Hindemith claims that 'the music of
all styles and periods may be analysed by the methods proposed in this
book' [: 202]. His premises include the derivation of two chord
categories depending on the presence or absence of the tritone as an
intervallic constituent, the derivation of values of root progression
from combination tones of the overtone series, and the derivation
of harmonic fluctuation in terms of a categorical increase and
decrease in tension. Much may be gleaned from example 16, the
beginning of his analysis of the first 44 bars of *Tristan* [: 210–11].

In the melodic analysis, D means passing note (*Durchgang*), N

Ex.16 Wagner: *Tristan und Isolde*, Prelude

an unprepared neighbouring note. 'Fluctuation' derives from Hindemith's chord groups, calculated by interval: I_2 refers to chords without the tritone or seconds or sevenths where the root lies above the bass note; II_{b2} refers to chords containing the tritone and major seconds or minor sevenths or both where the root lies above the bass note; and so on. V (in bar 10) is worth noting, an indeterminate chord-group comprising the augmented triad or added fourth chord (in the pitch-class set notation discussed in Part III, 0, 4, 8 and 0, 2, 7 trichords, 3–12 and 3–9). Degree-progression is calculated partly in relation to Hindemith's Series 1, 'the chromatically arranged twelve-tone series born of the tensions set up by the juxtaposition of vibrating units in the proportions of the simple numbers from 1–6' (: 53 – the notes of Series 1 are, in pitch-class notation, 0 7 5 9 4 3 8 2 10 1 11 6; see the table of Derivation of Tones, pp. 48–9, which represents 'the significant order in which the twelve tones of the chromatic scale . . . appear, in diminishing degree of relationship to the given tone', : 56). Hindemith draws attention to, for example, bar 9, where 'the d^1 of measure 8 has to be taken into account, and thus beneath the a^1 . . . there is a root, d^{1}' [: 214].

It must be stressed that the process of calculation and systematic derivation in Hindemith's theory makes a particular analysis hard to assimilate without close knowledge of his theoretical work, as explained economically enough in his two hundred pages of argument and exposition. The resulting picture shares consistency of method with Schoenberg's very different approach. Hindemith's analyses of extracts from Stravinsky's Piano Sonata, Schoenberg's Piano Piece, Op. 33a, and his own *Mathis der Maler* (following pp. 216, 217 and 220) are highly recommended as comparative studies.

Réti

Comprehensive though Hindemith's theory is with respect to harmony, it is concerned almost exclusively with the musical surface. In contrast, Rudolph Réti assumed the need for reduction in analysis and concentrated on the relationship between theme and structure. His aim was 'to lay bare a principle: to give a description, or at least a first outline, of *the thematic process in musical composition*' [Réti, 1962: 6]. Like Hindemith, Réti took little account of previous theory and, writing in 1950, he was frank about why: 'No real attempt has ever been made to comprehend in a systematic analysis the working of this most essential process of musical composition.' [: 3–4] And like Hindemith, he succeeded in gaining only limited influence with what he regarded as a novel and critical approach. Nevertheless, he publicized an area of inquiry that was taken up in significant contributions to the general understanding of tonal music, notably in the work of Rosen (who disavows Réti's own work), Keller and Walker. In Britain especially, analysis of theme and motive, underpinned by conventional formal and harmonic theory, has been the essence of what is understood by post-Toveyan 'analysis' in secondary and tertiary education.

Many readers will know that Réti's work has often been condemned for revealing no principles – it is widely adduced to epitomize the perils of lack of method. As far as the simple facts of thematic transformation are concerned, Réti could rightly claim that his empirical approach was the only possible one. There is no doubt that the categories of transformation he mentions are reasonable analytical premises: inversions, reversions, interversions, change of tempo, rhythm and accent, thinning and filling of thematic shapes, cutting of thematic parts, thematic contour and compression, change of harmony, pitch identity, and change of accidentals [: 68–105]. Equally, however, as with Schoenberg's guidelines in *Fundamentals of Musical Composition*, there is no question here of a literally sufficient theory of thematic relationships. Réti argues that composers constantly invent new kinds of thematic transformation, so that 'no real list . . . can be made, as is done with the contrapuntal devices . . . In fact, it is, above all, the examples rather than the definitions that count . . .' [: 67] The broad sweep of what counts in Réti's examples is nowhere more evident than in the analysis of Schumann's *Kinderszenen*, Chapter 2 of *The Thematic Process in Music*. His summary is given in example 17. It shows how Schumann's thirteen pieces are unified partly by an initial motive which becomes a 'prime thought'; in Nos. 1–4 the motive is shown at original pitch; in Nos. 5–9 it is transposed; in Nos. 10–12 it is 'sharpened', given at 'regular' pitch, then regular and sharpened; in No. 13 there is a 'new and transposed version' but the original motive appears at the end (No. 13*b*). Later in the book, Réti claims that there is a 'thematic key relation' in *Kinderszenen* as a whole. After listing the keys (example 18), he observes that these tonics fall into three groups each expressing the interval of a sixth 'on which the work's main theme is centred', while the G sharp/G

Ex.17 Schumann: *Kinderszenen*, Op.15

Ex.18 Schumann: *Kinderszenen*, Op.15

natural corresponds to the sharpened and regular pitch of the 'prime thought' [: 228].

Such analysis may seem to authorize an alarming freedom in determining which notes of a theme represent an underlying motive; nearly three decades after this study, Epstein needed to emphasize the arbitrary nature of the approach, especially when it is taken so far as to allow 'the mere existence of two notes relevant to a theme . . . as proof that they generate key relations on the same roots' [Epstein, 1979: 10].

Nevertheless, the student must bear in mind how primitive Réti himself considered his work to be at the level of theory; how much he regarded it, not as wilful in the interests of proving a point, but as tentative, as a sketch of the overwhelming evidence for why some future theory of thematic unity would be helpful. In summarizing degrees of thematic identity, Réti follows Schoenberg (and common sense) in listing imitation, variation and transformation; but he adds 'indirect affinity', noting that this concerns 'producing an affinity between independent shapes through contributory features' [Réti, 1962: 240]. We can take the large noteheads in the Schumann examples to represent such contributory features. Yet Réti did not pretend to have formulated thoroughly how any feature does actually contribute in any context. In fact, he admits that 'strong musical effects' may be produced by 'remote affinities, which analysis often has difficulty in making credible' [: 241]. This is typical of the way Réti unwittingly prepared the ground on which he was to be attacked by theorists. He seems to lack confidence in his musical judgement in suggesting that analysis can somehow make a musical effect more credible, and such defensiveness is hardly necessary in view of the degree of perception in his illustrations, which are not only acute, but also remarkably extensive (including, for instance, studies of examples from Liszt's *Les Préludes*, Debussy's *La Cathédrale engloutie*, Wagner, Strauss and Bartók). The affinities that Réti found so striking are surely, even in the absence of a systematic theory of affinity, legitimate quarry for the analyst. Indeed Hans Keller, who did feel that Réti 'exaggerates the melodic aspect', argued forcefully that 'as soon as you have analysed the unity of a great work, its variety explains itself' [Keller, 1965: 93 and 91].

It is inevitable that Réti's historical diagnoses are undervalued, in view of the particular bias of nineteenth-century studies. Buried among his lengthy analytical illustrations is the claim, and the

Ex.19   Beethoven: Piano Sonata in C minor, Op.13 (*Pathétique*)

(contrary motion of *Grave* shapes)

beginnings of a demonstration, that works such as *Kinderszenen* and the Brahms Rhapsodies, Op. 79, represent a genre that had not been properly identified before 1950, a genre midway, as he notes, between the suite and variations. These startling readings of Romantic music were a consequence for Réti of his studies of Beethoven, which had led him to the conclusion that 'the different movements of a Classical symphony are built from one identical thought' [Réti, 1962: 13], traced through pitch 'cells' and rhythmic cells that recur as 'patterns'. In *Thematic Patterns in Sonatas of Beethoven* Réti's terminology is ill-defined and inconsistent (the terms 'are chosen almost at random, for the sake of conciseness only', p. 20), and the two main studies, of the *Pathétique* and *Appassionata* sonatas, do not offer clear models for analysis. Yet the results, which might have been achieved by various analytical routes, can carry great conviction. Perhaps the best-known example is his reading of the *Grave* and *Allegro* of the *Pathétique*, (example 19), which proves for Réti that the Introduction is an 'improvised draft of the *Allegro*, outlining the plan of the work to be' [: 49]. No special analytical technique is used here. If 'technique' is to be found at all in Réti, it consists of gauging the relevance of cellular combination both at the level of smallest detail and of greatest prolongation. This can be illustrated from his reading of the *Appassionata*. In the first theme, Réti picks out, as usual, a cluster of cells, shown in example 20. By the time he has considered the whole first movement, the combination of a neighbouring-note figure and thirds and fifths has been shown to saturate the texture – not surprisingly perhaps. But the fact that the Coda prolongs the fifth degree, C, rather than the tonic in the melody leads Réti to speculate on a two-part structural framework covering the whole work in what he calls an 'amazing design' (example 21). The student's final verdict on such an analysis might be that, were the prolonged pitches to be demonstrable through a full voice-leading graph, the correspondence of detail and structure would indeed be amazing.

Ex.20 Beethoven: Piano Sonata in F minor, Op.57/1 (*Appassionata*)

Ex.21 Beethoven: Piano Sonata in F minor, Op.57

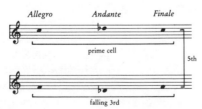

In Réti's books on thematic process and patterns, the actual mechanism of hierarchical correspondence is not revealed. There is no explanation, either of how we are to prove a correspondence, or of how we are able to perceive it. Réti shares with Schenker, Schoenberg and Hindemith a tendency to rely on the immanence of musical meaning; it is something assumed, and something the effects of which are the object of analytical study. Whether the meaning investigated by the analyst is the same as the meaning, as it were, injected into the music by a composer was not a difficult or even a valid question for these writers. Nor did they concern themselves with whether a piece of music means the same to different people – the Germanic inclination was to believe that there is an inherent meaning, an essence, in a masterpiece. Nor did it seem interesting to ask just how musical information is transmitted to the listener. This last matter in particular is traditionally a question of aesthetics rather than analysis. Yet we cannot escape from the intimate connection between claims about musical function and assumptions about how any such function is perceived. This connection is examined explicitly in the work of Leonard Meyer. The results of his inquiries fall, as we shall discover, squarely within the field of thematic analysis, but the thinking behind his analytical technique derives from sources sharply opposed to the kinds of approach discussed so far.

Meyer

The mechanism and transmission of musical information is best understood, Meyer believes, and as he had learned from information theory based on mid-century American research into 'behavioural' science, in terms of a binary switching mechanism. Something is either meaningful in music or it is not. If we respond to a stimulus, information has passed from the medium to the recipient, meaning has been established. This produces an affective response: that is, we are affected by the stimulus and we expect it to be continued (and if this affect is absent, no stimulus has been recorded in our minds). Logically, it will either be continued or not continued, and it is in dealing with this 'implication' that information theory applied to music makes a superficially attractive model. First, non-continuance is unexpected, that is, it 'means' more to us than would the expected succession, and thus information is again transmitted.

This would seem to explain why what we may informally call 'contrast' is in fact meaningful. Meyer's initial category for this (in *Emotion and Meaning in Music*) was 'frustration'. On the other hand, obviously some response, some satisfaction at the arrival of the expected, is to be discerned when an expectation is 'realized'. With such a theory Meyer has a rich model at his disposal: meaning is a function both of what we expect and of what we do not expect. Technically, information can be measured as a 'flux' between frustration and realization. This seems, psychologically, readily acceptable. If something is repeated, it becomes boring. But if it is repeated significantly more than, culturally or stylistically, we can recognize as being 'normal', the situation becomes more interesting, and the longer repetition goes on, the more excited we become by the expectation that it will be disrupted. Then we begin to accept that perhaps it will not be disrupted: a new time-scale, Meyer would claim, is brought into play, and a certain satisfaction is generated through our recognition of a new kind of normality.

The adequacy of this theory of perception is certainly question-able, for all its attractiveness, and some basic reservations should be made clear in advance of analytical discussion. One commentator argues that to explain music in terms of an 'emotional' mechanism is a fallacy of reasoning, since that mechanism is itself more obscure than the meaning first at issue [Stopford, 1983: 4]. More prag-matically, it has been observed that Meyer implies a quite unrealistic picture of actual human musical behaviour on at least four points of principle (see E. Dunsby, 1983). Analytically, for the present purpose, it must be remembered that Meyer's stance implies no more refined a picture of the components of tonal musical structure than is to be found in the informal critical literature, in Tovey for instance, and on these grounds it may surely be considered, as a mid-twentieth-century theory, a reversion, bypassing new analytical methods. This suggests that it is not the assumption of a mechanism of perception alone that should be questioned in this approach, but the relevance of that assumption in a set of assumptions about our response to musical structure which do not actually represent that structure, so much as a musically irrelevant abstraction from it (which would be the dismissive Schenkerian reaction to Meyer).

Nevertheless, many musicians have been impressed by the analytical apparatus Meyer brings to bear on melodic analysis. It is reasonably reproducible and, if intellectually confusing, none the less able to articulate the modest perception of simple music. As an

Ex.22 Beethoven: Piano Sonata in Eb major, Op.81a/1 (*Les Adieux*)

illustration of Meyer's results, example 22 shows part of his analysis of Beethoven's *Les Adieux* sonata, first movement, in *Explaining Music*. An arrowhead denotes an 'implication' (his later term for expectation) leading to realization: it does not of necessity lead there, and indeed any musical event, according to Meyer, may carry many implications of which only some are realized. The different levels show, in general, longer- and shorter-term implications and their consequences. The whole adds up to a picture of information flux peaking somewhere in the middle of the passage where there is an accretion of unrealized implications. Obviously, the

extent of the extract chosen determines the scope of the analysis; most of the implications set up here could be seen, in an analysis of a longer extract, as unrealized in the Introduction. The fact that the nature of the analysis depends on the length of time of the music in question does not, however, make it 'dynamic', and Meyer's may properly be regarded as a peculiarly static theory in that it can never escape from the terms of description imposed by the object chosen: one cannot always tell from a Meyer analysis whether a piece or merely an extract of a piece is the object of analysis, a feature it shares with Schenkerian analysis.

Although Meyer restricts his comments on Schenker to incidental and mostly misconceived references, his teaching has spawned an extensive attempt to criticize Schenkerian analysis, which succeeds only in refuting a theory not actually to be found in Schenker [Narmour, 1977, undermined in Keiler, 1978]. To the extent that we take a Meyer-type analysis to be adequately descriptive of motivic relationships, however, his work may be viewed as a substantial complement to Schenkerian theory in one respect. A Schenkerian analysis is weak in the attention it can draw to intra-hierarchical relationships of theme or motive. Such relationships, the motivic parallelisms that were so significant in the formation of Schenker's theory of structural levels, are left to observation rather than explanation in most cases. Meyer offers the chance to explain some of these factors. Example 23(a) presents a Schenkerian graphic analysis of the music analysed by Meyer in example 22. In example 23(b), abstracts from Meyer's melodic analysis explain some of these events as having their origin in implicative ideas, all of which are on different hierarchical levels from their realizations. In a fully laid out Schenkerian graph (with foreground, middleground and background) we could indeed draw attention to these intra-

Ex.23 Beethoven: Piano Sonata in Eb major, Op.81a/1

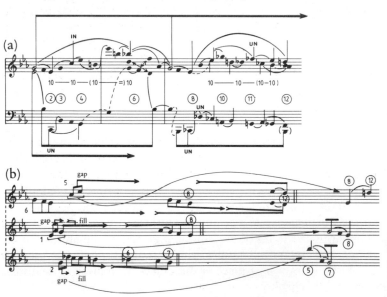

hierarchical relationships, but not explain them graphically, as does Meyer, in terms of the tendency of stepwise progressions to be continued, or the tendency of 'gaps' to be filled, usually by stepwise motion. Probably all such perceptions are implicit in Schenkerian theory (for example, the concept of intervallic unfolding underlying foreground stepwise progression is vastly more sophisticated than Meyer's idea of a tendency for melodic gaps to be filled), but Meyer has found an effective supplement for their notation. (For further commentary on Meyer's work, see Diepert, 1983, and E. Dunsby, 1983.)

Guidelines for Further Study

Schenkerian Analysis

The primary source, Schenker's *Free Composition* (*Der freie Satz*), is essential study for musically advanced students. Even though it may be used most fully and effectively at postgraduate level, the teacher can find stimulating selections from the text and examples to enrich earlier stages of tonal analysis courses. Forte's and Gilbert's *Introduction to Schenkerian Analysis* provides a variety of schedules for the study of this subject from rudiments to an advanced level, and both beginning teachers and students can work the graded assignments, checking many of their solutions against the authors' discussions in the companion volume, *Instructor's Manual*. One particular advantage of these authors' approach is their emphasis on 'rhythmic reduction': this preserves the music's durational and proportional characteristics in the first stages of analytical reduction. A Schenkerian analyst will claim that rhythmic relationships in the musical foreground implicitly determine many aspects of a foreground 'reading' of voice-leading connections. The implicit role of rhythm thus assumed – as it is in much of our own discussion of Schenkerian techniques – is often deplored, or misunderstood. Forte's and Gilbert's attempt to encourage an explicit role for rhythmic structure in voice-leading analysis may become an important factor in future work in this field. Among introductory articles for teachers, Beach, 1983, will be found particularly helpful. Students will welcome the clarity and comprehensiveness of Forte, 1977, which, though somewhat out of date bibliographically, includes an enlightening survey of Schenker's analysis of Schumann's *Dichterliebe* No. 2.

Among points of advice (see also Chapter 4, 'Summary and Prospects', above) experience suggests that the following considerations are paramount:

(i)   The concepts of structural hierarchy and fundamental structure should be contemplated at as early a stage as their role in voice-leading theory can be grasped; the student who is able to accept musically the idea of diminution will welcome the secure overview of tonal structure represented in Schenker's limited set of background models.

(ii) It is essential to be specific about what aspect of music is addressed by voice-leading analysis; students should always consider (and be encouraged to consider) the explicit limitations in the kinds of feature it can explain. Antipathy and even animosity can result from misconceptions about the scope and aims of voice-leading analysis.

(iii) Sensitive choice of repertory includes not only considerations of the music's relative complexity, but also of its relevance for the student. Voice-leading analysis is not a good way to 'learn' music if it threatens to suppress the student's 'instinctive' musical response, memory and creativity. One should analyse music (and extracts) with which one is thoroughly familiar: since all music students are also performers at however basic a level, the ideal repertory is often self-evident, but equally often neglected because of the separation into 'academic' and 'practical' of fields of teaching.

Other Approaches

Schoenberg's pedagogical texts are used in many institutions. In the early stages of any course on tonal analysis *Fundamentals of Musical Composition* is a sound basis. Where the luxury of extensive analytical study over several years is available, *Fundamentals* can even be used as a 'foreground primer' for voice-leading analysis, providing the student with a useful picture of motivic connection, phrasing and form. It was through his ever-deepening awareness of how 'motive' functions in tonal structure that Schenker was encouraged to formulate his theory of organic coherence. As was indicated briefly in our discussion of Meyer, an awareness of the nature and function of motivic connection may be not only the starting-point for a voice-leading analysis, but also one of its most valuable results. Recent literature suggests that the combination of Schenkerian 'organicism' with 'thematicism' in its various forms is a trend for the future. (Teachers will appreciate the wider discussions of Schoenbergian thematicism in Epstein, 1979, and Frisch, 1984.)

Other approaches can be drawn in to the main line of study by careful choice of repertory. The books by Tovey, Réti and Meyer discussed above, and of course many other sources in the critical literature that contribute to an analytical approach (Rosen, 1972, is a well-known example), offer case studies for comparison with the objectives and results of Schenkerian and Schoenbergian inquiry. To run a comparative thread through a tonal analysis course is challenging for the teacher, yet it has the advantage of allowing concrete expression of students' awareness of non-voice-leading issues and will lead to a sharper view in each student of the boundaries between analysis and criticism: indeed, the student's growing ability to move freely but consciously across these boundaries is a measure of the effectiveness and overall relevance of analytical study.

PART III

The Elements of Atonality

9

Introduction

The term 'atonality' has never won universal acceptance. It is, after all, a negative rather than a positive expression, and Schoenberg himself strongly disliked it. In a famous footnote to the 1921 edition of the *Theory of Harmony*, he wrote that 'I am a musician and have nothing to do with things atonal. The word "atonal" could only signify something entirely inconsistent with the nature of tone.' [Schoenberg, 1978: 432] Schoenberg's own preferred term was 'pantonal': 'by this we can signify the relation of all tones to one another, regardless of occasional occurrences, assured by the circumstance of a common origin' [Schoenberg, 1975: 284]; but the composer's somewhat opaque definition has not encouraged its adoption. By eliminating the 'tonal' component altogether, 'motivic' might seem a preferable term (see Boretz, 1972; Benjamin, 1979) and may well be chosen by those who like its flexibility – both tonal and atonal music can be motivic – and its ambiguity: at what point, if any, does music become 'amotivic'? 'Non-tonal' and 'post-tonal' are probably the least problematic terms, and the easiest to take literally; and to the extent that 'post-tonal' is less absolute than 'non-tonal' – as will be seen in the next chapter, to claim something as 'completely non-tonal' is never easy – it may well be the term to gain the greatest support in the future.

At the moment, nevertheless, 'atonality' is the term most commonly used for the kind of music with which Part III of this book is concerned, and the contention that the negative prefix imposes an inevitable connotation of disapproval for the absence of tonality is, perhaps, less pertinent than the belief, which we share, that freedom from the constraints of tonality in much twentieth-century music is actually a good thing: in other words, to describe an unregretted absence is scarcely negative at all. Nor will it do any harm to think of the word as a (positive) compression of the phrase 'all tones in equality', representing not so much the absence of something as the continuous presence of everything. Of course, atonal music does not literally work like that. Yet it is an inevitable consequence of the abandonment of hierarchic tonal structuring, not so much that all twelve pitch classes are likely to occur and recur with equal frequency, but that, even in atonal compositions where one or two pitches are given greater emphasis than others through repetition, they will by no means establish an unambiguously diatonic framework within which all the other pitches may be felt to function.

Part III of this book is called 'The Elements of Atonality', and a reader who comes to it with a wide general knowledge of, and enthusiasm for, the major masterpieces of twentieth-century music, from *Erwartung* and *Wozzeck* to *Pli selon pli*, *Mantra* and the *Symphony of three orchestras*, may be disconcerted to find the range of reference so restricted. The limitations of what can be deduced from a handful of brief compositions will be obvious. The justification is that our approach is more technical than historical, although 'history' has clearly been acknowledged to the extent that compositions from the earlier phases of atonal and twelve-note music have been elected in preference to later miniatures, on grounds of their greater accessibility and familiarity. Nor can the reader be offered the comforting promise that the pieces discussed have been chosen because they provide models for the analysis of all kinds of atonal composition, long or short, recent or early. The intention is not to over-simplify a complex historical process in the interests of technical generalization, but, more modestly, to indicate to what extent certain basic technical issues can be elucidated through application to particular compositions. The technical issues are those which we believe no would-be analyst of atonal music can evade; and we also believe that those issues are best explored initially through the close study of short but masterly compositions.

10

Harmony and Voice-leading

The years spanned by Schenker's major theoretical publications, 1904 to 1935, were not, to put it mildly, years of consolidation or fulfilment for the kind of composition Schenker most admired. Schenker the theorist (see chapter 3) reaffirmed in *Free Composition* his long-held belief that Brahms was 'the last master of German tonal art' [Schenker, 1979: 94]. Meanwhile, atonality, neo-classicism and the twelve-note method had emerged, during the period of Schenker's most significant theoretical explorations, as witness to the common belief of many composers that, as Schoenberg put it, the principle of tonality was 'no longer applicable' [Schoenberg, 1964: 104], and to the common dissatisfaction with 'the framework of classic tonality' [Stravinsky, 1947: 37].

Schenker analysed none of Schoenberg's compositions, finding ample ammunition for his attack in that composer's theoretical writings, which revealed a 'strange exuberance', and a desire to be at all costs 'the godfather of new chords' (see Kalib, 1973: vol. II, 208). And although Schenker did publish an interpretation of a few bars from Stravinsky's Piano Concerto [: 212–16], he could find in them only the most powerful confirmation of his belief that the art of true composition had gone into irreversible decline. For Schenker, the failure of composition was the direct consequence of a failure of theory. It was not that Schenker was opposed to chromaticism as such, but he remained faithful to his own admonition in *Harmony* that 'the musician must never sacrifice and destroy the primary element of his art, which is the diatonic system, for the sake of a merely secondary element, that is chromatic change' [Schenker, 1954: 290]. Schenker and Schoenberg agreed that the increase in chromaticism during the nineteenth century and the tendency to abandon the sonata principle were the result of those 'extra-musical influences' whereby composers were seduced into setting texts (especially librettos) and writing programme music (see Schoenberg, 1969: 76). But what, for Schoenberg, was an 'extended tonality', in which 'remote transformations and successions of harmonies were understood as remaining within the tonality' (Schoenberg's first examples of such harmonies were from *Tristan* and *Salome*), was for Schenker a clear indication of secondary factors overwhelming and destroying music's primary substance, the diatonic system, and although Schenker was no more tolerant of Stravinsky's music than he was of Schoenberg's theories, he would surely have endorsed the great neo-classicist's condemnation of Wagner's later works as 'more improvised than constructed, in the specific musical sense' [Stravinsky, 1947: 64]. Schenker was scathing about Wagner's assessment of himself as the heir to Beethoven (see Schenker, 1979: 137): in his view, 'Wagner's inability to achieve diminutions like those of the masters made it necessary for him to turn away from diminution, and, in the service of drama, to make expressiveness, indeed over-expressiveness, the guiding principle of music' [Schenker, 1979: 106].

Schenker's uncompromising attitude to the compositions he disliked might seem to have rendered permanently and totally implausible any attempt to extend his analytical techniques to such music. Yet many later writers have found the challenge of the Schenkerian polemic – in essence, that much of what is most highly regarded in the music of the nineteenth and twentieth centuries is not music at all – irresistible. As Part II of this book has noted, the two earliest extended studies in English to be influenced by Schenker diverged drastically in their attitude. Katz's *Challenge to Musical Tradition* attempts to demonstrate the limited applicability of orthodox Schenkerian techniques to the music of Wagner, Debussy, Schoenberg and Stravinsky, whereas Salzer's *Structural Hearing* aims to show that the music of Debussy, Stravinsky, Bartók and Hindemith, among others, can have its true coherence definitively illuminated by the adaptation and extension of Schenkerian structural principles. Such discussions of the relevance of Schenkerian analytical techniques to post-tonal music were the more difficult to evaluate in the absence of a comprehensive, textbook-like presentation of Schenkerian analytical techniques themselves. The appearance of such a book, 48 years after Schenker's death (Forte and Gilbert, 1983), should in due course promote a more thoroughgoing exploration of these issues than has so far been undertaken.

The argument in favour of extending and adapting Schenker is an evolutionary one. Just as 'extended tonality' (see Schoenberg, 1969, chapter X: 76–113) evolved naturally and inevitably out of diatonicism, so the voice-leading characteristics of diatonic music may be expected to evolve, and continue to function, even in music commonly considered so radically post-tonal as to be completely atonal. Since, the argument runs, all non-monodic music must combine linear and vertical elements, it is quite wrong for theorists to propose a complete break in techniques and procedures between the evidently tonal and the apparently atonal. Even if compositional systems appear to be mutually exclusive, compositional techniques for achieving connection and elaboration are likely to be held in common.

This argument has been widely debated, not so much as an immediate response to the work of Katz and Salzer, but starting in earnest a decade or so later, when two new journals were launched in America (*Journal of Music Theory* in 1957, *Perspectives of New Music* in 1962). The initial impulse for this debate was provided less by analysts who continued to operate within the boundaries of extended tonality as set by Salzer than by one who advanced boldly into the music of Schoenberg and Webern. With possible ironic intent, Roy Travis took up Katz's subtitle – 'A New Concept of Tonality' – and applied it to an attempt to demonstrate that Schoenberg and Webern were not composing atonally at all, but – in a new way – tonally (see Travis, 1966 and 1974).

Such notions have won support (see, for example, Morgan, 1976, and Lewis, 1981), but they have also come under strong attack, both from those who contend that Schenker's spirit is betrayed by such distortions, and also from those who claim to demonstrate the true atonality of such works as Schoenberg's opus 19 and Webern's opus 27, using methods of analysis that avoid the Schenkerian vocabulary deriving from strict counterpoint (see J. Baker, 1983: 153–83). Nowhere are the difficulties of drawing generally acceptable technical conclusions about the development of music since the middle of the nineteenth century more apparent than in the matter of identifying some kind of fundamental structure (which can be said to determine, through composing out, the entire surface of the piece in question). As long as the material for study is drawn from certain areas of the Bach-to-Brahms repertory, the Schenkerian analyst does not even need to invoke the possibility of substitution or implication at the background level with any great consistency: fundamental structures are usually explicit enough, and complete enough, for the general theory of their existence and function to be both testable and acceptable. In *Free*

Composition, Schenker does provide for the possibility of substitution at middleground as well as foreground level: 'even at the first level, a tone which is not part of the fundamental line can substitute for a fundamental-line tone' [Schenker, 1979: 51] – and he illustrates the absence of the structural $\hat{2}$ in short pieces by Brahms and Schubert (figure 46). He also implicitly acknowledges that a composer may, on rare occasions, employ a substitute for the initial I of the bass arpeggiation (figure 110 d3); or use an incomplete fundamental structure (figure 110 a3). Nevertheless, such exceptional instances cannot be interpreted as covert evolutionism on Schenker's part. In his view these were not factors destined to change the entire nature of the tonal system from within, but exceptional deviations within that system which could be justified only because the system normally functioned without them.

The Schenkerian analyst is faced with the need to determine when a fundamental structure may be said, definitively, to have disappeared; and music theory has yet to propose a comprehensive, consistent set of principles that can be applied analytically, and effectively, to the large amount of music whose tonality is extended rather than diatonic, yet whose points of contact with diatonicism still remain, to the ear, evident and vital. This, it must be stressed, is music in which some kind of tonic (or dominant) functionality seems still to survive. Such functionality is not to be confused with those 'pitch centricities' or 'pitch-class priorities' (see Berger, 1963: 123) that may be established by simple emphasis or repetition in works that remain, in their most basic essentials, atonal (see also Schmalfeldt, 1983: 249). As will be argued later in this chapter, particular problems arise when analysts attempt to demonstrate the presence of orthodox voice-leading techniques in compositions that are held to centre on a 'tonic sonority' that is precisely *not* a tonic triad, but may be anything from a single note to a more complex construct which need not even include all the elements of the tonic triad alongside other elements. It is often all too easy to identify such sonorities, very much more difficult to analyse the piece in which they occur entirely by means of coherent 'composings out' of that sonority. And so what is called 'implicit tonality' in the following paragraphs refers to implicit tonal function, not just explicit pitch-class priority. 'Implicit tonality' suggests that voice-leading analysis, however 'post-Schenkerian', may still provide a viable approach, and that the piece in question cannot simply be categorized as an example of 'atonality with pitch-class priority'.

Ex.24 Skryabin: *Enigme*, Op.52/2

James Baker's study of 'Schenkerian Analysis and Post-Tonal Music' (in Beach, 1983) ends with an analysis of Skryabin's *Enigme* (Op. 52 No. 2), which represents Baker's conclusions about the extent to which a diatonic background may be plausibly modified by implication and substitution. (Comparison of the background level of Baker's analysis (example 24(a)) with that of the same piece in Morgan, 1976 (example 24(b)) is instructive.) As his analysis indicates, Baker accepts that whatever the faults of Salzer's actual interpretations of examples of extended tonality, his basic principle is acceptable: extension or adaptation of Schenker is not necessarily distortion. Baker makes every effort not to exaggerate or over-simplify: he argues that 'tonal forces . . . are responsible in large part for the overall coherence' of *Enigme*, and that 'a tonal structure is implicitly contained within the piece . . . at least to the extent that a dominant function is prolonged' [Baker, 1983: 179, 178]. But he also accepts that 'the retention of whole-tone elements participates in the prolongation of the dominant function, while other non-tonal relationships, in particular those based on complementation, are important in establishing structural bonds between the contrasting sections of the piece'. The justification for voice-leading analysis therefore seems to be primarily through reference to an implied diatonicism: more precisely, a dominant triad is implied by the whole-tone and seventh formations present in the piece, and motion from this to a tonic triad is also implied, though this 'must be assumed to take place, if at all, after the piece has ended' as the square brackets in example 24(a) show. The fact that it is a 'whole-tone dominant chord on A flat', however, rather than an A flat major triad which is 'prolonged throughout', raises a fundamental issue: what is ambiguous, if not actually enigmatic, about the piece is whether the sonority prolonged throughout is consonant or dissonant. Of course, it may be 'actually' dissonant while strongly implying consonance through its 'dominant function'. But a tonality without either a tonic triad or any actual, diatonic consonance is inherently highly unstable, even in a composition like *Enigme* where the bass, as Baker rightly notes, remains 'an organizing force'. It is worth noting at this point that Baker's 'implicit tonality', in the specific case of *Enigme*, is equivalent to Schoenberg's '*schwebende Tonalität*', a term translated by Roy E. Carter as 'fluctuating (suspended, not yet decided)', and applied by Schoenberg to his song 'Lockung' (Op. 6 No. 7), which 'expresses an E flat major tonality without once in the course of the piece giving an E flat major triad in such a way that one could regard it as a pure tonic' [Schoenberg, 1978: 383]. Later, Schoenberg claimed simply that 'the tonic, E flat, does not appear through the whole piece' [Schoenberg, 1969: 111]. There is, then, some point in suggesting that 'extended tonality' should be used for compositions in which a tonic chord is present (for example, Bartók's *Bourrée* from *Mikrokosmos* Book IV, as analysed in Salzer, 1952, example 504), and 'implicit tonality' reserved for pieces, like *Enigme*, that lack a clearly stated tonic. It follows, of course, that examples of 'extended tonality' can be made the subject of voice-leading analysis, even though Schoenberg himself never explored the technique.

The reader may well have encountered several other terms for music that is other than, in essence, diatonic. A modality based on the octatonic scale (of alternate tones and semitones, or vice versa) has been shown to have widespread relevance to many late nineteenth- and twentieth-century composers, and its pervasiveness is a measure of its adaptability, the fact that it can serve equally well to promote extended tonality, or something much closer to atonality. Many analysts employ the notions of bi- or polytonality in an effort to elucidate the traditional bases of the music. We believe that, while it is perfectly possible for a composer to juxtapose tonality (diatonic, extended or implied) with atonality within one composition, the superimposition of one tonality on another actually creates atonality. One tonality cannot integrate with another, and the notion of simultaneous, independent functionalities is a contradiction, not an enhancement, of tonality's true, unitary nature.

To return to Skryabin: Baker's position may be summarized as follows. Even though Skryabin interprets his basic dominant chord more as the generator of purely whole-tone formations than as a diatonic triad that must ultimately resolve on to a tonic triad, its presentation and prolongation are close enough to those of tonal orthodoxy for it to be defined as a D flat major dominant, despite the absence of the D flat major tonic. The music therefore makes sense through reference to an implied diatonicism. Even though it might be cited as an example of the consistent emancipation of the dissonance, systematic reduction to a prolonged background is still plausible. In Baker's judgement, *Enigme* is not atonal, but rather the 'furthest extension of implicit tonality in the music of his [Skryabin's] transitional period' [Baker, 1983: 179].

It is clear from Baker's commentary that he nevertheless wishes his analysis to include other factors – in particular, those 'non-tonal relationships' which can be represented as 'pitch-class sets' (a concept fully discussed in chapter 12). In this respect, and in his observation that Skryabin 'made a gradual transition from tonality to atonality over a period of years', Baker establishes a parallel with Allen Forte's interpretation of Schoenberg's 'creative path to atonality' [Forte, 1978a]. Forte's analysis of 'Lockung' involves a considerable amount of voice-leading, and it also indicates passages which 'although not completely organized in the manner of the full atonal piece . . . do exhibit certain structural characteristics that resemble those of atonal music' [: 157]. It is indeed beyond dispute that Schoenberg and others did tread such a transitional path: yet the music in question hardly makes it easy to establish the precise point at which 'implicit' tonality yields to 'actual' atonality. If the analyst is prepared to approach all such transitional works as containing elements of both, then the immediate problem of how to decide in favour of one or the other may disappear, and a useful acknowledgement of the symbiotic presence of distinct rather than synthesized features may be reinforced. The whole point of the music of this transitional period is that it cannot adequately be analysed with reference to one type of pitch-structuring alone. As Adorno observed in connection with Schoenberg's *Das Buch der hängenden Gärten* (1908–9) a 'field of tension' exists between tonal elements and their negation [Adorno, 1959, 78–9; cited in Regener, 1974 : 193]. Nevertheless, even if the analyst need no longer decide that a particular piece is *either* tonal *or* atonal, the need to apply suitable analytical techniques correctly remains. The student analyst may well concur, after reading this chapter, with our view that the close study of such transitional works, with all their necessary and fascinating ambiguities, is best postponed until considerable experience in 'purer' tonal and atonal analysis has been acquired (see Guidelines for Further Study, pp. 205–7).

The matter is all the more complex since the analyst must decide, not only whether or not both tonal and atonal elements are present, but also how best to deal with each phenomenon analytically. For example, while there is probably wide agreement that Forte's actual tracing of the process of transition in Schoenberg is correct – as is

Ex.25   Schoenberg: Six Little Piano Pieces, Op.19/2

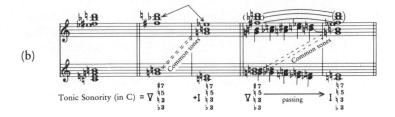

Baker's in Skryabin – there is hardly a consensus about the value of explaining that process through the shift from voice-leading (rather than functional harmony) to pitch-class sets (rather than motives). Most would argue that Roy Travis went too far in seeking to demonstrate a pure, two-voice G major fundamental structure in one of Webern's 1913 Orchestral Pieces [Travis, 1974]. Yet not everyone dissatisfied by Travis will accept that the pitch-class-set analysis by Forte that appears alongside Travis's provides the 'right' answer. And there is even wider disagreement as to whether other studies by Travis are as plausible as the Webern – for example, his work on Schoenberg's piano piece, Op. 19 No. 2 [Travis, 1966, with ensuing correspondence, Travis/Goode/Wuorinen, 1967]. Travis uses this piece as an instance of what he calls 'directed motion', and his analysis is directed very firmly towards the claim that the piece does *not* display what is sometimes called 'atonal voice-leading'. Rather, the music refers to a diatonic, tonal background, which is, in the absence of a fundamental structure, never explicit. Travis interprets the piece in terms of an overall motion from V to I in C major, and this progression is itself the result of partitioning a 'tonic sonority' that embraces the seven pitch-classes of the major and minor tonic and dominant triads, as well as an F sharp – eight notes altogether. (Example 25 (a) shows the piece, example 25(b) the 'higher levels' of Travis's interpretation.)

It is certainly possible to take issue with Travis's interpretation without rejecting the notion of a tonal background – if only an implicit one – out of hand (see Travis/Goode/Wuorinen, 1967). For example, why prefer a C major V–I progression to a G major I–(IV)–I progression? If *Enigme* prolongs a dominant without a tonic, may not the Schoenberg prolong a tonic without a dominant? As for the argument that Travis is verticalizing what, in the actual music, Schoenberg is careful to keep apart – the 'dominant triad' is never sounded as a simultaneity, the 'tonic' C does not actually underpin the final chord – it might be claimed that the higher levels of orthodox voice-leading analyses often effect such verticalizations.

Such issues bring out the dangers of making unwary comparisons between diatonic and non-diatonic music. We must be on guard, for instance, when generation of the harmony is interpreted as being the function of a bass line, and distinguish with care between the non-synchronized diatonic events (which can be legitimately verticalized in a middleground reduction) and the actual non-overlap of atonal events in an essentially non-hierarchic structure. Even a strong bass line like the one in Op. 19 No. 2 may not have the power to focus atonal elements into diatonic functions.

Even though voice-leading was not a part of Schoenberg's own analytical armoury, however, the concepts that voice-leading analysis makes available cannot simply be set aside unconsidered as long as a piece retains links with tonal procedures. Even when the functional distinction between consonance and dissonance seems to have disappeared, there may still be linear connections, still the sense of the degree of hierarchy that always obtains as long as some relatively stable, persistent features are heard to be decorated by other, relatively incidental features. The more distant the texture of an atonal piece is from that of a tonal piece, however, the less perceptible such local hierarchic events are likely to be. For example: the insistent repetitions of the G/B dyad in Op. 19 No. 2 may help to ensure that many of the other events in the piece sound as in some sense subordinate to it – but such statistical subordination is scarcely equivalent to contrapuntal prolongation. In Op. 19 No. 6 (see example 26) the presentation of E and D sharp in bars 3 and 4 may encourage the observation that the D sharp is 'prolonged' by the motion to its upper neighbouring note E; and it may indeed be possible to sense an allusion to the upper-neighbouring-note technique at this point. But without a framework founded on the consonance/dissonance distinction, and without the consistent use of this and other voice-leading techniques throughout the piece, it is difficult to feel that the analysis of the composition is greatly advanced by such an observation. Such local, and relatively superficial 'prolongations' may indeed be evident, but they cannot be deemed part of a fully integrated contrapuntal structure of the kind that obtains when a plausible diatonic background can be demonstrated – whether this background is actual, or implied, as in

Ex.26 Schoenberg: Six Little Piano Pieces, Op.19/6

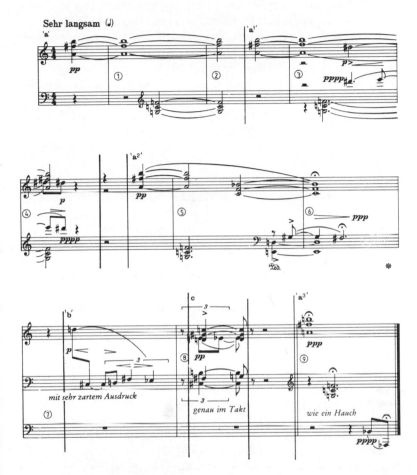

Enigme. Similarly, the movements of particular intervals or pitches to different octave positions in the two Schoenberg pieces are hardly the linear transfers or couplings of diatonic music. In Schoenberg their function is not so much to prolong particular structural entities as to define those areas of musical space within which motivic statements lie. In an atonal piece, repetition is likely to increase the possibility of an event being relatively more 'essential', relatively less 'inessential', if only in a motivic sense; but this is still in decisive contrast to tonal voice-leading, in which the essential structural forces, the tones of the fundamental line and bass arpeggiation, need not be greatly emphasized on the musical surface.

As noted above, Travis's interpretation of Op. 19 No. 2 (shown in part in example 25(b)) involves the 'composing out' of a C major tonic sonority, first by separating out its dominant and tonic components (linked, of course, by common tones), and then by connecting those components with the passing and embellishing motions shown in abstracted form in the third stage of the example. These motions are then variously dispersed and displaced in the actual music. It would be to reinterpret rather than reject Travis's analytical approach to follow the suggestion made above (p. 115) that the piece was 'composed out' from a G major rather than a C major sonority – represented by the final chord of the piece, and without the C and E natural that Travis retains in it. Even with this change, however, the principal structural feature of the piece remains an enriched rather than a pure triad; comparison is still possible with the prolonged dominant sonority (altered to a whole-tone chord) of *Enigme*, and it is only when that comparison is pursued in all necessary detail that we can appreciate the differences between Skryabin's 'implicit tonality' and Schoenberg's 'atonality with pitch-class priority'. The structural features in the Skryabin that support a tonal interpretation are evident and consistent: in the Schoenberg they are so dispersed and overlaid with other elements that a tonal interpretation, if not quite implausible, is much more difficult to demonstrate conclusively.

Travis's approach to Op. 19 No. 2 may well have been inspired by Schenker's example of an incomplete fundamental structure in *Free Composition* (figure 110a; although Chopin's dominant and tonic do not first need to be disentangled from a more complex 'tonic sonority'), and the elements of C major/minor and G major/minor triads are certainly prominent in Schoenberg's piece. Op. 19 No. 6 (example 26) is much more radical in the sense that, even if the principal chord is interpreted as an altered and enriched G major tonic, none of that tonic's diatonic relatives is given a comparable degree of clarity. The most plausible kind of tonal background for this piece is not that of the incomplete fundamental structure but that of a tonality extended through motion to more distant relatives along the minor third 'axis'. Example 27 provides an appropriately rudimentary reduction of the piece to four chords (the first and last identical) in which the bass notes represent an incomplete 'tonic axis' of this kind. To see this as a distant

Ex.27 Schoenberg: Six Little Piano Pieces, Op.19/6

derivation from the kind of symmetrical harmonic structure illustrated in example 29 below is not to argue for a significant degree
of literal similarity, though, as will be suggested shortly, the
principle of symmetry may be at work in both cases. The G tonic
axis is completed by the B flat in bar 9, but the connection of that
pitch to the final A flat in the actual music suggests that a rather
different type of completion may have been in Schoenberg's mind.
The reduction in example 27 shows a high proportion of stepwise –
half or whole – linear connections in the upper parts between
chords 1 and 2, and 3 and 4 respectively (shown by dotted lines in
example 27), as well as the presence of common tones. In view of
the fact that the first pair of chords represents an eleven-note
collection, and the second pair a twelve-note collection, it might be
thought that Schoenberg had in mind, as 'background', two twelve-
note complexes. This issue is also considered more fully below: but
it cannot be accepted at this stage that a purely chordal, and
therefore harmonic, background of the kind just described is a
satisfactory explanation of the piece's most essential processes.

In view of the analytical dilemmas just explored, other ways of
interpreting and determining atonal structures may be invoked –
for example, it might be worth attempting to apply or adapt the
kind of harmonic analysis that Schoenberg himself favoured for his
more explicitly tonal compositions (see Schoenberg, 1969: 110–13),
analysis that confines itself to the identification of chords and tonal
regions. There is no record that Schoenberg himself ever applied
this technique to opus 19, but the consequences of doing so are not
without interest. For example, five of the six notes of the initial
chord of Op. 19 No. 6 belong to the scale of G major (or E minor),
and, even including the F natural, the spacing of the six-note
construct may suggest that it represents the tonic of an extended
tonal region of G major. Although this chord employs half the

twelve possible pitch classes (as does any so-called 'dominant eleventh'), it is far from neutral as far as tonal association is concerned. Moreover, it may be claimed that Schoenberg refers to the tonal polarity that can be set up between the initial six-note unit and that formed by the remaining six pitch classes, G sharp, A sharp, C sharp, D, D sharp, and E, whose most likely tonal region would be that around E (or B) major, with possible reference to C sharp minor. The two areas of tonal polarity could then be interpreted as deriving from those third-related schemes that were so important a part of the tonal extensions of nineteenth-century music – schemes involving the major or minor thirds on either side of the main tonic, and beyond them, the octave-bisecting tritone. (As noted in chapter 7, Schoenberg gave these various regions specific designations: to a G major tonic, E minor was 'direct and close'; E major 'indirect, but close', and C sharp minor 'distant'. See Schoenberg, 1969 : 68.) In Op. 19 No. 6, the tendency for the various regions to intersect around E major/minor might be felt to account for the harmony between bars 3 and 6, even though it is less a matter of various regions in turn being established by harmonic progressions than of regions being represented, or suggested, by a single chord. The lowest notes throughout the piece can scarcely be said to function as a bass line, but they do seem to support the polar contrast between G and C sharp (C sharp is the last of the pitch classes to be introduced) with E as median point between them, and therefore to extend (if not to prolong) the basic tonic of G in a manner deriving from the kind of third- – and tritone- – based extensions that Schoenberg noted in Wagner and others (see Schoenberg, 1969 : 104, and below, p. 123). Any argument in favour of an E major/minor background to the piece would be strengthened, of course, had Schoenberg notated the last two notes as A sharp and G sharp, and the way in which the notation here emphasizes 'contrast' rather than 'similarity' is an important factor in deflecting glib assumptions about tonal backgrounds when not a single diatonic triad is explicitly stated. Even so, a comprehensive analysis of opus 19 can scarcely ignore the issue of extended, or implicit, tonality, any more than it can ignore Schoenberg's own attempts to deal with the question of harmonic 'logic' in such music.

Opus 19 was completed in May 1911, and that same year the first edition of Schoenberg's *Theory of Harmony* was published. In the final chapter, 'Aesthetic Evaluation of Chords with Six or More Tones', Schoenberg refers to a variety of examples, including an eleven-note construct or accumulation from *Erwartung*, and extracts from Webern, Berg, Bartók and Schreker. Schoenberg's argument is that, however complex the harmony – however emancipated the dissonance – the ear will still expect it to *function* as a dissonance, and therefore to resolve. If it does not actually resolve, however, it need not be a question of musical illogicality – in fact the distinction between consonance and dissonance has indeed become unreal. Frustrated expectation need not, therefore, lead to incomprehension.

Schoenberg, secure in his belief in the inevitably evolving forces at work in music, is content to rely on the aural adaptability of the listener to justify procedures whose logic he can sense but whose laws he cannot explain.

It is striking, and suggestive of conclusions, that I and those who write in a similar vein distinguish precisely when a five- or six-note chord should appear, when a chord of yet more parts. It would not be possible without impairing the effect to omit a tone in an eight-part chord, or to add one to a five-part chord. Even the spacing is obligatory; as soon as a tone is misplaced the meaning changes, the logic and utility is lost, coherence seems destroyed. Laws apparently prevail here. What they are, I do not know. Perhaps I shall know in a few years. Perhaps someone after me will find them. For the present the most we can do is describe. [Schoenberg, 1978: 421]

It would seem that, simply because Schoenberg was never able to discover the harmonic 'laws' that determined the processes of pieces like those of opus 19, he was stimulated to develop the *motivic* laws that ultimately determined the nature of the twelve-note method as he understood and practised it in later decades. In the final chapter of *Structural Functions of Harmony*, he wrote in the context of a discussion of the basic features of twelve-note music that:

evaluation of (quasi-) harmonic progressions in such music is obviously a necessity, though more for the teacher than for the composer. But as such progressions do not derive from roots, harmony [tonal harmony?] is not under discussion and evaluation of structural functions cannot be considered. They are vertical projections of the basic set, or parts of it, and their combination is justified by its logic. This occurred to me even before the introduction of the basic set, when I was composing *Pierrot lunaire*, *Die glückliche Hand*, and other works of this period. Tones of the accompaniment often came to my mind like broken chords, successively rather than simultaneously, in the manner of a melody.

And Schoenberg concluded that:

one day there will be a theory which abstracts rules from these compositions. Certainly, the structural evaluation of these sounds will again be based upon their functional potentialities. But it is improbable that the quality of sharpness or mildness of the dissonances – which, in fact, is nothing more than a gradation according to lesser or greater beauty – is the appropriate foundation for a theory which explores, explains and teaches. From such gradations one cannot deduce principles of construction. Which dissonances should come first? Which later? Should one begin with the sharp ones and end with the mild ones, or vice versa? Yet the concept of 'first' or 'later' plays a role in musical construction, and 'later' should always be the consequence of 'first'. [Schoenberg, 1969: 194–5]

It seems clear from this that Schoenberg himself was never convinced that harmonic identity in atonal composition could be equated with harmonic *function* – a term that remained more comprehensible in relation to tonal procedures founded in diatonicism. After all, even the way in which the initial sonority of Op. 19 No. 6 is built up suggests a technique fundamentally at odds with tonal convention. In the final chapter of the *Theory of Harmony* Schoenberg has this to say about how what he calls a 'chord progression' – the statement of one chord which is then sustained while a second chord is added to it – may be constructed: 'The chord progression seems to be regulated by the tendency to include in the second chord tones that were missing in the first, generally those a half-step higher or lower.' [Schoenberg, 1978: 420] In Op. 19 No. 6 the F and G of the second chord are indeed, as pitch classes, a half-step from the F sharp of the first, and the C is a half-step from the B. But it is less a case of 'progression' from the first chord to the second than of the second chord *complementing* the first, and such a principle of complementation becomes of major importance as the twelve-note technique evolves out of 'free' atonality. It is also an indication that the function of such complementation may be as much, if not more, 'motivic' than 'harmonic' – even when (as will be argued in the next chapter) such accumulations as the one that begins Op. 19 No. 6 are strongly if not totally symmetrical.

11

Harmony – and Symmetry

The extended tonality of the nineteenth century increased the incidence of chromaticism, and also of dissonance: but both were still ultimately subject to fundamental consonance and diatonicism. As a result, chords that were constructed as literal symmetrical entities, or projected from such entities (whether literally or in the abstract), were seen as ultimately subordinate to their often long-delayed, occasionally omitted but still implied chords of resolution. (Such symmetrical chords were most commonly the diminished and augmented triads, the diminished seventh, and the chord using elements from the whole-tone scale – for example E flat, G, A, D flat – sometimes known as the French sixth.) Similarly, the potentially disruptive contrasts between tonal regions located symmetrically on either side of a tonic – at the major or minor third, the tritone, even the major or minor second – were contained by the subordination of such regions to the central tonic; or, on the larger scale in such throughcomposed structures as the acts of Wagner's music dramas, they were part of the long-term progress towards a final, all-powerful goal of resolution. (For discussion of this latter technique in *Parsifal*, see Whittall, 1981.) In *Structural Functions of Harmony*, Schoenberg illustrates an eight-bar phrase from *Lohengrin* which extends its tonic as far as the 'distant' region ⑤, the 'lowered mediant of the Mediant', at its mid-point: that is, it moves from A flat major to D major via C flat major, and back again via F major – a perfect encapsulation of third-related triadic harmony extending a single tonal region (example 28; see Schoenberg, 1969: 104). Such processes are often quite explicit on both the small and large scale in post-Wagnerian tonal music, where the tritonal axis of symmetry is most decisively located either exclusively in the bass, with the poles functioning as roots of triads (or alternative tonics) or – as in Debussy's predominantly whole-tone prelude *Voiles* – with the axis evident between a pedal bass (as overall 'tonic') and the upper lines. In atonal music, by contrast, the

Ex.28 Wagner: *Lohengrin*

lower line loses its bass, root or tonic function, and it becomes possible for the pivot or axis of an inversionally symmetrical structure to be located literally at the centre.*

Jonathan Harvey has expressed the nature and consequences of this possibility with arresting clarity:

The bass moves into the middle: this is our musical revolution. Several composers after Webern, myself included, have been fascinated by harmonic structures which radiate out from either side of a central axis in reflecting intervals. Unless a strong contrary line is taken in atonal music the bass will remain at the bottom of what sounds like dissonant music. But in symmetrical mirroring structures it is *forced*, focal attention is forced, into the axial middle, because all relationships converge there: the sounds point to it. [Harvey, 1982: 2; see also Harvey, 1984]

Some of the implications for atonal music of this 'revolution' will be considered in later chapters. But it must be emphasized again that the kind of 'polarity' that Schoenberg's Wagner example illustrated is very different from the atonal polarities to be considered below, where the centre, and its potentially or literally symmetrical counterpoles, function not in relation to a tonal,

---

*A fascinating example of a theorist's early recognition of the compositional potential of symmetrical inversions, first published in 1912, may be found in Ziehn, 1976.

triadic music but rather to define the registral space within which the music moves motivically: and even, if the symmetry is strict and all-pervading, to determine the nature and order of the musical events themselves.

The importance of symmetry in atonal music has long been recognized by commentators, who often take their cue from Webern's celebrated statement that 'considerations of symmetry, regularity, are now to the fore, as against the emphasis formerly laid on the principal intervals – dominant, subdominant, mediant etc.' [Webern, 1963: 54]. Symmetrical pitch constructs are often held to offer a stabilizing focus, to stem the atonal flux, and to achieve a satisfying degree of control, even of pitch-class priority, without creating incongruous tonal allusions (see Perle, 1977: 26–9; and also Burkhart, 1980). However, the kind of literal, predictable symmetry that finds expression in the palindrome is normally less appealing to composers than symmetries that play a vital but not all-determining role in the atonal chain of events.* For example, Schoenberg's Op. 19 No. 2 can be seen as a 'composing out' of the model shown in example 29, not as some kind of compound C major tonic, but as a symmetrical construct radiating outwards from the central G and bounded by D a twelfth above and C a twelfth below. Just as tonal pieces do not normally confine them-selves to the notes of the tonic triad, so by no means all the pitches or placements of pitches in Op. 19 No. 2 are determined by reference to a single fundamental symmetrical model. Example 29 does suggest that a symmetrical framework for the piece is provided by a fifteen-note collection made up of minor seconds and major or

Ex.29 Schoenberg: Six Little Piano Pieces, Op.19/2

N.B. The presence of an A♯ a diminished third below the low C would symmetrically balance the highest note, F♭.

*Only very rarely are totally symmetrical compositions to be found in the pre-twelve-note atonal repertory: one example is Webern's two-voice canon by inversion at the tritone (Op. 16, No. 2). Palindromes are even more rare, and when Webern uses them within larger movements of his twelve-note works (Symphony Op. 21, second movement, Cantata No. 1, Op. 29, second movement) they avoid mechanical literalness, usually in quite subtle ways.

minor thirds – the open notes in example 29. But there are 26 different pitches in the piece altogether (27 if the low B sharp should read A sharp – see the reproduction of the manuscript in Brinkmann, 1975: vii, and Forte, 1983: 267, n. 1), and not all of these can be derived by registral displacement from the 'open-note' model, since this contains no D flat, F or A. (As example 29 indicates, if there is an A sharp a major third above the lowest note, as might be the case on manuscript evidence, then this mirrors the highest note, the F flat, and both could be incorporated into the open-note model.)

For compositions as short as Op. 19 No. 2 it is a simple matter to write out all the notes employed (conventionally, in ascending order) in order to test for the presence of one (or more) axes of symmetry. But such models are obviously an abstraction from the music of quite a different kind to Schenkerian fundamental structures. Example 29 does not represent the order of events in the piece itself, even though the open notes suggest certain prominent invariants which are of both harmonic and motivic significance, and the analyst should always be prepared to explore connections between model and piece, if only to establish the extent to which the notion of 'composing out' is justified or not.

In Op. 19 No. 6 the abstraction of symmetrical models yields some interesting results, as example 30 demonstrates. In example 30(a) Schoenberg's initial six-note chord is shown, not as 'rooted' on G but as centred on A, even though, as initially presented in the composition, the sequence of pitches and intervals is not symmetrically complete – a C sharp (shown in brackets) is needed to mirror the F: as it happens, the delayed presentation of C sharp (to be discussed later) can be seen as structurally significant in the piece. Example 30(b) concerns the piece's second event, (a^1),* the music between the second half of bar 2 and the second half of bar 4. Here the symmetrical model is modified in two ways: by the omission of C sharp and D (again shown in brackets) and by the octave transposition of two pitches: the first D sharp is shifted up by two octaves (alternatively, both D sharps are shifted up by one octave) and the E is shifted up by one octave. These transposed, displaced or shifted elements are circled in example 30(b). It

---

*Rather than call these various parts of the piece 'phrase' or even 'section', we have chosen the relatively neutral terms 'event' and 'segment', to avoid association with the articulatory functions familiar from discussion of diatonic tonal music.

Ex.30 Schoenberg: Six Little Piano Pieces, Op.19/6

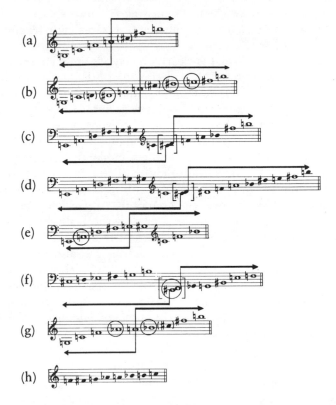

follows, of course, that example 30(b) can be regarded as representing the complete piece so far since it includes the material of 'a'.

Example 30(c) presents all the pitches used in the piece's third event (a^2) (last beat of bar 4 to end of bar 6) as a linear sequence, and it is clear at once that, if Schoenberg had happened to conceive the piece in terms of systematic mirroring procedures, this would have been the point at which he began to modify and break down those procedures. Even if we were to accept a change from a single central axis to a double one (C sharp/D, shown in brackets on the example because they are not literally present in the music), it is still a fact that only the two lowest and two highest pitches in example 30(c) are in a symmetrical relation to that double axis. Rather more pitches can be accounted for if a complete model for the first six bars of the piece is assembled (example 30(d)). Another possibility is to designate as axis a pitch that is actually present – the G – in which case a model results that contains all the new elements in bars 5 and 6, and from which the missing A and F sharp can be derived by octave transposition: only the B is unavailable (example 30(e)).

When we proceed to what is clearly the piece's main contrasting event – the monody in bar 7 (b) – derivation of the pitches from a symmetrical model is even more improbable, and the value of the contrast may lie as much in that difference as in the simple textural opposition here with the rest of the piece. Nevertheless, in view of the fact that bar 8 (c) repeats two of the actual pitches and all the pitch classes of bar 7, it is worth testing a model that covers both bars (example 30(f)). Once again the literal axis is a double one, C sharp/D, and this time those pitches are represented, in octave transposition. The model gives eight out of the twelve actual pitches used in bars 7 and 8, and only one pitch – the F sharp – is not present in the model at any register. After this, bar 9 (a^3) marks not only a return to the piece's principal material, but also to a more symmetrical mode of procedure. As example 30(g) shows, a symmetrical model for bar 9, which presents the six initial pitches in their actual registers, can include an A flat and a B flat as shown, or in any equivalent octave positions – but not as Schoenberg actually places them. His decision to displace them so dramatically may have to do with his desire for a cadential, bell-like sonority: also, perhaps, with a desire to disguise the sense in which those pitches complete an unbroken segment of pitch classes running from F up to C (example 30(h)).

As this discussion has demonstrated, the principle of symmetrical structuring does not provide Op. 19 No. 6 with an all-embracing unity. If all twenty-five pitches used are set out in relation to an axis of A (example 31(a)), only fifteen of those twenty-five pitches are accounted for, though in pitch-class terms the tally is more impressive, in that ten of the twelve are present: the absentees are C sharp and F. A model using C as the axis of symmetry (example 31(b)) may look initially more convincing, since it embraces the highest and lowest pitches of the piece. But only nine pitch classes are included here: C sharp, F sharp and B are all missing. Once again, the 'foreignness' of the C sharp to the piece may be reinforced by the fact that both comprehensive symmetrical models fail to include it. But if we set symmetry aside, and consider the pitch materials – pre-twelve-tonally – in their linear order, and also in relation to the

Ex.31 Schoenberg: Six Little Piano Pieces Op. 19/6

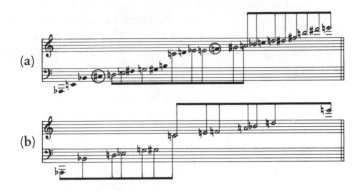

(a)

(b)

accumulation of twelve-note collections, which saturate the texture atonally without requiring any of the systematic orderings of twelve-note music proper, then the C sharp becomes pivotal. As example 32 indicates, the piece's atonality is expressed through the gradual unfolding of two twelve-note collections: the first is completed by the C sharp in bar 7: the second begins either on the same note (in which case the C sharp in bar 8 is a repetition) or with the D that immediately succeeds it. Both collections include various repetitions of previously stated pitches or pitch classes that obey no obvious rules of procedure.

To establish the extent to which a composition accumulates twelve-note collections, or appears to relate to particular symmetrical formations, is to demonstrate degrees of logic in the use of musical space. When tonal harmony no longer determines linear connection, twelve-note collections, or aggregates and symmetrical relationships offer means of observing balance and equilibrium. But both may do so without governing linear ordering, and it is perfectly possible for atonal compositions to make sense as evolving

Ex.32 Schoenberg: Six Little Piano Pieces, Op.19/6

Pitch-class repetitions shown in brackets,
pitch repetitions not shown.

structures without the presence of either. Collection-completion and pitch-symmetry are therefore secondary factors (unless, as already noted, the piece in question is strictly inversional and palindromic): they concern the organization of musical material, but do not help us to define those materials as such. As far as opus 19 is concerned, of course, the question of defining materials is a rather different matter if the analyst insists on considering all six pieces as a unified whole, and refuses to take single items out of context in the way we have done here. Whether wholes or parts are in question, however, Schoenberg's own fundamental concern in musical composition of all periods was the 'idea' as expressed as a relatively small musical unit — a motive or group of motives.

12

Pitch-class Sets

The last two chapters were concerned with analytical issues which arise when compositions that do not present the most fundamental features of diatonic tonal structures in their purest form are nevertheless felt to demand consideration, in essentially harmonic terms, as examples of implied or extended tonality – as music whose harmony, even if derived in whole or in part from symmetrical constructs, might seem to remain in certain respects hierarchic. In this chapter the main theme is quite different: what issues arise when the pitch materials of compositions are considered as representative of total chromaticism – of atonality? It might indeed seem a good deal easier to regard, and describe, the pitch components of the two pieces from Schoenberg's opus 19 as segments of the chromatic scale than to attempt to devise labels appropriate to the notion of extended tonality, such as 'an altered tonic eleventh in G major' for the initial sonority of Op. 19 No. 6. And in atonal compositions that consist largely of repetitions and easily detectable variations of an initial sonority, it might also seem perfectly acceptable – using musical intuition rather than a theory of atonal structure – to describe the ways in which that sonority is modified in the remainder of the composition – transposed, inverted, reversed, shortened, extended, and so on: 'remainders' from this procedure, and their variations, may be described as 'contrasting'.

This process is akin to certain aspects of motivic analysis, to be discussed in the next chapter. But another matter demands attention first, since it involves a more challenging notion of how pitch relationships can be defined and represented than is conventionally taken account of in motivic analysis. In Op. 19 No. 6, it is easy to identify repetitions and transpositions: for example, the initial left-hand chord G/C/F appears transposed in bar 5 as C/F/B flat, and in bar 8 as C sharp/F sharp/B. The three chords appear in different contexts, but there is an undeniable similarity between them: the intervals remain the same, but the pitches change, partially in the first transposition, totally in the second. We will now compare two other elements from the piece, the chords formed from the last three notes of bar 5 – E/D/G sharp – and the last three left-hand notes of bar 8 – C sharp/G/B. This time the second chord is not a literal transposition of the first, and if they occurred in a tonal piece there might well seem little point in seeking to establish any equivalence between an 'incomplete dominant seventh' and an 'incomplete secondary seventh'. Yet even the tonal analyst habitually and legitimately makes comparisons between elements on other than a purely literal basis, if only to the extent (hallowed by thoroughbass) of regarding intervals larger than an octave as projections – compounds – of smaller intervals within the octave: for example, to describe the interval between E and G sharp in the first chord as a 'major third' is universally understood as analytical shorthand for 'an octave and a major third'; and it is also understood that intervals larger than the tritone *within* the octave can be described as inversions of smaller intervals: for example, the minor seventh E to D is an 'inversion' of the major second D to E, and while in a tonal context that act of inversion may have very specific consequences for the nature and function of chords and counterpoint, no such constraint appears to operate in atonal music. For the moment, it may seem to be jumping to a dubious conclusion to assert that the collection D/E/G sharp is a transposed inversion of the collection C sharp/B/G – and vice versa – but it would be difficult for any analyst to complain that the act of abstraction, which makes that direct comparison and equivalence possible, was either incomprehensible or illegitimate. What the analyst will wish to keep clearly in mind is that in performing this particular exercise of 'reduction' it has become possible to relate two items of compositional material to something that is not specifically present in the composition at all – the collection formed from a major second and a tritone on the same 'bass' note. However, if that major second and tritone are regarded, not as literal intervals, but as interval classes, representing the smallest possible form of all their possible projections, then their power and validity as legitimate abstractions from specific compositional events is greatly enhanced.

It is to facilitate and systematize the fundamental distinction between 'pitch' and 'pitch class', 'interval' and 'interval class', that integer notation has been introduced as an analytical tool. Thus, if the twelve pitch classes from C (an arbitrary base) to B are numbered from 0 to 11, the collection D/E/G sharp – however it is projected in an actual composition – will be identified as 2, 4, 8: and its transposed inversion – C sharp/B/G will be 1, 11, 7. For the moment, the simplest way to confirm the equivalence of the collections as pitch-class sets is to note that the distances between the three elements of each set (with reference to the cycle of twelve pitch classes set out below) are the same – 2 and 4:

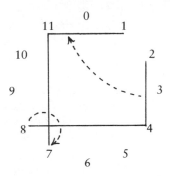

In a pitch-class collection, or set, matters of register and interval do not arise. Pitches are separated from one another by intervals, but pitch classes are separated from one another by interval classes – so that just as the pitch classes 2 and 4 could be D and E in any and every octave position, so the interval class 2, which separates 2 and 4, can be inverted and compounded to generate the minor sevenths, major ninths, and all larger spans of actual music. The fact, noted above, that there are twelve different pitch classes but only six different interval classes (if the notion of inversional equivalence on either side of the tritone is accepted) remains the cause of much theoretical debate, but it will do no great harm to our present purposes to accept it: the extensive literature on pitch-class-set analysis includes the possibility of certain alternatives in terminology and analytical practice, but they do not invalidate the elementary features considered here.

Readers who know something of the twelve-note method will have no difficulty in accepting the idea of several transposed inversions deriving from a single source. In one not very interesting sense, all twelve-note sets are 'the same'; they are all permutations of the same twelve pitch classes: or, a little more formally, there is a single source set – the 'chromatic scale', or 'universal set', of twelve pitch classes for all the many millions (479,001,600) of possible twelve-note sets. Clearly, the chromatic scale, if represented as an abstract ascending sequence of twelve different pitch classes, is far removed from a living musical organism. But to assert its function as a 'background' to all differently ordered twelve-note formations is to make certain kinds of analytical comparison possible, and to facilitate the demonstration that certain types of twelve-note formation have special properties which can be of considerable significance for the composer. The compositional significance of the relation between such 'tropes', or source sets, and the specific melodic orderings and chordal entities that they can generate in twelve-note music is well attested (see, for example, Babbitt, 1955: 58, and Perle, 1977: 129f.), and it is this concept of the source set as a succession, or selection, from the complete collection of twelve pitch classes that has provided an important stimulus for the use of pitch-class sets in the analysis of pre-twelve-note atonal music.

The Structure of Atonal Music by Allen Forte (1973) was the first book to offer a systematic study of 'non-twelve-note' pitch-class sets, a comprehensive terminology, and an account of their possible functions. And although this book has inspired much critical debate* it raises issues that remain central to any attempt to analyse an atonal piece, not as an isolated phenomenon, but as part of a larger whole – the general repertory of atonal compositions, large and small, vocal and instrumental, early and recent. *The Structure of Atonal Music* is a theoretical exposition, not a textbook, and it is indicative of the importance attached – at least in America – to the possible analytical consequences of the theory that a textbook by John Rahn (1980) is now available that provides a graded guide to what the author sees as the basic principles of atonal theory and analysis in the light of, though not in complete agreement with, Forte's work. Any student, or any course, proposing to explore the connection between note and number and such fundamental types of invariance as inversion, transposition and inclusion by way of systematic definitions and theorems will find Rahn a considerate guide.

At first glance, what is most unusual and forbidding about a pitch-class-set analysis of an atonal composition is the prominence of numbers, which seem to give an arid, mathematical aura to the whole enterprise. Numbers do have a role to play in the analysis of tonal music, of course: the Arabic numerals of figured bass, the Roman numerals of functional harmony, or the mixture of the two

---

*For a wide-ranging consideration of the implications for analysis of the concept of the pitch-class set, see Benjamin, 1979.

(with additional symbols) employed by the voice-leading analyst. Moreover, as suggested earlier, numbers are used in tonal and atonal analysis for the same basic reason: to provide the kind of notational shorthand that enables the analyst to bring into full focus the similarities and differences between various elements and events. In tonal analysis a number will be equivalent to, and translatable into, a particular function for which a form of words exists: mediant degree, structural $\hat{2}$, diminished 7th, and so on. And these functions will obtain whatever the tonality in question: the notation stresses the identity and function of the mediant degree, rather than its particular pitch. In atonal analysis, there are no comparable functions to be identified, and the most basic use of number, as already indicated, is to identify a pitch-class location, or the size of an interval class from 1 (minor second) to 6 (tritone).

Forte's theory and technique operate with particular reference to three sequences of numbers: first, the collection representing the twelve different pitch classes, from 0 to 11, where C is designated 0; second, the collection representing the six different interval classes, from 1 to 6; third, the sequence of 'prime-form' pitch-class sets (see p. 137 below), which total 224, or 208 if the sets of cardinality (= number of pitch classes) 0, 1, 2, 10, 11 and 12 are excluded.* It must again be stressed that these sequences are all abstractions in the sense that they cannot, by definition, represent directly the actual pitches, still less the actual character, of compositional events: rather they provide reductions from, and backgrounds to, the enormously large number of different collections and combinations a composer can employ. Thus the sequence of twelve pitch-class integers may seem a crude alternative to the sequence of eighty-five pitch integers that would be needed for the seven octaves within which music normally moves, and it would be a poor analysis that at no stage took some account of the fact that pitch classes may occur (as pitches) in different registers – as well as using different durations, tone colours, and so on. But since the process of analysis depends on systematic and strictly controlled types of description and comparison, it is extremely useful to have a terminology of manageable proportions available – manageable,

---

*Forte's decision to include only sets of cardinality 3 to 9 in his definitive list (Forte, 1973: Appendix 1) is the result of his general view of atonal compositional techniques, and indicates among other things that small-scale motivic factors are not in his judgement the most essential in determining the structure of atonal music. This point is returned to on p. 151 below.

Ex.33 Webern: Three Little Pieces for Cello and Piano, Op.11/3

Segments I   II   III

The four cello harmonics sound as follows:

that is, by the human brain; the computer is, in this respect at least, already less limited.

Simply to translate pitch into pitch class and pitch class into integer notation is of little analytical consequence, however. To take a rudimentary example, consider the very short atonal piece, Webern's Op. 11 No. 3 (example 33). Translating the pitch classes of the piece into integers, with C as 0, the following sequence emerges:

Bar	1	2		3	4	5		7	8	9	10
Cello:	3	4	0	11 10				5		9 2 1	
Piano:			2		6	8 7		11			
			1				3	6			
			5				4	0			
								10			

Reading numbers on a textural map of this kind will certainly draw attention to various recurrences, as well as suggesting that Webern tended to associate near neighbours in the numerical sequence. But this information will be scarcely less evident in a simple transcription of pitch into pitch class. Clearly, a more differentiated means of making comparisons between the various distinct events in the piece is needed if any process of translating pitch, via pitch class, into number is to be justified – and making comparisons means observing all possible degrees of difference and similarity so that, in the end, their relative musical significance may be evaluated.

It is precisely through recognition of the possibility and desirability of demonstrating invariance – the underlying similarities of pitch organization – as succinctly as possible that the specific techniques of pitch-class-set analysis have been devised. Atonal compositions can be described not so much as successions of integers representing pitch classes, as shown above, but rather as successions of events, which use collections of pitch classes, and which group those collections into musically significant statements. 'Grouping' inevitably involves a notion of form, but matters of pitch organization will for the moment be considered separately from any notion of form other than that of segmental identity. In order to facilitate comparison of the collections that comprise atonal compositions, therefore – collections that, as selections from and orderings of segments of the total chromatic, can total many millions – they are, the pitch-class-set analyst argues, best represented and compared not in their diverse compositional characters, but in a presentation arrived at through a uniform ordering procedure. The constituent pitch classes of each collection are therefore translated into integers and arranged into a 'normal order' – 'the order that groups the integers within the smallest distance from left to right and with the smallest successive intervals on the left' [Forte 1978b: 3]. If the normal order is then transposed and inverted, if necessary, so that its first term is 0, the 'prime form' can be identified, by reference to such complete lists of prime forms as that provided in *The Structure of Atonal Music*, Appendix 1. For example, the piano chord in bars 2 and 3 of the Webern cello piece has pitches in ascending order – F, C sharp, D. As a linear succession of pitch classes within the octave C to C, their order is C sharp, D, F, the smaller interval class preceding the larger. Normal order is therefore 1, 2, 5: prime form – subtracting 1 from each member of the normal order – 0, 1, 4.*

This is pitch-class set 3–3 – the third in the sequence of twelve

---

*The prime form represents the total pitch-class content of the set, and in Forte's theory it also represents an 'interval vector', the total of all possible interval classes, that is, all the intervals between any pair of elements within a set. In the case of pitch-class set 3–3, the interval vector is 101100: one each of interval classes 1, 3 and 4, and no instances of interval classes 2, 5 and 6. This is another aspect of Forte's pitch-class-set theory that continues to be widely debated.

possible sets of three pitch classes. Two bars further on, the piano chord E, E flat, G proves to be a different transposition of the same prime form as the first chord: normal order E flat, E, G (3, 4, 7): prime form 0, 1, 4. This example already shows how the process of determining prime forms makes it possible to identify invariants which underpin the evolving surface of the music itself – though the analyst will never want to forget that such invariants may also represent strong surface contrasts.

It will be evident from examples to be discussed later that more factors are involved in the determination of prime forms than those illustrated so far: for example, not only are different transpositions of the same set – different normal orders – regarded as equivalent, but so are inversions: 0, 1, 4 can refer to an ascending or descending sequence of pitch classes. It will also be clear that since pitch-class sets are in question, it makes no difference whether or not a particular pitch occurs more than once in any given segment, or in more than one octave position: the argument is that transposition, inversion, permutation, expansion by pitch-class repetition, and other compositional operations, are significant precisely because they are performed on an existing entity, a set, rather than being part of that entity in its most fundamental form. Indeed, one of the most controversial aspects of pitch-class-set analysis is the claim that it reveals an actual compositional process (see Forte, 1973; 1978b; 1981). The suggestion is not that Webern literally thought of those two chords in Op. 11 No. 3 as pitch-class set 3–3 in two transpositions interval class 2 apart, but that he, like Schoenberg and others, built his atonal compositions from the manipulation (not simply the statement) of 'unordered' collections of pitch classes (see p. 153 below).

It was stated earlier that 'a more differentiated means of making comparisons between the various distinct elements' of atonal pieces is needed than is provided by the translation of pitch classes into strings and bundles of integers. Pitch-class-set analysis involves the segmentation of the piece in question into a sequence of distinct events before the analyst determines the prime forms of the pitch-class collections within each event. The relative brevity and simplicity of Webern's Op. 11 No. 3 make this task unusually straightforward. The small number of notes and the presence of rests make the initial decision to establish three principal segments, as shown in example 33, an uncomplicated one. In more typical, more complex textures, however, a clearly defined principle for segmentation will be difficult to establish and can (as shown later) involve either the separation or overlap of intuitive musical judgements and the more objective but arguably mechanical application of 'blanket' segmentations (Forte's 'imbrication'; see Forte, 1973: 83). In 1973, Forte conceded that 'it seems virtually impossible to systematize' contextual criteria for segment determination 'in any useful way' [: 91]. Since then, one scholar at least has made a serious attempt to tackle this problem (see Hasty, 1981). Nevertheless, for the beginner it is usually best to proceed from the largest, relatively self-contained units – Forte's 'composite segments' – even if these contain all twelve pitch classes, down to the events within those units which retain a distinct identity of some kind – Forte's 'primary segments'. Even in Op. 11 No. 3, each of the three composite segments can be subdivided according to the promptings of the texture. Thus in composite segment 1 the five pitches in the cello form one primary segment; the chord in the piano another; and the vertical alignment of the piano chord with three different cello notes provides three more. And just as these events are subsegments of the main composite segment, so their pitch-class sets will be subsets of the overall set, the 'superset'.

Webern: Op. 11 No. 3
Composite segment I (see example 33)
Primary Segment 1. Cello: pitch classes

Eb	Fb	C	B	Bb
3	4	0	11	10

Normal order: 10, 11, 0, 3, 4 – 'the order that groups the integers within the smallest distance from left to right and with the smallest successive intervals on the left' [Forte, 1978b: 3]. This ordering underlines the need to consider the integers 0–11 as a circular sequence, in which 0 can follow 11 (see the 'clock' on p. 133 above). To establish the prime form of this normal order we transpose to '0' by adding 2 to each integer.
Prime form: 0, 1, 2, 5, 6
Set name: 5–6

Primary Segment 2. Piano: pitch-class set 3–3 (see above, p. 137)

Primary Segments 3, 4 and 5. Piano plus cello:

Pitch classes	Normal order	Prime form	Set name
(3) F, C♯, D, C			
5, 1, 2, 0	0, 1, 2, 5	0, 1, 2, 5	4–4
(4) F, C♯, D, B			
5, 1, 2, 11	11, 1, 2, 5	0, 2, 3, 6	4–12
(5) F, C♯, D, B♭			
5, 1, 2, 10	10, 1, 2, 5	0, 3, 4, 7	4–17

In both (4) and (5) the first interval class is larger than the second, but the complete sequence of interval classes occupies the smallest possible space: in (5) a descending form of the set would be identical in interval class terms to an ascending form – in other words, this is an example of a set that is inversionally symmetrical about its central interval class.

Composite Segment I

Pitch classes:	E♭, F♭, C, F, C♯, D, B, B♭
	3 4 0 5 1 2 11 10
Normal order:	10, 11, 0, 1, 2, 3, 4, 5
Prime form:	0, 1, 2, 3, 4, 5, 6, 7
Set name:	8–1

The first composite segment of Op. 11 No. 3 is therefore revealed as the 'composing out' of a complete, eight-note sequence from the total chromatic, an interesting comparison with the last bar of Schoenberg's Op. 19 No. 6 (see p. 127 above).

   Examples 34 and 35 show two of Allen Forte's segmentations of short atonal pieces, one (Schoenberg's Op. 19 No. 6) already familiar from chapter 10, the other (Webern's Op. 7 No. 3) to be discussed more fully in later sections. It will be clear at a glance that, while the more diverse linear texture of the Webern produces a more elaborate segmentation, in both cases pitches function simultaneously as part of smaller and larger pitch-class collections.

   Simply to establish and list the prime-form pitch-class sets in an atonal composition may, as has already been indicated, reveal certain 'background' similarities: but the pitch-class-set analyst seeks to extend the concept of invariance beyond mere identities between prime forms. Since, in Forte's theory, a set is not just a

Ex.34 Schoenberg: Six Little Piano Pieces, Op.19/6

collection of pitch and interval classes, but can be represented by an interval vector (see p. 137n) there are various kinds of 'similarity relations', reflecting both pitch-class and interval-class content, which can be demonstrated with reference to the prime forms.* It will be obvious that, in terms of the finite system employed, some

---

*These types of similarity relations are four in number: 'Maximum similarity with respect to pitch class (R_p); Minimum similarity with respect to interval class (R_0); Maximum similarity with respect to interval class (with interchange feature, R_1; without interchange feature, R_2)' [Forte, 1973: 49]. For pitch-class relations between a particular set and each of its own transformations, see Rahn's discussion of 'common-tone theorems' [Rahn, 1980: 97f.].

Ex.35 Webern: Four Pieces for Violin and Piano, Op.7/3

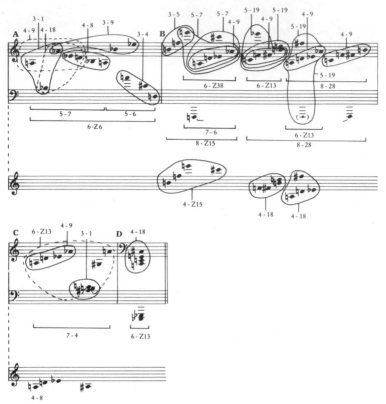

sets will be more similar than others, both with respect to pitch-class content, and to interval-class content as represented by the interval vector. Only comparison between sets of the same cardinality is involved here, of course, and some degree of similarity (if only the presence of interval class 1) is all-pervasive. Hence the importance Forte attaches to types of relation that are rare within the system, like maximal similarity of both pitch and interval class: for example, of the twenty-nine sets of cardinality 4, only two have this relation:

$$
\begin{array}{lll}
4\text{–}2 & 0,1,2,4 & 221100 \\
4\text{–}3 & 0,1,3,4 & 212100
\end{array}
$$

Three of the four pitch classes are the same, and, allowing for the 'interchange feature' between the second and third vector entries, those vectors are identical.

The analytical relevance of similarity relations will naturally vary according to the composition under consideration (see Forte, 1973: 158–66 and 1978b: 13–17). Nor will similarity relations on their own normally represent the fullest ramifications of set structure, for the simple reason that a composition is unlikely to segment solely into sets of a single cardinality. Hence the importance of a technique for comparing sets of different sizes, to define relations that are, in one sense, all-pervading. For example, pitch-class set 3–1 (0, 1, 2) is a subset of no fewer than 94 larger sets, or wellnigh half the total possible number of sets of cardinality 3 to 9 (208). The point is not that the recurrence of a particular trichord, whether as a separate set – a primary segment – or as a subset, must invariably be seen as compositionally insignificant, and treated with disdain by the analyst, but that, in making comparisons between prime forms of different cardinalities, the analyst may find it useful to distinguish between those types of inclusion that are common and those that are much more rare.

In considering similarity and inclusion relations, it becomes possible to envisage a totally unified atonal structure in which not only are all the sets related to each other through similarity or inclusion procedures, but the whole composition may be regarded as being controlled by one or very few sets. In other words, a piece may employ what Forte terms 'nexus' sets, and through such collections it becomes possible for a notion of hierarchy to enter the vocabulary of pitch-class-set analysis. Some indication of the importance of complementation in atonal music was given in Chapter 10 and it is this notion of complementation that is central to Forte's theory of the 'set complex' as an association that relates to a referential nexus set. Not only can a set be repeated, transposed, inverted, reversed, broken down into subsets; it can actually be complemented by the one other set that provides those members of the total chromatic – the universal set – not present in the first set. This means that the cardinalities of a set and its complement always sum to 12: for example, the complement of 5–24 is 7–24, and that of 4–Z15 is 8–Z15. But it will be clear as soon as we write down the prime forms of such complementary pairs that prime forms themselves do not express the literal complementation just described. For example:

5–24   0, 1, 3, 5, 7
7–24   0, 1, 2, 3, 5, 7, 9

In this case the prime forms have five pitch classes in common, and the total number of different pitch classes is seven, not twelve. For literal complementation to be demonstrated, therefore, one member of the pair must be transformed – transposed, inverted, or both. If we (a) present the larger member of the 5–24/7–24 pair as a sequence of pitch classes, we can then (b) identify the missing pitch classes and (c) form them into a normal order which represents the necessary complement (d):

(a) 7–24: C, C♯, D, D♯, F, G, A
(b) *Missing pitch classes:* E, F♯, G♯, A♯, B
                               4, 6, 8, 10, 11
(c) *Normal order:* 11, 10, 8, 6, 4
(d) Prime form: 0, 1, 3, 5, 7

Exponents of set theory argue that to confine the principle of complement relation to such literal pairings is an unnecessary restriction, and so the pitch-class-set analyst will 'accept as complement of a given set not only the literal pitch-class complement of that set but also any transposed or inverted-and-transposed form of the literal complement' [Schmalfeldt, 1983: 70].

With hexachords, of course, a larger–smaller complement pairing is not possible, but hexachordal complementation is still possible, and is of two types. The first type of hexachord is self-complementary – thus in the case of 6–22 (0, 1, 2, 4, 6, 8), the missing pitch classes are 3, 5, 7, 9, 10, 11 – an inverted transposition of 6–22 itself: 11, 10, 9, 7, 5, 3 = 0, 1, 2, 4, 6, 8. The other type of hexachord will be complemented by a different set, for example:

6–Z6   0, 1, 2, 5, 6, 7 (C, C♯, D, F, F♯, G)
6–Z38   0, 1, 2, 3, 7, 8

The prime form of 6–Z38, given here, is transposed and inverted from this normal form: 11, 10, 9, 8, 4, 3 – that is, B, A sharp, A, G sharp, E, D sharp.*

---

*The letter Z as prefix to some of the set numbers given in this paragraph indicates that the set has the same interval vector as another set while not being reducible to the same prime form: in these cases the complements are the related sets in question.

Forte has devised a characteristically systematic process for describing complementation and testing for its presence or absence. Once a piece has been segmented, and the prime forms determined, it will often be evident that many if not all of the smaller sets are subsets of one of the larger sets, either literally, or through transposition. Moreover, as already noted, some of the smaller sets, particularly the trichords, will probably be subsets of *all* the larger sets. Would that situation justify arguing that those trichords and their complements are in Forte's terms, the 'nexus sets' of the whole piece, in a sense generating all the other material? Once more, Forte argues that such relationships are too widespread – and perhaps more motivic than harmonic – to be of major structural significance. Forte's 'nexus sets' are governors, rather than generators; that is, they seem to control the flow of events by reference to their own invariant properties, rather than by setting in motion a sequence of transformations that may become progressively more remote from the original nucleus, as in an evolutionary, motivic structure. For Forte, the most interesting structural function is identified when it is possible to establish that a particular set *and its complement* are both in an inclusion relation with a significant number of the other sets that segmentation reveals in the work. And this is where the idea of the 'set complex' comes into play.

Two basic types of set-complex relation are possible: 'K' and 'Kh' (both terms are arbitrary). The K relation holds between a pair of sets when one – at any level of transposition or inversion – is included *either* in the other *or* its complement: thus, in Webern's Op. 7 No. 3, 3–1 (0, 1, 2) is in a K-relation to 4–8 (0, 1, 5, 6), even though the relation is with 4–8's complement – 8–8 (0, 1, 2, 3, 4, 7, 8, 9) – a set not actually present in the piece as segmented by Forte. (The point is that, while there is no way in which 0, 1, 2 can be mapped on to 0, 1, 5, 6 – by transposition or inversion – it can be found no fewer than four times in 8–8, as 0, 1, 2/1, 2, 3/2, 3, 4 and 7, 8, 9.) The Kh-relation is more exclusive, since it involves the inclusion of a set in *both* another set and also in the complement of that other set, *whether or not that complement is actually present in the composition.* For example, 3–4 (0, 1, 4) can be in a K-relation to 4–8 (0, 1, 5, 6): 0, 1, 4, transposed and inverted to 6, 5, 1, is a subset of 0, 1, 5, 6. But 3–4 can be considered to be in a Kh-relation to 4–8 only if it is also included as a subset in the complement of 4–8, 8–8. Since 8–8 consists of 0, 1, 2, 3, 4, 7, 8, 9, it will be seen that the inclusion relation holds: 3–4 is a subset of both 4–8 and

8–8 (it actually appears no fewer than six times in 8–8: 0, 1, 4/3, 4, 7/8, 7, 4/4, 3, 0/8, 9, 0 and 1, 0, 9) and is therefore, in Forte's terms, a member of the set-complex Kh about 4–8/8–8.

If all the sets in a particular composition are in a K- or Kh-relation to one of their company (other than a trichord or its complement), then that set may be designated the 'nexus set', which Forte defines simply as 'a referential set for a particular set complex' [Forte, 1973: 210]. More often than not, however, no such clear-cut hierarchy can be found – in other words, a single set complex may not be equivalent to the entire piece – and it becomes necessary to consider the presence of more than one set complex, and more than one nexus set. Just as Forte regards the more exclusive Kh-relation as more significant structurally than the more common K-relation, so, in seeking to establish the presence of nexus sets, he works downwards from sets with the largest cardinality (allowing for 'complement equivalence'): that is, from hexachords through pentachords to tetrachords. In Forte's terms, a set-complex structure may be 'connected' if all the sets are related through one or more nexus sets, but it is of course perfectly possible for an atonal composition to lack such 'connections' altogether – indicating, perhaps, that the composer has a less integrated sense of atonal structure than Forte and other theorists have since identified in some music, especially Schoenberg's.

In order for the various types of set-complex relation to be determined it is necessary to draw up a table of the kind illustrated in example 36, for Webern's Op. 7 No. 3. The horizontal axis lists in ascending numerical order from left to right all the sets considered by the analyst to be identifiable in the piece, and the vertical axis lists in numerical order from top to bottom all those sets which are considered suitable candidates for the role of nexus set: the vertical axis always excludes trichords, which cannot themselves function as nexus sets but which can be part of K or Kh set complexes. The larger complements of sets are not normally shown separately, even when they are actually employed in the piece. It will also be noted that, because sets of the same cardinality cannot be compared for the inclusion relation, the table is 'stepped' in shape.

In a relatively short, simple piece like the Webern, the analyst can, with a little practice, work out the K- or Kh-relations from the prime-form details alone (all that is needed is reference to Appendix I of *The Structure of Atonal Music*). An example – in order to check

Example 36

Webern: Four Pieces for Violin and Piano, Op. 7/3

Table of Set-complex relations

	3–1	3–4	3–5	3–9	4–8	4–9	4–Z15	4–18	8–28	7–4	5–6	5–7	5–19
4–8	K	Kh	Kh	K									
4–9	K	K	Kh	K									
4–Z15/8–Z15	K	K	Kh	K									
4–18	K	K	Kh	K									
8–28			K		K	K	K						
7–4	Kh	Kh		K	K	K	K						
5–6/7–6	Kh	Kh		K	Kh	K	Kh						
5–7	Kh	Kh		Kh	Kh	Kh	Kh						
5–19	K	K		K	K	Kh	Kh	Kh	K	K	K	Kh	
6–Z6/6–Z38	Kh	Kh		Kh	Kh	Kh	K					Kh	
6–Z13	K	K		Kh		K*	K*	K*	K*	K*	K*		K*

Table adapted from Forte 1973: 128.

'The asterisk attached to K indicates that the inclusion relation holds. This is used in case of a single Z-type hexachord.' [Forte 1973: 98] the relations between 5–7 and all the other sets established in the initial segmentation, we first determine the pitch-class content of 5–7 (0, 1, 2, 6, 7) and its complement 7–7 (0, 1, 2, 3, 6, 7, 8). We then check the pitch-class sequences of all the other sets against both 5–7 and 7–7. First, the trichords: 3–1 (0, 1, 2) is a subset of both 5–7 and 7–7: the relation is therefore Kh. 3–4 (0, 1, 5) is a subset of both through transposition, so the relation is, again, Kh. Both the other trichords, 3–5 (0, 1, 6) and 3–9 (0, 2,7) are Kh with 5–7/7–7. Next, the tetrachords: 4–8 (0, 1, 5, 6) and 4–9 (0, 1, 6, 7) have the Kh-relation (4–8 being a subset of 5–7 by transposition as 1, 2, 6, 7). 4–Z15 (0, 1, 4, 6) is a subset of 7–7 at t2 (as 2, 3, 6, 8: 't2' means transposed by two semitones or interval class 2) but not of 5–7: the relation is therefore K. Similarly 4–18 (0, 1, 4, 7) is a subset of 7–7 at t2, but not of 5–7, and the relation is again K. The first blank entry in the table comes at 8–28 (0, 1, 3, 4, 6, 7, 9, 10): although 5–7 is related to 8–28 through their common tetrachord (0, 1, 6, 7), 5–7 as a whole is not included in 8–28; nor is 4–28 (0, 3, 6, 9) included in 5–7: there is therefore no K- or Kh-relation. Finally, the hexachords: 5–7 is a subset of both 6–Z6 (0, 1, 2, 5, 6, 7) and 6–Z38 (0, 1, 3, 7, 8) – the latter by t1, so the relation is Kh. But 5–7 is a subset neither of 6–Z13 (0, 1, 3, 4, 6, 7) nor of its complement 6–Z42 (0, 1, 2, 3, 6, 9), so the entry in the table is blank.

When the table of set-complex relations has been completed, the total of K- and Kh-relations for each of the sets in the vertical axis is calculated, starting with the largest independent set and working 'upwards'. The totals for Op. 7 No. 3 are as follows – and it will be seen at once that, of the eleven entries in the vertical axis, none includes, or is included in, all other sets of different cardinality:

	Kh	K	Blank	Kh/K totals
6–Z6/6–Z38	7	2	4	9
6–Z13	1	8	4	9
7–4	4	5	2	9
5–6/7–6	6	3	2	9
5–7	7	2	2	9
5–19	5	5	1	10
4–8	5	4	1	9
4–9	4	6	0	10
4–Z15/8–Z15	3	7	0	10
4–18	2	7	1	9
8–28	0	3	7	3

Forte comments that 'from the table of set-complex relations . . . it can be ascertained that the structure is connected, with nexus sets 6–Z6/38, 6–Z13 and 4–9' [Forte, 1973: 126]. In other words, the set or sets with the largest K/Kh totals, or the largest single Kh entry, do not automatically become nexus sets. Here, 6–Z6/38 and 6–Z13 each have a total of 9 K/Kh-relations, and, as example 36 shows, those sets which are not related to both hexachords – 3–9, 4–8, 4–18, 8–28, 7–4, 5–6, 5–7 and 5–19 – are related to one or the other. The details are as follows:

		4–8	4–9	4–Z15	4–18	8–28	7–4	5–6	5–7	5–19
6–Z6	(0, 1, 2, 5, 6, 7):		K					K		
6–Z38	(0, 1, 2, 3, 7, 8):	Kh	Kh						Kh	
6–Z13	(0, 1, 3, 4, 6, 7):		K	K	K	K	K			K
6–Z42	(0, 1, 2, 3, 6, 9]:									

Notes: 4–8 is t2 in 6–Z38 (2, 3, 7, 8)
4–9 is t1 in 6–Z38 (1, 2, 7, 8)
4–Z15 is t1 in 6–Z6 (1, 2, 5, 7)
5–7 is t1 in 6–Z38 (1, 2, 3, 7, 8)
6–Z42, the complement of 6–Z13, is not used in the piece: those sets (other than trichords) which would have a Kh-relation with 6–Z13/42 are only three in number: 4–12, 4–13 and 4–18 (see Forte, 1973: 206).

As Forte concludes, 'excluding the trichords, every set but one relates primarily either to 6–Z6/38 or to 6–Z13. The sole exception is 4–9, which relates to both, thus linking two distinct hexachordal complexes.' [: 126] The table shows that 4–9 is the only set (other than a trichord) to be included in all three of the piece's hexachords: 4–Z15 is included in only two (6–Z6 and 6–Z13). For this reason, therefore, Forte regards 4–9 as a secondary nexus set. Such is the harmonic significance of the hexachords, however, that these have priority as nexuses, even though their K/Kh totals are smaller than those of 5–19 and 4–Z15/8–Z15. Although 5–19 has 5 Ks and 5 Khs, the fact that it is included in only one of the piece's three hexachords shows how limited its deeper connections actually are. Similarly, although 4–Z15 registers no blanks in the table of set-complex relations, the fact that it does not relate to 6–Z38 prevents it from functioning as a secondary nexus set.

It will be evident that Forte's tables of set-complex relations involve a good deal of shorthand. In particular, it is not evident from the table alone what level of transposition or inversion, if any, the K- or Kh-relation represents, or whether the smaller set is a literal subset of the larger as presented in the piece or not. And although in example 36 the asterisks attached to six of the Ks in the bottom line indicate that the inclusion relation in question is actually with 6−Z13, rather than with its (absent) complement 6−Z42 (the first two Ks, 3−1 and 3−4, are present *only* in 6−Z42), the table does not tell us how literally, or at what levels, the relations actually operate.

The many qualifications attached to the table of set-complex relations should reassure those who would rightly be suspicious of a simple equation between the relative numbers of set relations and relative musical importance. That a set has ten rather than nine K- or Kh-relations in a 'connected' structure would hardly seem to tip the balance in determining the most significant characteristics of an atonal piece. Nevertheless, it will be seen from Forte's segmentation (example 35) that all four nexus sets are of considerable *musical* importance in this composition (a factor to be considered again in Part IV).

6−Z6 is the superset for Section A, while its complement 6−Z13 is the superset for section D, and is prominent in sections B and C. As for 4−9, it provides the ostinato motive in section B, having been anticipated, in Forte's segmentation, in section A. Needless to say, some of these occurrences overlap: in section A, 4−9 is a subset of 6−Z6, and, in section B, of 6−Z13. Indeed, 4−9 is the subset that all three hexachords have in common, since 0, 1, 6, 7 is literally present in 6−Z6 and 6−Z13, and at t1 (1, 2, 7, 8) in 6−Z38: the nexus sets therefore account between them for a fair proportion of the pitches in the piece. Nevertheless, since the set-complex analysis deals only in prime forms, the reader should remember that the 'identities' revealed in this analysis are not necessarily identities on the musical surface: for example, the first 6−Z13 from section B − B, C, D, E flat, F, F sharp − is quite different from that of section D − C, C sharp, E flat E, G flat, G: these two forms of 6−Z13, interval class 1 apart, have only three pitch classes in common.

For most analysts, even those intrigued by the theoretical and compositional potential of the theory of set-complex relations, the degree of abstraction demonstrated in the above account will be self-defeating if it does not ultimately relate to events that can be shown to be relevant or significant on the musical surface. Much depends on how we define 'significant'. In tonal music, although dissonances and passing decorations may well be most significant expressively, structural significance is another matter. So, in atonal music, the fact that a nexus set may not be prominent chordally or thematically, and that the determination of its existence may involve considering elements (complements) not present in the piece itself, need not automatically create a sense of musical unreality. For Forte, any single atonal composition is significantly analysable primarily as one instance of a language, of a harmonic, structural process that can be paralleled in all atonal compositions. It follows that pitch-class-set analysis is seen to best advantage when several different compositions are compared, or when the apparently disparate sections of large single compositions are analysed in order to yield a thorough determination of their differences and similarities, in relation to 'the structure of atonal music', understood as 'the structural principles represented in all atonal compositions'.

As Forte's own work has developed, it has become increasingly clear that he seeks to distinguish between an account of 'successive segments' in an atonal composition that stresses their motivic or thematic characteristics, and an account motivated by the conviction that the most important segments and sets are the means whereby atonal music achieves harmonic coherence. There is, then, a challenging parallel with the Schenkerian interpretation of tonal music as structured most fundamentally by the interaction of contrapuntal and harmonic forces, with motivic processes relatively superficial. With respect to what he calls 'Schoenberg's first atonal masterwork' (itself an unambiguously Schenkerian expression!) Forte claims that the elements of coherence of the Piano Piece, Op. 11 No. 1, 'as well as its special elusive quality, are provided by the dynamic and kaleidoscopic transformations beneath what appears to be a conventional musical surface composed of themes and motives' [Forte, 1981: 137]. Thus, while an analysis of Op. 11 No. 1 of the kind that Perle introduces [Perle, 1977: 10–15] can demonstrate relationships between motives and chords that use a common three-note cell or trichord, this, in Forte's view, focuses on a relatively superficial aspect of structure, for such trichords 'play a role analogous to dyadic motives in tonal music' [Forte 1981: 136]. By contrast, Forte designates as the most significant structural components of this piece 'six hexachords and their complements, six pentachords and their complements, and two tetrachords and their complements' [: 133], all of which extend beyond those components that assume specific thematic shapes. It therefore follows that even when (as suggested below, p. 158) the concept of the pitch-class set can be invoked as part of a kind of motivic analysis, the results of such analysis will be quite different from an analysis of pitch structure using the techniques developed by Forte himself.

Forte's own segmentations can be controversial: in Op. 7 No. 3, for example, he does not take the piano melody that runs from bars 5 to 8, with its bass note, as a distinct segment, and the set formed – 7–2 – is not part of his analysis. In the absence of hard and fast rules for segmentation, and given the sheer variety of texture typical of atonal music, differences of opinion and emphasis in segmentation are inevitable. So it is a valuable exercise in itself to compare the results of different segmentations of the same piece, given that segmentations, and the conclusions drawn from them, can only be part of the technical interpretation of the music – a much more varied and diverse activity than pitch-class-set manipulation on its own. Nevertheless, as a means of demonstrating concisely how it is possible to present an interpretation of the interacting, underlying pitch-class collections of atonal compositions, the table of set-complex relations is a fascinating phenomenon. It should be stressed that Forte himself has never sought to use the notion of the nexus set to imply an overriding unity – something equivalent to the diatonic fundamental structure – in atonal music. For example, in his analysis of Schoenberg's orchestral piece, Op. 16 No. 3, Forte divides the piece into three strata, each of which has different nexus sets, and while stratum 1 can be linked to stratum 3, and stratum 2 to stratum 3, stratum 1 and stratum 2 remain, in Forte's interpretation, 'essentially detached from one another' [Forte, 1973: 177]. Similarly, in his controversial and stimulating *The Harmonic Organisation of 'The Rite of Spring'*, Forte, while naturally arriving at important conclusions about the incidence and significance of recurrent harmonic configurations, does not seek to reduce these to fewer than three seven-element sets and four eight-element sets [Forte 1978: 132].

Apart from Forte, several other writers have published pitch-class-set analyses of large-scale atonal compositions. One of the most interesting is Janet Schmalfeldt's study of *Wozzeck*, not least because students who are disappointed to find that a work as brief as Webern's Op. 7 No. 3 requires three nexus sets can contemplate the argument that 'the fundamental pitch-structural components of *Wozzeck* share complex interrelationships that can be formally summarized in terms of the interaction of just three subcomplex Kh families – Kh (6–Z19/Z44), Kh (6–34), and Kh (4–18)' [Schmalfeldt, 1983: 237]. Another is James Baker's article on Webern's Op. 6, with its conclusion that a single nexus set for the whole work can be demonstrated, in the shape of the hexachord pair 6–Z19/44. Baker notes that

the fact that 6–Z19/44 is the main link among important motivic sets in the *Six Pieces* . . . takes on particular meaning when one considers the dedication of the piece – 'To Arnold Schoenberg, my teacher and friend, with greatest admiration' . . . It happens that the nexus set, 6–Z44, is the Schoenberg motto, the hexachord resulting from the notes associated with the musical letters of the name: Es (E flat) – C natural – H (B natural) – B (B flat) – E natural and G natural. [Baker, 1982: 26–7]

This collection is of particular interest to pitch-class-set analysts, since it seems to offer conclusive evidence that the early atonal composers did think in terms of pitch-class collections prior to any special ordering that they might be given compositionally, and as such not restricted to linear, thematic presentation. Such a harmonic conception – apart from its anticipation of the kind of complementation that pervades twelve-note music – is evidently the source of many different musical events, rather than just a 'motive' in itself, and its occurrence in so many different contexts in early atonal music argues strongly for the kind of consideration of the music against the background of pitch-class sets that Forte's system makes possible.

13

Motives

Pitch-class sets are finite in number and can be arranged into an ordered sequence. It is on the basis of such a sequence, and the ways in which certain types of connection between its members can be demonstrated, that Forte justifies his claim to be able to describe the structure of atonal compositions; and in the most fundamental sense that description is unaffected by textural considerations – whether a composition is predominantly chordal or melodic in character (homophonic or contrapuntal), whether any distinction can be made between melody and accompaniment. Such textural factors are likely to be reflected in the segmentation, of course, but there is not one kind of pitch-class set for a melody and another for accompanimental chords. It follows that the emergence and development of pitch-class-set analysis has heightened the challenge to those who believe that the most basic element in a study of an atonal composition should be the infinite diversity of specific textural phenomena and, in particular, the most essential compositional idea as represented by a basic motive. And if such a motive is not reduced to its possible 'prime form', but is itself seen as the source for those transformations which analysis can show the composer to have employed in the composition in question, it may then be argued that the particular qualities of that composition are likely to be more directly expounded in motivic analysis than by means of the powerful abstractions of pitch-class-set analysis. The directness comes from the fact that the basis for transformation – the motive, the gesture, or the concrete musical 'idea' – is literally present in the music. Just as we noted earlier that the presence of symmetrical constructs in a composition may well not help to identify the actual musical material being organized, so we may contrast the concept of a pitch-class set with the fact of some actual, musical material to which later transformations refer.

Simply because motives are compositional ideas rather than the abstracted sources of compositional materials, there is (as yet) no 'theory of motivic analysis' to place alongside the theory of pitch-class sets. When Réti, as quoted above (p. 89), observed about the thematic process that 'no real attempt has ever been made to comprehend in a systematic analysis the working of this most essential process of musical composition' he was describing a situation that his own work did little to change. Yet, as argued above (p. 91), the absence of 'a systematic theory of affinity' cannot and should not prevent the analyst pursuing instincts and ideas about unifying connections – if only, in atonal music, as a way of testing the extent to which such ideas remain relevant. Another reason to persist with motivic analysis of atonal music, even when the contrasting virtues of pitch-class-set analysis are acknowledged, is the importance attached to that activity by the seminal master of atonality. This is how one Schoenberg pupil described the activity:

The evaluation of musical ideas, their character and elaboration was discussed; symmetry, contrast, structural balance between sections and overall organization were dealt with. The study of the smallest musical unit, the motive, was the point of departure. Its logical development makes coherence in music possible, not only by exact repetition, subtle changes in melody, rhythm, or harmony, but by altering sound and character. These procedures comprise the basic compositional technique: variation. The variation should be perpetual to make the organization of a piece natural, for in spite of contrasts, a common denominator in every composition must be established. [Pisk, 1976: 40]

The question of whether or not Schoenberg, Webern and other early atonal composers actually thought in terms of the unordered collections now known as pitch-class sets will continue to provide the basis for vigorous debate. But nothing is more explicit in Schoenberg's work, as composer or teacher, than his belief that motivic processes are more fundamental than harmonic or contrapuntal procedures:

One may sooner sacrifice logic and unity in the harmony than in the thematic substance, in the motives, in the thought-content . . . It is difficult to conceive that a piece of music has meaning unless there is meaning in the motive and thematic presentation of ideas. On the other hand a piece whose harmony is not unified, but which develops its motive and thematic material logically, should, to a certain degree, have intelligent meaning. [Schoenberg, 1975: 280]

Nevertheless, as already indicated in this book, Schoenberg offered more comprehensive guidance for analysing the 'structural functions of harmony' in tonal compositions than he did for determining the possible nature and extent of thematic unity as it operated in either tonal or atonal music through the pervasive transformations of motives or basic shapes (see chapters 7 and 10 above). The distinction between these two thematic elements must now be pursued, although Schoenberg himself defined the former more clearly than the latter. In essence, the motive is smaller than the basic shape, it is the 'smallest common multiple', the 'greatest common factor', which 'generally appears in a characteristic and impressive manner at the beginning of a piece' and whose 'features . . . are intervals and rhythms, combined to produce a memorable shape or contour' [Shoenberg, 1970b: 8–9]. It is 'a unit which contains one or more features of interval and rhythm' [Schoenberg, 1972: 15], and it seems clear that Schoenberg was willing to abstract a single interval class or interval type from a more varied line in order to propose an underlying generating motive of a single interval (see his discussion of Brahms's Symphony No. 4 in Schoenberg, 1975; 405–6). The basic shape, according to Schoenberg's pupil Josef Rufer, is the next largest formal unit after the motive, a phrase that may be several bars long and that consists of the 'firm connection of one or more motives and their more or less varied repetitions' (see Epstein, 1979: 18, and Appendix A; also above, chapter 7). And what Schoenberg himself said on the subject – for example, 'a shape usually consists of more than one statement of the motive' [Schoenberg in Goehr, 1977: 22] – certainly confirms the contrast between the two concepts, without necessarily discouraging the analyst of atonal music from using the notion of basic shape even when the idea of 'a phrase that may be several bars long' seems less appropriate, as it is bound to do in small-scale atonal compositions.*

If the analyst does seek a hard and fast distinction between motive and basic shape, then the relative proportions of the two must obviously be stressed. With respect to his Op. 22 No. 1, Schoenberg spoke of a minor third and minor second being 'combined to yield the following "shape"' (*Gestalt*) (example 37(a)) [Schoenberg, 1968: 28–9]. Of example 37(b), referring to Op. 22 No. 2, Schoenberg said that this is 'to be found almost everywhere and may well be considered as the "common

---

* For the argument that an eight-bar *Grundgestalt* is possible in a tonal piece – Chopin's C minor *Etude*, Op. 10 No. 12 – see Phipps, 1983.

Ex.37 (a) Schoenberg: Four Orchestral Songs, Op.22/1

(b) Schoenberg: Four Orchestral Songs, Op.22/2

Al-le wel-che dich

denominator" of all the shapes in this piece' [: 37]. Schoenberg's examples of such derivations in Op. 22 Nos. 1 and 2 are extensive, though by no means comprehensive: and he later confesses that 'the third and fourth songs afford their analysis far greater difficulties . . . I know that these songs do not dispense with logic – but I cannot prove it' [: 39; and see Dunsby, 1977b].

The matter of terminology is further complicated by the fact that the expression 'motivic analysis' tends to be used whether or not the essential material is more appropriately defined as 'motive' or 'basic shape', and whether or not the unity between thematic elements is best represented as the variation of a single common element (something Schoenberg himself classified as 'modified repetition' (in 1970b: 9) or as the more thoroughgoing transformation of elements – Réti's 'indirect affinity' – which can nevertheless be regarded as (in Pisk's phrase) a 'logical development' of the motive.

Schoenberg sought to distinguish between 'variation' of the basic motive, with 'changes of subordinate meaning which . . . have only the local effect of embellishment' and 'developing variation', meaning that 'in the succession of motive-forms produced through variation of the basic motive, there is something which can be compared to development, to growth' [: 8]. This is by no means Schoenberg's only attempt to define the concept. As Walter Frisch argues, with some justification, 'perhaps the clearest single definition is one of the last he attempted, in a 1950 esssay entitled "Bach"':

Music of the homophonic-melodic style of composition, that is, music with a main theme, accompanied by and based on harmony, produces its material by, as I call it, developing variation. This means that variation of the features of a basic unit produces all the thematic formulations which provide for fluency, contrasts, variety, logic and unity on the one hand, and character, mood, expression, and every needed differentiation, on the other hand – thus elaborating the *idea* of the piece. [Schoenberg, 1975: 397; quoted in Frisch, 1984: 1–2].

Elsewhere, Schoenberg states that 'variation . . . is repetition in which some features are changed and the rest preserved' [1970b: 9]. 'Development' allows for the possibility of transformation: it implies, even on the smallest scale, 'not only growth, augmentation, extension and expansion, but also reduction, condensation and intensification' [: 58]. Clearly, the process of development brings with it the possibility of relationship and connection crossing the border into separation and contrast, and the point at which this occurs will often be obscure, as the following analysis of Op. 19 No. 6 will confirm. Motivic analysis is not a discipline with absolute categories, and it is necessary to recall that Schoenberg's own aim as a theorist was to stimulate composers, not to promote analysis as an academic discipline in its own right.

Practically speaking, when the material in question is provided by atonal miniatures, there are two distinct types of motivic analysis: the first is expressed primarily through the actual pitches, intervals, durations and other features present in the music; the second tends to concentrate on pitch, and to reduce the pitches and intervals to classes, as in the early stages of a pitch-class-set analysis; then, instead of proceeding to establish 'unordered' collections and to explore the harmonic significance of the various collections by means of similarity relations and set-complex relations, the analyst will determine an 'abstract' motive, or basic shape, and trace processes of variation and transformation, in ways that might not, in the end, account for literally every pitch in the piece. In addition, the first type of motivic analysis may tend in one of several different directions, according to the nature of the music concerned. It may be able to account for the relationships within the piece wholly or predominantly by means of a series of modified repetitions, or variations, of one or more motives: or the emphasis may be more on derivations – developed transformations.

As far as the atonal miniatures considered here are concerned, it is clear that 'motive' may be understood as referring to vertical as well as linear musical statements, or to statements distributed in fragmented fashion in both planes. After all,.what Schoenberg, in connection with twelve-note music, called 'working with the tones of the motive' [Schoenberg, 1975: 248] certainly did not rule out such non-melodic formations, as if some concept of 'implicit' or 'extended' motivicism might be allowed. So, in the analysis of Op. 19 No. 6 which follows (example 38(a)) the principal motive is formed from the two three-note chords that begin the piece. As the

Ex.38 (a) Schoenberg: Six Little Piano Pieces, Op.19/6

'a'

Features: duration – 7 crotchets
: dynamic – uniform *pp*

'a¹'

Varied repeat of 'a'
Variants: duration extended to
8 crotchets
: expansion of pitch-content and
register
: differentiation of dynamic levels
The 'minor ninth' D♯/E may be derived
from the F/F♯ of 'a'.

'a²'

Modified repeat of 'a¹'
Variants: duration extended to a minimum of
9 crotchets
: pitch-content expanded by (i) partial
transposition of initial LH chord,
(ii) further transposition of that
chord's boundary interval to E/D,
(iii) addition of linear major second,
varying ⓧ in 'a¹'
: dynamic – general *diminuendo*

'b'

This is 'a motive-form too foreign to the basic motive' to be derived
from the literal features of that motive. The initial D/C♯/D may be
derived by inversion and interval-expansion from the minor ninths
of 'a²' and 'a¹', while the D and F♯ are pitches repeated from 'a²'.
But these relationships do not justify defining this statement as a
whole as a modified repeat of any previous statement.
dynamic – the loudest of the whole piece
duration – shorter than any 'a' statement

mit sehr zartem Ausdruck

'c'

Not a modified repeat of 'a', but derivable by variation from the LH
chord of 'a' and from the vertical/linear texture of 'a¹'. 'c' comprises
(i) a transposition of the LH chord (C♯/F♯/B), (ii) two alterations
of that chord – D/G♯/C and C♯/G̲/B, (iii) an additional RH line
(E/E♭) which mirrors the LH F♯/G. A literal precedent for the
descending half-step is in 'a¹'.
dynamic – reverts to the basic *pp*
duration – shortest of the whole piece

genau im Takt

'a³'

A modified repeat of 'a'
Variants: duration reduced to a minimum of crotchets
: dynamics reduced to *ppp/pppp*
: pitch-content expanded with LH Bb/Ab. As a distinct
motivic element this is derivable either literally from the
span of the first 3-note chord of 'a', or by alteration from
the linear G♯/F♯ of 'a²'.

wie ein Hauch

example and its annotations indicate, this composition is formed mainly from development of the initial statement, and even the two events designated as contrasts, rather than as variants of the principal motive, have points of contact with that motive or its variants. The distinction between the 'a'-type segments and the remainder is therefore based more on the closeness of the 'a' statements to each other than on the principle that 'b' and 'c' are totally independent of 'a'. But at least one alternative segmentation, which eliminates that distinction altogether, might be worth consideration:

Segment	Alternative	
a	a	chord+chord
a^1	a^1	chords+linear statement
a^2	a^2	chords+linear statement
b ⎤ c ⎦	a^3	linear statement: chords+linear statements
a^3	a^4	chords+linear statement

It is a matter of opinion as to how literally exhaustive motivic analyses of this type can be, and we shall discuss more generally in Part IV the question of how analysis is to deal with the variety of results that derive from a variety of criteria for segmentation. Clearly, the line between tediously stating the obvious and overlooking significant if slight nuances is a fine one, and example 38(a) should be seen as comprehensive rather than exhaustive. Example 38(b), a motivic analysis of the 'abstract' type, is obviously more economical, and, in dispensing with the piece's actual order of events, gives still greater emphasis to fundamental invariants, especially interval class 2, which would be of little significance in a pitch-class-set analysis. It will also be clear, comparing example 38(b) with a pitch-class-set analysis, that even if the latter were to be presented in such a manner as to identify the use of pitch-class set 3–9 (0, 2, 7) as an *expansion* of pitch-class set 3–7 (0, 2, 5), there remain segments in the motivic analysis – 'b' and 'b^2' – that are not presented in the normal order appropriate to pitch-class sets.

Both motivic analyses draw attention to the point at which development or derivation might turn into contrast, or even conflict. Example 38(b) is limited to matters of pitch class; example 38(a), by attempting to describe the piece's materials as motives subject to repetition, development and transformation in both time and space, inevitably raises the question of form, and, with form, duration.

Ex.38 (b) Schoenberg: Six Little Piano Pieces, Op.19/6

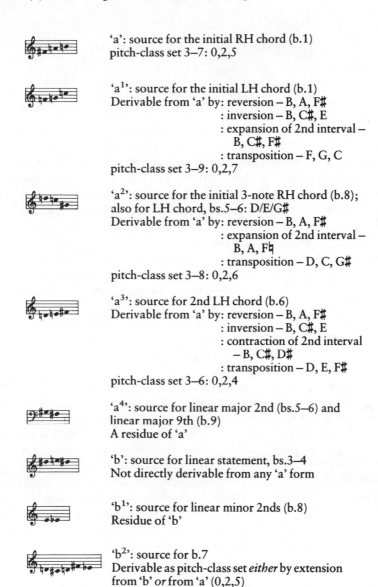

'a': source for the initial RH chord (b.1)
pitch-class set 3–7: 0,2,5

'a¹': source for the initial LH chord (b.1)
Derivable from 'a' by: reversion – B, A, F♯
                 : inversion – B, C♯, E
                 : expansion of 2nd interval –
                   B, C♯, F♯
                 : transposition – F, G, C
pitch-class set 3–9: 0,2,7

'a²': source for the initial 3-note RH chord (b.8);
also for LH chord, bs.5–6: D/E/G♯
Derivable from 'a' by: reversion – B, A, F♯
                 : expansion of 2nd interval –
                   B, A, F♮
                 : transposition – D, C, G♯
pitch-class set 3–8: 0,2,6

'a³': source for 2nd LH chord (b.6)
Derivable from 'a' by: reversion – B, A, F♯
                 : inversion – B, C♯, E
                 : contraction of 2nd interval
                   – B, C♯, D♯
                 : transposition – D, E, F♯
pitch-class set 3–6: 0,2,4

'a⁴': source for linear major 2nd (bs.5–6) and
linear major 9th (b.9)
A residue of 'a'

'b': source for linear statement, bs.3–4
Not directly derivable from any 'a' form

'b¹': source for linear minor 2nds (b.8)
Residue of 'b'

'b²': source for b.7
Derivable as pitch-class set *either* by extension
from 'b' *or* from 'a' (0,2,5)
pitch-class set 4–4: 0,1,2,5

14

Form – and Duration

So far, this study of the elements of atonality has concentrated on pitch relations, examining the successive events, statements or segments of compositions in an attempt to establish the extent to which connections (explicit or implicit) may be revealed. By considering such events essentially as collections of pitches or pitch classes (even when the determination of such collections involves an intuitive response to other features, as part of the process of grouping that listening to music inevitably brings with it) it has been possible to postpone the discussion of form as such. Segments have been established by observing degrees of similarity and contrast, connection and separation, and no formal principles or models have been adduced. Nevertheless it will already be clear from the compositions considered that a brief atonal piece may involve a large measure of exact or modified repetition (as in Schoenberg Op. 19 Nos. 2 and 6), or it may involve a strategy in which repetitions (similarities) are either more rudimentary (in the sense of involving only single intervals or interval classes), or more submerged, in ways that pitch-class-set analysis enables one to indicate (as in the discussion above of Webern's Op. 7 No. 3 and Op. 11 No. 3). There may also be the kind of obvious surface contrasts between 'regular' and 'irregular' factors which involve the rhythmic profile of a segment, and which might set up contrasts between fragmentation and consolidation, expansion and contraction, dissolution and 'resolution' (in the sense of 'completion' applied to Op. 19 No. 6; see pp. 129–30 above). All these processes can contribute to the overall organization normally termed the 'form', but they do not in themselves define that form in any conventional way.

'Form', according to Schoenberg,

means that a piece is *organized*; i.e. that it consists of elements functioning like those of a living organism. Without organization music would be an amorphous mass, as unintelligible as an essay without punctuation, or as disconnected as a conversation which leaps purposelessly from one subject to another. The chief requirements for the creation of a comprehensible form are *logic* and *coherence*. The presentation, development and interconnection of ideas must be based on relationship. Ideas must be differentiated according to their importance and function. Moreover, one can comprehend only what one can keep in mind. Man's mental limitations prevent him from grasping anything which is too extended. Thus appropriate subdivision facilitates understanding and determines the *form*. [Schoenberg, 1970b: 1]

Of course, Schoenberg's concern in *Fundamentals of Musical Composition* is entirely with tonal music, and, as we have already shown, the Schenkerian analyst is not likely to regard the traditional formal categories that Schoenberg retained as truly 'fundamental' at all. Indeed, it was Schenker's belief that 'true form . . . lies in the presence of either an undivided or divided fundamental structure' which rendered 'defunct' the Schoenbergian view that – in tonal music – 'an overwhelming proportion of musical forms is structurally composed of three parts' (see chapter 4, pp. 38–40). But another obvious difference between the two theorists is that, while Schenker was concerned solely with tonality, Schoenberg – in other writings – did not rule out the possibility of analogies between the forms of tonal and atonal compositions.

One of the best-known 'facts' of twentieth-century music history is that the change from tonal to atonal composition did not, of necessity, involve the complete rejection of those principles of formal organization which Schoenberg and others regarded as basic to tonal music. Hence the 'atonal sonata', which many commentators and composers have regarded with horror as the ultimate contradiction in terms (see, for example, Boulez, 1976: 30f.). Yet the fact that Schoenberg, for one, saw no contradiction between atonality and the sonata principle emphasizes yet again the primacy of the motive, and of thematic processes, over tonal, harmonic factors in his thinking. As late as 1949 Schoenberg was able to write that

coherence in classic composition is based – broadly speaking – on the unifying qualities of such structural factors as rhythms, motives, phrases, and the constant reference of all melodic and harmonic features to the centre of gravitation – the tonic. Renouncement of the unifying power of the tonic still leaves all the other factors in operation. [Schoenberg, 1975: 87]

Schoenberg undoubtedly came to believe that, in those early, pre-twelve-note atonal miniatures with which Part III of this book has so far been concerned, 'all the other factors' did *not* automatically remain 'in operation'. In his essay on opus 22 he wrote that 'in the new direction my music had taken I was compelled, in the first place, to renounce not only the construction of larger forms, but to avoid the employment of larger melodies – as well as all formal elements dependent on the frequent repetition of motives' [Schoenberg, 1968: 27]. That in itself may well be evidence of the peripheral importance he ultimately attached to a work as brief as opus 19, but it is not in itself an argument that opus 19 lacks form. After all, Schoenberg's most fundamental formal requirements, as quoted above, involve logic and coherence, the differentiation and connection of ideas, and a 'punctuated' design, such as can be achieved perfectly adequately on a very small scale indeed. What is missing in opus 19 is something comparable to the balance of large- and small-scale formal factors found in the extended (textless) symphonic forms of the tonal era, and Schoenberg himself was evidently not satisfied until it was possible to create atonal (usually twelve-note) structures on a scale comparable with the symphonic movements of Beethoven and Brahms. It is undeniable that analogies between the forms of tonal and atonal compositions make most sense when it is not necessary to take account of the particular kinds of ambiguity that can arise when a process of 'miniaturization' takes place. After all, in atonal miniatures (like those under consideration here) the principal unit of structure is not the 'phrase', or even the 'period' or 'sentence', as such terms are normally understood, but a self-contained segment of texture, or an event that seems to function as a 'motive' even when it may be more chordal than melodic in character.

This point needs such emphasis simply because our consideration of form is much less wide-ranging than it would be if the materials involved were, say, Schoenberg's later string quartets or concertos or those large-scale atonal (if not twelve-note) symphonic works of later generations which have profited from awareness of Schoenberg's (and Webern's) commitment to the 'atonal sonata'. In many such works, analysis of form (and duration) could indeed involve the notion of phrase-structure even if the criteria for such analysis were more motivic than harmonic. But in the field of early atonal miniatures, even when analogies between their design and that of strophic, binary or ternary models are possible, significant ambiguities are likely to arise. Of course, we might prefer to believe that it is part of the necessary radicalism of such pieces that they parade their freedom from such models. Yet Webern, for one, saw no incongruity in establishing connections: he wrote of his opus 6 Pieces that they 'represent short song forms, in that they are mostly tripartite' [Moldenhauer, 1978: 128]. When even 'the frequent repetition of motives' is difficult to detect, then one can see how Schoenberg could have come to regard his own early atonal music as in some respects a necessary but relatively primitive phase in the evolutionary chain. Nevertheless, our ensuing discussion, which considers form and duration together, accepts the premiss that the student analyst, whose prime objective is a deeper understanding of the elements of atonality, still needs to consider how such pieces are assembled, and to what degree their structures may relate to familiar models, or to more flexible schemes of succession involving specified degrees of contrast and similarity. (Even in the chapter on twelve-note composition (see p. 186 below) little space is devoted to large-scale structures, not least because these tend to receive the lion's share of the available space in more general accounts.) To say, as Schoenberg did, that 'form means that a piece is *organized*' implies the organization of time as well as space, rhythm as well as pitch. For whether or not we agree with the argument occasionally advanced that rhythm – duration, pulse, proportion – is more essential to music than pitch, no argument is needed to justify the evident fact that, while music may escape both tonality and harmony, it cannot escape duration. The time factor is, ultimately, the most potent connection between music of all eras and all civilizations: yet that great thought should not permit us to assume that a metrical structure will be as perceptible in twentieth-century music as it is in that of earlier centuries. Lerdahl and Jackendoff argue that 'though all music groups into units of various kinds, some music does not have metrical structure at all, in the specific sense that the listener is unable to extrapolate from the musical signal a hierarchy of beats', and they instance 'Gregorian chant, the alap [opening section] of a North Indian raga, and much contemporary music' [Lerdahl and Jackendoff, 1983: 18]. This is probably something of an overstatement. In the act of composition, at least, it is surely untrue that 'much contemporary music' is conceived without reference to a hierarchy of beats, or of time spans, however suppressed. The problem is rather that recent developments in the organization of temporal grouping are of so radical a nature that it is still extremely difficult to theorize about them.

As far as the music under consideration here is concerned, it is clear that Schoenberg for one never intentionally abandoned periodic metre. He noted in the unpublished *Gedanke* writings (see chapter 7, pp. 74–7) his need to write against an implied periodicity. And yet it can be argued that, even in a piece like Op. 19 No. 2, where a (fairly) regular quaver beat is marked, the listener is not encouraged 'to extrapolate . . . a hierarchy' so much as to register an evolving motivic succession, since the miniature form promotes the avoidance of larger-scale repetitions. If the resultant rhythms of the piece's nine bars are compared, it will be seen that they are all different, and the effect of the two points in the piece where one bar is linked to the next by a tied event is to suggest a simple symmetrical structuring of the bar-units:

Of course, repetitions within the resultant rhythms can be observed on a smaller scale than that of the one- or two-bar segment, but it will be noted that the most obvious of these – the succession of three quavers (x) – loses its fixed position in the bar after bar 2. Though containing plentiful articulations of duple elements – quaver, crotchet, minim – this composition can scarcely be claimed to possess a consistent periodicity, whether or not such periodicity is implied.

Some of the issues raised in the attempt to integrate rhythmic and pitch analysis in tonal music have been aired in Part II. Here we will offer no theory of atonal rhythmic structure, although Allen Forte has argued that an interaction of rhythm- and pitch-structures can be demonstrated, so that 'pitch-class-set structure – both in the simple and complex segmentations – is intimately allied to the fundamental rhythmic structures of the work' [Forte, 1980: 109; see also Forte, 1983]. Such a theory may well gain credibility and support through further study. For the moment, however, the discussion here will be confined to consideration of matters of form and duration in two of the compositions that provide the basic materials for these chapters: Schoenberg's Op. 19 No. 6 and Webern's Op. 11 No. 3. The emergence of 'musical prose' out of 'musical verse' – the dissolution of the regular-period structure conceived most basically as successions of four-bar units which could be modified without the sense of their fundamental forming presence being lost – is familiar from studies of nineteenth-century music, especially of Brahms and Wagner (see Dahlhaus, 1979; 1980). And yet the evolution away from tonal structure conceived in terms of consonance, dissonance and goal-direction was not immediately paralleled by an evolution away from rhythmic organ-ization conceived as sequences of balancing phrases even if those phrases themselves differ greatly in their actual duration. Such balance is naturally most evident in compositions where repetition is most explicit. For example, in Schoenberg's Op. 19 No. 6, most of the successive statements relate directly to the first, and the piece consists of a sequence of events whose character and order are determined not by the presence of an instinctively understood syntax of tonal harmony and regular, periodic phrase structure, but by motivic expansions and contractions, similarities and contrasts, which can be experienced as such even though it is very difficult to sense a 'hierarchy of beats'. This music is indeed free of the harmonic constraints imposed by the traditional distinction between consonance and dissonance, yet it still recognizes the need to balance motivic differences and similarities, and to do so in respect of duration and tone colour, as well as of pitch content: the principal contrast (bar 7) is significantly shorter and louder, as well as texturally differentiated from the main material and its variants.

As indicated above in our motivic analysis, the piece can be subdivided into six separate events, each new event beginning either with repetition of a previously stated element, or after a silence. Of the six events, the first three and the last evidently have common elements, and possible associations with both binary and ternary form might therefore be explored. A ternary model would involve a very strong contrast of proportions between section A (bars 1–6), and B (7–8) with A^1(9); while a binary model – section A (bars 1–6), and section A^1 (bars 7–9) at least has some points of contact with Schoenberg's definition of binary form as 'characterized by two balanced segments, built from closely related but differentiated motive-forms, so that the second section is in some respects a contrast' [Schoenberg, 1970b: 168]. The binary interpretation is perhaps also suggested by the piece's division into two large pitch-class collections – 11 + 12 (see p.129). Yet it remains distinctly at odds with more orthodox examples of both traditional formal schemes, and we might therefore prefer not to advance the description of the piece's form beyond that of the 'six separate segments'. Given this approach, the form of the piece is equivalent to the motivic interpretation already provided above (example 38(a), p. 159). Clearly, such a rudimentary 'form-plan' is of value only if it provides the basis for fuller consideration of its contents. But however the analyst decides to group or label the separate segments of the piece, their individual time-structures need to be considered in as much detail as their pitch-content.

The first segment is the most basic, the only one without some melodic addition to the two three-note chords. It is also basic in the way it avoids strong accents and regular pulsation. The 7 slow crotchets that it spans make, in conventional terms, an 'irrational' value, but once we know the piece well we are likely to sense this not simply as a means of avoiding regularity, but as a means of initiating an evolutionary process in which that basic unit of value, divided as it is into 3 + 4, is a significant structural component in itself.*

The second segment of Op. 19 No. 6 is not just an expansion of the first in terms of pitch materials, adding two new pitch classes to the initial six, but also an extension in time: 3 + 4 becomes 3 + 5, and the additional pitch-material creates a more complex attack-point sequence: calculated in quaver values, it is 6 + 2 + 3 + 2 + 3 – assuming that the last attack counts through the next crotchet beat. In the second segment, then, the extension of pitch and time brings with it an increase in the rate of rhythmic activity, and a more specifically articulated interaction between 'odd' and 'even' units.

The third segment, which follows after one crotchet beat's silence, continues the process of extension. Its minimum duration is nine crotchets, with the first two attacks brought closer together than before. And Schoenberg underlines the effect of the piece's first departure from its initial harmonic base by allowing this cadence to

---

* '3 + 4' represents the distance between the two attacks in the segment and the second attack and the joint 'release point' at the end of the segment. '3 + 4' is therefore also a description of the 'resultant rhythm' of the segment, and in the discussion that follows it is resultant rhythms as sequences of attack points that form the basis of analysis. Clearly, whenever release points are not immediately adjacent to attack points they create further subdivisions of the rhythmic profile of a segment, but without modifying the resultant rhythm as a pattern of attacks. Indeed, it might be argued that release points affect tone colour and texture more directly than rhythm (see in this connection Batstone, 1969).

die away naturally on a pause. Calculating the distance between attack-points in quaver values, the sequence for segment 3 is $2 + 4 + 2 + 1 + 3 + 6$. In contrast with segment 2, the longest unit is the last.

If we consider 'a^3' (bar 9) at this point, it is evidently a varied recapitulation of 'a', compressed in time, and with an attack-point pattern of $2 + 4 + 1 + 1$ quavers. It should be noted that the pauses in the piece do not serve to delay the actual entry of any element: the final bar, however long its actual duration, is still a distinct compression of earlier events, as if in response to the much shorter duration of the piece's two principal contrasts, segments 'b' and 'c', the materials in bars 7 and 8.

Whether or not Schoenberg ultimately derived the monody in bar 7 from his initial event, as both motivic and pitch-class-set analysis enable us to claim, and whether or not the F sharp and D, which segment 'c' shares with segment 'b', are of any especial significance, bar 7 offers what in the context of this piece as a whole is a notable reduction, texturally and proportionally; a reduction that seems all the more remarkable in view of the extravagant leap with which it begins, motivically paralleling (it may be) the E/D sharp of bars 3 and 4 (see example 38(a)). Segment 'b' occupies only three crotchet beats, less than half the span of the smallest event so far (1), and within that span it is a good deal more active than its predecessors. In order to calculate the distances between attacks as whole numbers – that is, to accommodate the association of duple quaver with triplet crotchet – it is necessary to take the triplet semiquaver as the prime unit of value: in which case, the sequence of values for segment 'b' is $3 + 5 + 2 + 4 + 4$ (a total of 18 triplet semiquavers). This may seem of no consequence beyond confirming the increasingly aperiodic, 'prosodic' quality of Schoenberg's atonal thought. Yet it does recall segment 'a^2', at least in the sense that this also spans 18 durational units (quavers in segment 'a^2'). Broadly speaking, there-fore, segment 'b' reduces the duration of segment 'a^2' by two-thirds (excluding, as always, the possible effects of bar 6's pause).

The greatest sense of compression in the piece comes with segment 'c', in the penultimate bar, whose formal function seems to be that of a transition from monody back to the density of pairs of three-note chords. The durational values can be seen as a 'subset' of those of segment 'b':

Segment 'b': ♪♪♪ ♪   Segment 'c': ♪♪♪ ♪
       ⊗   ⊗ – (retrograde)

here, again, the triplet semiquaver is the unifying unit of value, and the total length of segment 'c' is 7, with the triplet semiquaver proportions within the bar as a whole dividing as 2 (rest) + 2 + 2 + 3 + 15 (rest). The piece's essential duple/triple contrasts are therefore encapsulated in segment 'c', and may even be felt to refer back to the initial contrast within segment 'a', whose total value was also 7 (crotchets).

Expressed entirely in terms of triplet semiquaver values – that is, expressing the distances between all attacks in the piece as whole numbers – the basic durational structure of Op. 19 No. 6 is:

Segment

'a'	'a¹'	silence	'a²'	silence	'b'	silence	'c'	silence	'a'
1	2		3		4		5		6
42+	48+	6+	54+	6+	18+	2+	7+	15+	24

(Total 222)

This analysis indicates how fundamentally the opposition of duple and triple values is projected, and how important contrast and diversity are between the various events. The slow tempo and use of pauses may additionally encourage us to assume that relative proportions matter more than exact durations. Yet at the crucial point of the smallest values (and the shortest rest) in the piece – bar 8 – Schoenberg writes 'genau im Takt', 'strictly in time'. The motivic processes and formal layout of this piece could hardly be simpler, but the durational structuring ensures that this simplicity achieves an intriguing and precarious balance between the extremes of short and long.

The evident repetitions and relations in Op. 19 No. 6 inevitably influence the discussion of form and rhythm. In Webern's still more concentrated piece for cello and piano, Op. 11 No. 3, invariance in pitch-relations (beyond the ubiquitous 'semitones') is less self-evident; it might therefore be expected that little in the way of significant formal grouping will be discernible, and that the piece's succession of three separate segments might be best described as A B C rather than as 'A' 'A¹' 'A²', or as 'A' 'B' 'A¹'. It might also be expected that an analysis of durational patterning – simply by confirming a lack of similarity between segments – would support the thesis that significant connections in the piece are to be found only in the 'background' similarity relations between pitch-class sets. As it happens, however, things are not quite so simple.

The timespan on the page is a mere 10 bars of 2/4; with the triplet semiquaver as the highest common proportional factor (ignoring the trill), this timespan is expressed as 120 equal units:

Segment 1	*silence*	*2*	*silence*	*3*	*silence*	
33	1	38	8	34	6	(Total 120)

Naturally, attack-point profiles reveal a more complex interpretation of the actual musical surface:

Segment 1: $12 + {}_{\lceil}3 + 5 + 4_{\rfloor} + 9$ piano chord, duration 15 units
            $12 + 12 + 9$ cello line: $12 + 8 + 4 + 9$
   ($\div 3$) $4 + 4 + 3$

Segment 2: $\lceil 10 + 4 + 4 \rceil + 2 + 18$
   ($\div 2$) $5 + 2 + 2 + 1 + 9$

(Segment 2 can be summed to a symmetry of $9 + 1 + 9$ whose central axis is the two triplet-semiquaver distance between the fourth and fifth attacks.)

Segment 3: $10 + 9 \,(3 + 6) + 9\,(6 + 3) + \overset{\frown}{6}$

The actual duration of the piano chord is 22 units. If the silent triplet semiquaver from bar 7 and the last, silent crotchet beat are included, another symmetric model is created:

$$12 + 9 + 9 + 12$$
$$(\div 3) \quad 4 + 3 + 3 + 4$$

The analysis of relative proportions therefore supports an interpretation of the piece's form as a miniature ternary, not only by pointing out connections between the structures of the two 'A' sections, but by suggesting that the 'A's are in rhythmic contrast to 'B' – although 'B' is only fractionally shorter in total duration than each of the 'A's. Even so, however, it is probably true that 'A' and 'A^1' complement one another to a greater extent than would such sections in a traditional ternary scheme. In 'A' a connected melodic cello statement begins unaccompanied, and a piano chord is added at mid-point. In 'A¹' there is an initial piano chord, to which is added a cello statement, of three detached notes, which ends the piece unaccompanied. In these terms, 'A¹' is a free retrograde of 'A's basic textural features, while 'B' – piano melody plus piano/cello chord – is more a variant of 'A'. Nor would an analysis of form involving textural features wish to ignore the fact that, while the cello progresses from low to high registers during the course of the piece, the piano explores a relatively restricted, relatively low area, with the chord of segment 3 included within the span of the chord of segment 1. Even without carrying the analysis further at this stage, therefore, it is clear that the various claims of pitch-class-set, textural, formal and rhythmic aspects confirm that a piece of extreme brevity can be just as allusive and ambiguous, and as multifaceted in its technical processes, as any large scale design. (For further discussion of durational factors in Webern's Op. 11 No. 3, see Batstone, 1969 and Berry, 1976. Wintle 1975 discusses aspects of the piece that anticipate twelve-note technique.)

15

The Structure of Atonal Music:
Synthesis or Symbiosis?

All the analytical techniques discussed in this book have served, in various ways, a single aesthetic principle:

Unity is surely the indispensable thing if meaning is to exist. Unity, to be very general, is the establishment of the utmost relatedness between all component parts. So, in music, as in all other human utterance, the aim is to make as clear as possible the relationships between the parts of the unity: in short, to show how one thing leads to another. [Webern, 1963: 42].

The aim of the composer, as Webern described it, is also, normally, the aim of the analyst, and Part I of this book outlined the ways in which that aim gradually evolved into the terminologies and processes we call analytical. Yet the analyst needs to question whether there is a genuine continuity from tonal to atonal composition that justifies the belief that, in all circumstances, unity is 'the indispensable thing'. The point is not that, in genuinely atonal music, unity must logically be replaced by its opposite, utter chaos, but that 'to show how one thing leads to another' need not be the same as establishing 'the utmost relatedness between all component parts'. After all, unity in this sense has never been fundamental to all types of musical form, even in the tonal era, as Schenker clearly sensed in his various diatribes against music drama. But, if 'unity' is dispensable, coherence is not, and a shift from the unifying integration of contrasted but none the less related elements (synthesis) to the establishment of an equilibrium, a balance between elements that remain distinct (symbiosis), would not therefore entail a shift from sense to nonsense.

This is not the place for discussion of the historical and aesthetic issues that such a shift of perspective might involve (see Whittall, 1983). But some of the consequences for the analyst can be explored here, by means of a study of one of the more radical pieces included in this book. To describe Webern's Op. 7 No. 3 (see p.227) as 'more radical' than, for example, Schoenberg's Op. 19 No. 6, may already be to make a very large intuitive leap, but that description is the result of the belief that, while the Schoenberg is an example of an atonal piece that is governed more by unity than diversity, the Webern (certain repetitions notwithstanding) is not. This is not to say that there are no unifying factors in the Webern, but that those factors, in themselves, may not, under investigation, prove to promote 'the utmost relatedness between all component parts'.

So far, the only analysis of the Webern that has been presented in these pages is that by Allen Forte as part of his discussion of set-complex relations (see p. 142). Forte concludes that the piece is a 'connected' structure, but he also points out that 'although there is minimal change at the surface level of the music [in section B] there is a pronounced change in the underlying structure' [Forte, 1973: 128]. Even pitch-class-set analysis does not inevitably lead to a concern with unity at all costs, and the application of other analytical techniques can help to confirm the sense in which 'connection' – and contact – may be far from synonymous with synthesis and integration.

To explore the piece for evidence of implicit or extended tonality will seem a futile activity if a process as integrated and consistent as that traced by Baker in Skryabin's *Enigme* is sought (see pp. 111–3). But if the initial statement of the piece is seen as an opposition between two separate elements (two separate instruments) – not, primarily, as a single, motivic minor second – it is evident that such a separation is in certain respects sustained throughout, and sustained in such a way that particular pitch-priorities cannot be excluded from the discussion. The violin part is not merely more obviously unified (motivically) than the piano part, but it is more invariant in pitch-content. That content is not diatonic, but it is notably restricted, not so much in pitch-class terms – nine different pitch-classes are present – as in register. Only two of those nine pitch-classes – A and A flat/G sharp – occur in more than one octave position, and the violin part ends when those pitches achieve their 'voice exchange', a process prepared by the symmetrical presentation of the previous four-note group (see example 39(c) below). The fact that the first and last notes of the violin part are As, and that four of the instrument's other six statements begin or end on A, encourages the view that the violin part is centred on that pitch, and unified by reference to it. Even if we then go on to talk of an A/E flat polarity, which interlocks with a D/A flat polarity (moving into the more abstract region of discussing the two types of symmetrical pitch-class set that the violin part employs – 0, 1, 5, 6 and 0, 1, 6, 7) the priority of A seems a reasonable deduction on aural as well as structural grounds, though aurally the extremely attenuated tone quality – muted, on the bridge, *col legno* – and a dynamic that never rises above *ppp* can hardly be claimed to assert that priority.*

Compared with the violin part, the piano part is notably diverse, and it is correspondingly more difficult to argue a case for the pre-eminence of any pitch or pitches. It is true that the music from bars 5 to 8 has a hint of A minor/major about it, but the note A itself is given only the lightest emphasis in the piano part, and the relative prominence (linearly and vertically) of B flat/A sharp, A flat and E flat could even be an indication of Webern's decision to avoid A. The piano part lacks the single-pitch focus of the violin part, since, at the very least, any argument that it unfolds a 'progression' from B flat to E flat (with subsidiary emphasis on A flat and F) involves reasoning as selective as it is subjective. Moreover, while the musical materials might raise the possibility that the two parts would converge on a common emphasis on E flat/A flat, Webern seems intent on avoiding such convergence. At the very least, the subordination in the violin part of A flat to E flat, and of both to A, is reversed in the piano part, where A is less prominent than A flat, and both less prominent than B flat (A sharp) or E flat. But the contrast goes deeper than that: on its own, the violin part is audibly 'centred'; the piano part is not, for even if E flat is held to be the most 'significant' note, it is not used in ways that promote the recognition of its prominence. Nor is any other note; although of course if Webern had chosen to end the piece with a texture like that of bars 5 to 8 (the most integrated part of the composition) the low F in the piano, and the fact that this pitch class is doubled by the violin on two occasions, might have indicated a convergence of polarities on this (relatively neutral?) centre.

The more divorced discussions of pitch centricity are from either voice-leading or the chords of functional harmony, the more subjective and arbitrary they tend to become, and Webern has ultimately protected himself from incautious assumptions about tonal back-

---

* An alternative model for this structure would involve the 0, 3, 6, 9 collection, A, C, E flat, F sharp ('tonic axis' in Lendvai's terms: see Lendvai, 1971); D, F, A flat, B ('subdominant axis') with the briefly-heard B flat (bar 4) the only representative of the 'dominant' axis (E, G, B flat, C sharp).

ground by means of a final chord that very efficiently resists transformation into an 'altered higher dominant', or any other 'tonal' formation, despite the C major triad embedded within it. That chord, the formal function of which will be considered again later, seems to reinforce the complementary roles of the two instruments and their materials and to suggest that, here, complementation is promoting symbiosis rather than synthesis. But it is certainly possible to see such surface complementation as a composing out of a single 'background' process of pitch-structuring, and one less elaborate than that suggested by pitch-class-set analysis. The table below simply lists the pitch-class content of the piece's five main segments (Forte's 'section A' is here divided into two), without seeking to distinguish between pitch-classes that appear in one or other instrument only and those that appear in both.

Segment

A	A	Bb									
B	A	Bb	Ab	Eb	D	C♯					
C	A		Ab	Eb	D	C♯	E	F	C	F♯	B
D	A	A♯	G♯						C		B
E				Eb		C♯	E		C	Gb		G
	1	2	3	4	5	6	7	8	9	10	11	12

This table shows the very different interpretation that can arise if we transform consideration of the piece's harmony from the sphere of post-tonality to that of 'pre-twelve-note serialism'.* Expressed in such summary terms, the principal rationale of Op. 7 No. 3 seems to be a single statement of all twelve pitch classes. Yet although the twelfth note, G, may have been 'saved up' by Webern for the final chord, the gradual unfolding of the twelve-note collection – the 'universal set' – is embedded in a sequence of repetitions that do not appear to obey a single, consistent structuring principle when considered, as here, in pitch-class terms. As a 'pre-twelve-note atonal structure', therefore, the piece is again more coherent than 'unified'. And the use of symmetrical formations seems to confirm its freedom from strictly systematic procedures. While it is striking to note that the piece's initial A and B flat form the central axis

---

* One common and significant criticism of pitch-class-set analysis is that it can easily, if inadvertently, obscure the ways in which the early atonal repertory foreshadows twelve-note serialism by consistently accumulating twelve-note collections. See p. 129 above for discussion of the collections in Schoenberg's Op. 19 No. 6.

Ex.39 Webern: Four Pieces for Violin and Piano, Op.7/3

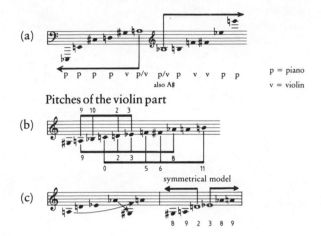

between the highest and lowest notes – the piano E in bar 6 and the piano E flat in bar 12 – there is no consistent mirror symmetry. Example 39(a) shows the pitches present in the piece (12 out of 29) which form a single symmetric pattern with the initial A/B flat, but symmetry is most evident on a smaller scale in the violin part in the presentation of the 3, 2, 10, 9 (E flat, D, B flat, A) motive and its transformation to 9, 2, 3, 8/0, 5, 6, 11 (examples 39(b) and (c)).

By confining the consideration of applied motivic analysis of the strictest kind to Schoenberg's Op. 19 No. 6 (see pp. 158–161 above), it was possible to postpone certain problematic issues: in particular, what happens when the first event of a piece is not self-evidently its principal motive (by virtue of later repetitions and variations), and how motivic analysis can best adapt itself to a piece in which, on the surface, repetition and variation are no more, or even less, evident than contrast and transformation. Most commentators on Webern's Op. 7 No. 3 – for example, Kolneder, 1968; Wildgans, 1966; and Döhl 1976 – endorse Perle's view that it is the kind of piece in which 'microcosmic elements are transposed, internally reordered, temporally or spatially expanded or contracted, and otherwise revised, in a fluctuating context that constantly transforms the unifying motive itself' [Perle, 1977: 9]. But just as the pitch-class-set analysis seeks to operate with units larger than the

Ex.40 (a) Webern: Four Pieces for Violin and Piano, Op.7/3

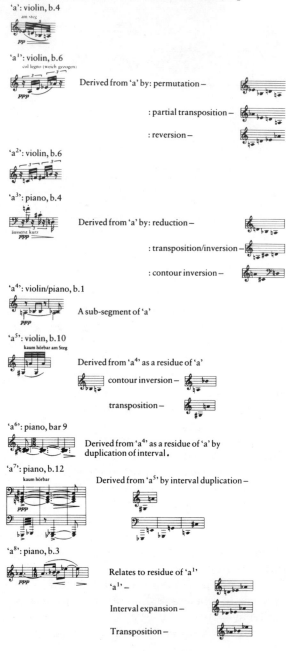

'a⁹': piano, b.5

Each successive interval of the melody is derived
thus: (i)   tritone – from 'a' (overall span)
      (ii) major 7th – 'a¹' (overall span)
      (iii) minor 3rd – 'a⁷'
      (iv) diminished 3rd – 'a⁶'
      (v)   minor 9th – 'a⁵'
      (vi) major 3rd – 'a'

single note or the dyad, so a motivic analysis must seek to do more than list the number of minor seconds and their compounds, if only as a way of *not* minimizing the significance of the diversity – in length, contour and register – of a piece's materials.

Example 40(a) selects as principal motive the first appearance of a figure which, miniscule though it is, provides the piece's most recurrent feature in the modified forms shown at 'a¹' and 'a²'. In this interpretation, all the segments in example 40(a) are shown to relate to, or derive from, the principal motive by specified procedures of variation. The descending order of connection is also, admittedly, an ascending order of improbability: in particular, 'a⁹' is shown thus simply to emphasize the difficulties of establishing a literal connection between this event as Webern characterizes it and its 'source'. The reader may well wish to propose an alternative principal motive for the piece, and even if our choice is endorsed the reader may prefer an interpretation that labels the elements from (at least) 'a⁶' onwards with different letters, as contrasts to 'a'. It would be surprising in the extreme if convincing alternatives to the proposed derivations shown could not be discovered, and in keeping with the provisional nature of the example, no attempt has been made to provide the kind of verbal listing of textural variants given in example 38(a) (see p. 159 above). But the important point here is not to offer an instance of that improbable phenomenon, the definitive motivic analysis: it is to indicate that an attempt at literal motivic analysis reinforces the ambiguity of the piece's 'unity', by focusing attention on those elements within the piece that contrast as much as they unify.

Example 40(b), a more abstract motivic analysis using collections of pitch classes, is of course less ambiguous, because it carries the process of reduction to common features that much further. Even at its most Schoenbergian, however, motivic analysis may not enable us to argue convincingly that the piece is literally 'monothematic': in particular, it emphasizes the sense in which the principal

Ex.40 (b) Webern: Four Pieces for Violin and Piano, Op.7/3

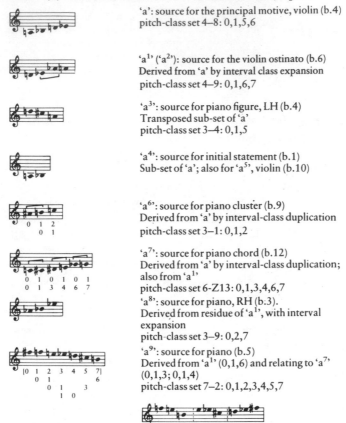

'a': source for the principal motive, violin (b.4)
pitch-class set 4–8: 0,1,5,6

'a[1]' ('a[2]'): source for the violin ostinato (b.6)
Derived from 'a' by interval class expansion
pitch-class set 4–9: 0,1,6,7

'a[3]': source for piano figure, LH (b.4)
Transposed sub-set of 'a'
pitch-class set 3–4: 0,1,5

'a[4]': source for initial statement (b.1)
Sub-set of 'a'; also for 'a[5]', violin (b.10)

'a[6]': source for piano cluster (b.9)
Derived from 'a' by interval-class duplication
pitch-class set 3–1: 0,1,2

'a[7]': source for piano chord (b.12)
Derived from 'a' by interval-class duplication;
also from 'a[1]'
pitch-class set 6-Z13: 0,1,3,4,6,7

'a[8]': source for piano, RH (b.3).
Derived from residue of 'a[1]', with interval
expansion
pitch-class set 3–9: 0,2,7

'a[9]': source for piano (b.5)
Derived from 'a[1]' (0,1,6) and relating to 'a[7]'
(0,1,3; 0,1,4)
pitch-class set 7–2: 0,1,2,3,4,5,7

contrasting event is the piano right-hand melody (bars 5–8). To see this as a 'free' extension of the 0, 1, 6 cell, or as made up of overlapping permutations of 0, 1, 6, 0, 1, 3 and 0, 1, 4, or, as shown in example 40(b), to trace every interval to another of the piece's transformations of its principal motive – is simply to stress the difference between events that need such laborious explanation and those that can be much more directly accounted for in terms of the 'rules' laid down. As far as the matter is taken here, however, it seems that both kinds of motivic analysis – simply by drawing attention to the difficulties involved in seeing the piece as literally monomotivic – can be used to support the argument that contrast plays a crucial role. It is still, however, a subordinate role; motivic analysis does not, of itself, demonstrate conclusively that a new, freer kind of coherence is present. A unifying motivic force predominates even if it is not, literally, all-generating. The relative radicalism of the processes at work in Op. 7 No. 3 is naturally reflected in the domain of rhythm. The background visible on the page is a timespan of 42 quaver beats at semiquaver *c.* 60 (actually 40 sounding and 2 silent quaver beats), with the characteristic 'atonal' contrast between duple and triple values and the repression of explicit periodicity carried into the time signatures themselves (see p. 170 above). The caesuras and silences that serve to mark off the principal divisions for formal and pitch-class-set analysis can serve here too.

Segment	Duration in quavers
A (bars 1 and 2)	8
B (to 1st beat, b. 5)	8
C (to 1st beat, b. 9)	10
D (to 1st quaver b. 12)	8
E (including final silent beat)	8

This interpretation obviously abstracts maximum durational symmetry from the piece, to the extent of suggesting an 'underlying' ternary form:

$$(A + B) \quad (C) \quad (D + E)$$
$$16 \quad + \quad 10 \quad + \quad 16$$

Nevertheless, in overlooking overlaps between segments A and B on the one hand, and C and D on the other, it inevitably oversimplifies, suggesting that a more detailed, more motivic examination of rhythmic organization is needed. After all, to regard segments as similar or even identical simply because they have the same overall duration is a distinctly primitive notion.

The justification for regarding Forte's section A as two segments, A and B, is that there is a strong contrast between them with respect to treatment of the basic pulse. The 8 quavers of segment A mark an initial downbeat and set up a clear quaver pulsation, with no cross-rhythms. But segment B – the first melodic statement in the piano, with its skeletal accompaniment – subdivides its 8 quavers in a notably anti-periodic fashion: the melody itself is built from 9 + 3 + 4 semiquavers, and it would seem that the changes of time signature are motivated primarily by Webern's desire for the first and last attacks of the accompanying counterpoints to occur on 'strong' downbeats.

Segments C and D are notable for their use of two forms of ostinato in the violin. The first and most extensive counterpoints the piano melody, of which more later. On its own, the first ostinato (bars 6–9) provides a model for the intersection of symmetrical pitch and rhythmic patterns, but not – as we need hardly say since Webern is the composer – with absolute regularity. Considered purely in terms of pitch, an 'a'/'b'/'a'/'b'/'a' pattern is evident, each unit itself inversionally symmetrical as a 9, 2, 3, 8 or 0, 5, 6, 11 sequence. Rhythmically, the basic unit of the ostinato pattern can be seen as four pitches plus the following triplet semiquaver rest – that is, a total of five triplet semiquavers. That pattern is maintained for four of the five statements, but an extra triplet semiquaver rest is inserted before the fifth and final statement. The effect of this extension is to place the final statement at the same point within the beat – starting on the second triplet semiquaver – as the first and fourth statements.

The successive rhythmic displacements of the ostinato become evident only when projected against the piano melody, which clearly marks the basic quaver pulse in bars 5, 6 and 7. Such definition is less explicit in segment D, which seems extraordinarily attenuated after the relative richness of activity in segment C, and functions to arrest the flow of the earlier material, preparing for the final cadence. The violin statements may, in the most basic sense, be 'symmetrical' on either side of a quaver rest, but the potential is not realized by the establishment of correspondences between the rhythmic patterns that end in bar 9 and those that begin in bar 12. The initial attacks of the two violin statements divide the time-span of the piano cluster into an irregular 5 + 4 + 6 semiquavers (attack/release pattern: 5 + 2 + 2 + 2 + 4); but this avoidance of regularity is arrested in segment E, where the 6-quaver time-span of the right-hand chord is divided 3 + 3 (attack/release pattern 2 + 1 + 3) by the two attacks.

The contrast between 'odd' and 'even' elements is therefore a basic attribute of this piece, and with it the interaction between 'rational' and 'irrational' values at various levels. Thus the demi-semiquaver quintuplet that fleetingly appears in bar 4 can be seen to foreshadow the pattern of 5 triplet semiquavers of the ostinato figure in segment C, while the triplet semiquavers from bar 4 help to prepare the actual rhythmic profile of that ostinato. It is indicative of Webern's highly refined attention to detail that the crucial point of the piece, rhythmically – the point where the two basic types of value, duple and triple, coincide – should be so unobtrusive. At that point of conflict, the unit of value, if all the durations of each of the five separate segments are to be calculated in whole numbers, becomes the triplet demisemiquaver, as shown in the following table:

Segment	Bars		Total duration (in triplet demisemiquavers)
A	1 and 2		48
B	3, 4, and 1st quaver of 5		48
C	2nd quaver of 5 to 2nd triplet semiquaver of 9	58 ⎤	
D	2nd semiquaver of 9 (piano) to end of 11	45 ⎦	102*
Silence	1st quaver of 10		6
E	2nd quaver of 10 to 1st quaver of 14		36
			240

* Segments C and D overlap by 1 triplet demisemiquaver.

If these totals are divided by six, the following scheme emerges:

Segment	A	B	⌞C	D⌟	Silence	E
	8	8	17		1	6

and this scheme, if compared with the more obviously symmetrical interpretation shown above (p. 181), has at least the virtue of making the tension between 'odd' and 'even' components present in the piece's background more explicit. After all, the fact that Webern notated the last five bars of the piece with a 3/8 signature could represent his own wish to demonstrate that the pervasive tensions between 3 and 2, odd and even, are not resolved so much as balanced out, to provide a coherent conclusion. The ending therefore reinforces the distinction between Webern's balanced contrasts and the synthesis of 'odd' and 'even' elements that a consistently periodic composition in triple time (a minuet, most obviously) would present.

The idea of a balance between different, irreducible elements can serve to lead us on to broader questions of form in Op. 7 No. 3.

Even more so than with the other atonal miniatures considered here, there seems little point in attempting to demonstrate that this piece is a small-scale binary or ternary form, rather than built from four sections identified in Forte or five segments as suggested here, which are best labelled A–B–C–D or A–B–C–D–E. But if we are to do justice to the notion that it is a balance of contrasts rather than 'the utmost relatedness between all the component parts' that matters in this piece, it is essential to bring that notion – the concept of non-convergent polarities – into the analysis at the most basic level: to synthesize observations about all the events around a central notion of symbiosis: the mutually beneficial partnership between elements of different kinds.

Any composition of any period for violin and piano is likely to exploit the evident and substantial differences between the instruments, and Op. 7 No. 3 is no exception, despite the uniformity of the extremely soft dynamics. At least one of the basic textural polarities present in the piece could equally well occur in a tonal composition – that involving 'sustaining' and 'punctuating' elements. A table points up the distinctions:

Segment

A	Violin sustains a single note	Piano punctuates (one note 3 times)
B	Piano sustains	Violin and piano (LH) punctuate
C	Piano sustains: legato phrase with sustained bass note	Violin punctuates: ostinato
D	Piano sustains: 3-note cluster	Violin punctuates
E	Piano sustains (RH)	Piano punctuates (LH)

This analysis, using minimal verbal description, focuses on the interaction of superimposed surface events. It is so laid out that only the final segment involves one instrument alone, and this stresses, in the simplest possible way, the sense in which the piece may be said to end with its strongest contrast. The next table, indicating further polarities, pursues this matter in relation to the registral and rhythmic profiles of the five segments.

Segment

A	Both instruments have single pitches close together
B	The piano line begins to ascend, without repeating pitches, and the violin is reduced to a subordinate role, of limited content
C	The piano employs a very wide span. The violin part, deriving from B, is persistent, and relatively regular in rhythm, but enclosed by the piano lines
D	This can be seen as a varied reversal of the roles of A, the piano sustaining, and the violin punctuating within a relatively narrow registral span
E	An 'inversion' of D, to the extent that a single sustained event is underpinned by a double, punctuating event

Although this table does not seek to divorce the final segment from all connection with its predecessors, it should by now be clear that its character is one of the most significant contributors to the piece's atonality. This goes further than the fact that, by analogy, we would be surprised if the last chord of a tonal piece contained a pitch not previously used in the composition, or consisted of six different pitch classes. The role of 'closure' performed by segment E is a mixture of pitch-class completion (the 'universal set') and textural, motivic complementation, especially with respect to segment A. But there is also a strong sense of contradiction. The final chord may be derivable motivically from the minor ninths in segment D, via the diminished octaves, major sevenths and minor seconds in segment C, from the minor second in segment A, and in these terms segment E may well have 'the most intimate relationship' with its predecessors. Yet at the same time it preserves 'the validity of the contradiction' between itself and those predecessors (see McFarlane, 1976: 88). It has the stability of those other segments which contain reiteration rather than motion, but in its density, and registral depth, it contrasts sharply with all that has gone before. In segment E one instrument has a dense but relatively widespread statement, and a texture that has grown from two to three strands, and on to the four pitches heard simultaneously in segment D, now reaches completion with 6 simultaneous pitches, and with a 6-quaver duration whose internal profile (2 + 1 + 3) neatly confirms the even–odd polarity, a particularly consistent feature of the music's concern with complementation.

16

Twelve-note Composition

When Webern made the remarks about unity quoted on p. 173 above, it was twelve-note music he had in mind. Like Schoenberg, Webern seemed to have no doubt by the 1930s that his earlier atonal but non-twelve-note compositions were preliminary (and even relatively primitive) steps on the path to the true new music. (As the discussion of Op. 7 No. 3 in chapter 15 suggests, 'twelve-note consciousness' was undoubtedly present some years before the twelve-note method itself emerged in the early 1920s.) But later generations have called this apparently blithe belief in the laws of progress into question. Some have argued that the twelve-note technique of Schoenberg and Webern is itself primitive in that it fails to draw the necessary radical conclusions about form and texture from the serial principle. Others, who see no purpose in extending those principles in the way that, for example, Babbitt and Boulez have done, have argued that pre-twelve-note atonality offers a more fruitful basis for new developments in its blend of strictness and freedom. Thus the matrices of more recent serial composers – for example, Peter Maxwell Davies – often contain fewer or more than twelve single pitches, and allow for a great diversity of routes through the basic pitch material (see Griffiths, 1982: 73f.)

However one reacts aesthetically to these issues, and the music that has resulted, the analyst is likely to be strongly aware of the contrast between works like those discussed so far under the heading of atonality, whose conscious principles of construction – as far as they can be deduced – are not highly systematized, and those twelve-note compositions whose basic materials and methods of organization are known, not least from the writings of the composers themselves. And it seems clear that when Schoenberg wrote of his search from about 1915 onwards for ways of constructing works 'on a unifying idea which produced not only all the other ideas, but regulated also their accompaniment and the chords, the "harmonies"' [Reich, 1971: 131], he was making a very clear distinction between the kind of motivic connectedness which he might have sensed in earlier atonal works, and that much more comprehensive control which comes about when a work's most vital elements – its thematic cells – are themselves subject to the control of an all-embracing, ordered presentation of the total chromatic.

There are many general historical and theoretical accounts of basic twelve-note principles and practices for the student to consult, even before advancing to more specialized articles and monographs (see for example the entries in such reference works as Vinton, 1974, and the *New Grove*). But the step from absorbing such basic information to acquiring actual analytical experience can still present problems, simply because there are technical aspects to the simplest twelve-note composition that are by no means self-evident. Even if a date and opus number, as well as some general historical account, proclaim a composition to be twelve-note, it may well not be immediately obvious from the music itself whether only a single form of its basic set is in use, or a succession of single set-forms, or whether the texture involves the superimposition of two or more set-forms. It is true that study scores of works by Schoenberg, Webern and others often contain prefaces that disclose the basic set, discuss some of its properties, and relate these to the overall formal organization of the music. Even with such cribs, though, a good deal of work is needed to complete an account of the piece's twelve-note materials and processes.

Not only do twelve-note compositions rarely consist solely of linear unfoldings of a single set-form (one that does is Webern's tiny *Kinderstück*, for piano, of 1924): they may well not begin with a clear indication of what the linear order of the set is. Yet if we assume that the student will begin to explore this subject by means of a work of Webern or Schoenberg that does offer a fairly clear initial statement, and that is already discussed, however generally, in the literature, it should be possible, without much difficulty, to determine the collection of eleven transpositions of the prime form, and the various transformations (inversions; with retrogrades and inverted retrogrades, where appropriate) which make up the set-group of the piece. By convention, the set-form that is most prominent at or near the beginning of a piece is designated the untransposed, untransformed prime (P–O). But general historical accounts, and studies of sketches, which indicate how often the composer's own 'original' prime does not actually begin a piece, will reinforce the point that it is usually the relative distance between all the versions of the set in question that is most significant: and the less hierarchic the composer's usage, the more difficult it may be to determine whether a particular form is truly 'untransposed', relative to the remainder, or not. This is not to imply that a twelve-note composer will necessarily seek to avoid certain types of preference for particular set-forms, and indeed for particular pitch classes within particular forms: examples of both types of invariance will be given below. But – and despite such comments as Webern's that 'the original form and pitch of the row occupy a position akin to that of the "main key" in earlier music' [Webern, 1963: 54] – a single, 'O' version of a twelve-note set is really not very similar to the scale of a tonic key within the tonal system. Full accounts of the contrasts between a work like Schoenberg's String Quartet No. 4, where particular regions of the set-group certainly do establish analogies with tonal areas, and a work like Webern's String Quartet, Op. 28, in which invariance is exploited without the slightest hint of such analogies, belong in comprehensive historical accounts of twentieth-century music (see, for example, Whittall, 1977). But such studies have often suffered from the failure of those under-taking them to provide adequate accounts of the twelve-note element itself.

The most economical and effective way of laying out the set-group of a twelve-note composition is as a numerical table, or matrix, whose horizontal axis presents the ordered elements of P–O and subsequent transpositions, and whose vertical axis presents the ordered elements of I–O and subsequent transpositions. (Note that 'O' need not necessarily be C.) Example 41 presents the set-group for Webern's Cantata No. 1, Op. 29, in this form. (If the sets are arranged in tables in simple numerical order, descending from 0, 1, 2, 3 . . ., then separate tables for primes and inversions will be needed.) Of course, a composer may construct a set that cannot be retrograded without reproducing itself in inversion, as Webern does here, since P–O^R is identical with I–5 (see below): nor is there any obligation to use all the members of a set-group within a com-position. A complete presentation of possibilities enables the analyst to study the various properties of the group more effectively (especially its invariant elements), and it is a good idea to do this before examining how the composer has actually used the material. But once the set-group has been established, and the sets actually used in the piece listed, the analyst can be confident that the

composer's own basic materials have been accurately revealed – a
very different state of affairs from that which obtains with a list of
pitch-class sets for an atonal piece such as Webern's Op. 7 No. 3.
And yet it hardly needs saying by now that a list of set-forms is not
an analysis. In atonal music, no less than in tonal music, the analyst
must not merely describe, but must also interpret.

Example 41

0	8	11	10	2	1	4	3	7	6	9	5
4	0	3	2	6	5	8	7	11	10	1	9
1	9	0	11	3	2	5	4	8	7	10	6
2	10	1	0	4	3	6	5	9	8	11	7
10	6	9	8	0	11	2	1	5	4	7	3
11	7	10	9	1	0	3	2	6	5	8	4
8	4	7	6	10	9	0	11	3	2	5	1
9	5	8	7	11	10	1	0	4	3	6	2
5	1	4	3	7	6	9	8	0	11	2	10
6	2	5	4	8	7	10	9	1	0	3	11
3	11	2	1	5	4	7	6	10	9	0	8
7	3	6	5	9	8	11	10	2	1	4	0

Prime forms: horizontal axis, left to right
Inversions: vertical axis, top to bottom

As was pointed out in chapter 12, the most significant property
of Forte's theory of set-complex relations is the emphasis given to
invariant elements: recurrences and relationships depending on
degrees of similarity. Even if the composition is in some sense as
much about differences (if not more) as about similarities, it is
important to have a systematic and convincing way of specifying
which is which. And so invariance, symmetry and complementation
– often interdependent as they are – are as important as analytical
tools in twelve-note music as they are in pre-twelve-note atonality.

There are two basic categories of twelve-note set. The first
contains sets that are symmetrical in the sense that the interval
classes of their second halves (hexachords) mirror those of the first,
while providing the complementary six pitch classes. The other
category contains sets that are not symmetrical in this sense: there is
no mirror relation between the two hexachords.

Webern's Cantata No. 1 employs a set of the first type, as can be
seen at a glance in example 42 where the hexachords of P–O and
I–5 are superimposed. This first hexachord on the lower stave is

Ex.42 Webern: Cantata No.1, Op.29

I–5 of the first hexachord on the upper stave, and this identifies the principal property of such symmetrical sets: they have no independent retrograde forms – that is, any apparent retrograde is identical with a transposed prime or inverted form. In the case of the opus 29 set, therefore, the 'retrograde' of the whole of P–O (P–O^R) is identical with I–5: and the 'retrograde' of I–5 (I–5^R) is identical with P–O.

P–O: A   F   G♯   G   B   Bb   C♯   C   E   Eb   F♯   D: P–O^R
1–5: D   F♯   Eb   E   C   C♯   Bb   B   G   G♯   F   A: I–5^R

This particular invariant relation naturally holds for all pairs of inverse-related sets separated by interval class 5 and, as a result, the group derived from this set contains only 24 distinct members. By contrast, the set of Webern's *Drei Lieder*, Op. 25, does have independent retrograde forms: P–O^R is not identical with I–1, even though, as example 43 shows, the first hexachord of I–1 does contain the same six pitch classes as the second hexachord of P–O *in a different order*. The set-group for opus 25 therefore contains the full complement of 48 members.

A composer who chooses to use the twelve-note method is by no means the prisoner of mathematical rules, but the most significant and pervasive techniques devised by Schoenberg, Berg and Webern do involve a recognition of that essential property of the method which generates invariants. In Schoenberg's case it is clear that his awareness of the absence of harmonic principles based on the distinction between consonance and dissonance, in an atonal idiom where melodic and contrapuntal factors are to the fore, led him to attach particular importance to the presentation of the material of the total chromatic in what is in the most basic sense a polarized or complementary rather than a focused or hierarchized fashion. Tonal harmony is not a matter of 'completion', still less of complementation. But Schoenberg's atonal harmony, in many of his

Ex.43 Webern: Drei Lieder, Op.25

twelve-note compositions, achieves its coherence through hexachordal complementation: the consistent juxtaposition or combination of one prime form of the set with one inversion in such a way that the pitch classes of the prime's hexachords are complemented by those of the inversion. Such a 'combinatorial' relationship has already been demonstrated above in connection with the set of Webern's opus 29. But Schoenberg's combinatorial pairs tend to involve inversions that are *not* equivalent to retrogrades of prime forms. In other words, they tend to present the pitch classes in a different order, as Webern does in the combinatorially related P–O/I–1 of opus 25 (not used as such in the actual music). Here are the P–O and 1–5 forms that Schoenberg *does* employ in his Piano Piece Op. 33a:

P–O: Bb F   C   B   A   F# C# D# G   Ab D   E: P–O^R
I–5: D# G# C# D   E   G   C   Bb Gb F   B   A: I–5^R

Since our concern here is with the first phase of twelve-note composition, the main point to reinforce is that the principle of comprehensive complementation as demonstrated above involved a vision of musical space as a superimposition of prime and inverted forms of the set, with all the potential for mirror symmetry that this affords, and with all the potential for tension between synthesis (completion of the twelve-note aggregate by means of combinatorial pairing) and symbiosis (contrast between mutually exclusive entities by avoidance of such combinatorial pairing). Such a super-imposition has been described above as more a matter of polarity than of focus or hierarchy: yet both Schoenberg and Webern were able to explore this total atonal space in ways that gave the complementary concepts of focus and polarity, hierarchy and symmetry, new structural force (see, for example, Phipps, 1984). Both composers were far too sophisticated not to relish and explore the different degrees of identity and overlap that invariance provides, and, as indicated above, an adequate analysis of any twelve-note piece needs first to explore the invariant properties of the set itself, as distinct from its compositional deployment. But however exhaustive the rationale that can be provided for the composer's choice of set-forms in sequence, the analyst must still confront and interpret the actual material to which the sets (as collections of integers or pitch classes) give rise: the ideas that may even have inspired the set in the first place.

The second movement of Webern's *Piano Variations*, Op. 27, (example 44) has frequently been discussed in the historical and theoretical literature (see especially Moldenhauer, 1978: 481–5; Westergaard, 1963; Travis, 1966). Our intention here is not to offer a comprehensive 'harmonic' analysis, but to concentrate on those aspects of the movement most directly concerned with its nature as a twelve-note composition. If we assume for the moment complete ignorance of the identity of the basic set (coupled with the knowledge that this is a twelve-note piece!), and also complete unawareness of the movement's canonic structure, which is after all hidden to the extent that the music neither looks nor sounds like the unfolding of two superimposed contrapuntal lines, we should begin the analysis with the attempt to identify the set and establish whether or not a succession of single set-forms is being used. Since the immediate repetition of the A in bar 1 is acceptable according to twelve-note theory, the following linear succession can be determined:

Bb	G#	A	C#	F	B	D	G	E	F#	C	F
1	2	3	4	5	6	7	8	9	10	11	5

In whatever order the pitches in the chord at the end of bar 3 are presented, there is a delayed repetition of F before a complete twelve-note cycle has been stated, and the missing pitch, E flat, does not occur until bar 6. So the only way in which the repetitions of pitches that occur before the apparent completion of a twelve-note cycle in bar 6 can be accounted for is by the presence of two simultaneously unfolding, and inversionally related, set-forms:

Bb	A	C#	B	D	C	F#	F	E	G#	G	Eb
G#	A	F	G	E	F#	C	C#	D	Bb	B	Eb

There are two ways in which Webern ensures that the disentangling

Ex.44 Webern: Piano Variations, Op.27/2

of these set-forms is not an absolutely straightforward matter of alternate pitches in alternate sets. First, he groups grace notes with their partners, so that any attempt to proceed by literal alternation in bar 2 will produce a sequence in which the inversional symmetry breaks down:

Bb	A	C#	B	G...
G#	A	F	D	E...

An even greater hindrance to the establishment of a correct linear ordering is the consistent placement of the three-note chords after the fifth linear pitch of each pair of set statements. Strictly speaking, in fact, the analyst does not need to know the 'correct' order of pitches within each chord, since Webern never uses a linear form of this trichord. The order can therefore be established only with reference to the other movements of opus 27.

Another favourite device of Webern's accounts for the way in which the pairs of superimposed set-forms, in the canon by inversion

Ex.45 Webern: Piano Variations, Op.27/2

* The boxes enclose the 3-note chords.

at the distance of interval class 2, and of a quaver, succeed each other. The last pitch of one set-form normally functions simultaneously as the first pitch of the next: the E flat and D sharp in bar 6 are the last notes of I–6 and P–4, *and also* the first notes of I–11 and P–11 (see example 45). Similarly, the B flat in bar 11 is the last note of P–11 and the first of P–6, while the G sharp is the last note of I–11 and the first note of I–4. Then the model breaks down, and the C sharp and F grace notes in bar 17 (the first pitches of the final set-pair P–9 and I–7) repeat the D flat and F that end the previous pair – I–4 and P–6. The twelve-note content of the movement therefore consists of four pairs of sets, eight different forms of a set that comes into the non-symmetrical category, but which all begin or end with the B flat/G sharp dyad. This material is laid out in abstract form in example 45; the transposition levels shown are those which result if the initial set of the work's first movement is designated P–0.

Presenting the basic material of the movement in this way emphasizes the existence of invariants, for although all eight sets occupy different positions in the set-group of the piece by virtue of the order of their pitch classes, each pair can be regarded as presenting a different permutation of the same collection of seven vertical dyads, as shown by the letters between the staves on example 45: a . . . e represent dyads of two different pitch classes, x, y dyads that duplicate a pitch class. The movement thus provides a particularly striking demonstration of the interaction between fixed and free elements that twelve-note music can exploit.

When the actual registral placement of pitches is taken into account, the 'fixed' aspect becomes even more notable. Not only is the movement a canon by inversion, but the entire pitch-structure is inversionally symmetrical about the axis of the A above middle C, as shown in example 46. This use of fixed registers, in combination with the systematic employment of varieties of accent and dynamics, encourages Westergaard to claim that 'here, as in tonal music, large-scale intervallic structure is the basis of form' [Westergaard, 1963: 118]. Undeniably, the effect of the symmetrically placed repetitions promotes the consistent placement of motives in space and time: but there is no voice-leading, any more than there is the absolute 'equality' between the twelve pitch classes that twelve-note theory may imply to be the ideal. And although the conjunctions of A and E flat (or D sharp) indicate that the movement is polarized around these pitches, if not literally centred on its axis of symmetry,

Ex.46 Webern: Piano Variations, Op.27/2

A, the effect is not of a Stravinskyan convergence on this or any other centre, but rather of polarities dispersed in space. (For a discussion of comparable issues in the second movement of Webern's opus 24, see Wintle, 1982.)

The function of this movement in opus 27 as a whole is as a short, sharp, scherzo-like explosion between two longer, more restrained movements. If Webern's ability to manipulate small musical 'molecules' were to be judged on the basis of this canon alone he would indeed rank as a primitive. But useful conclusions can still be drawn from it, and carried over into the analysis of the rather more explicitly motivic material that he normally employed. The way in which the motivic elements are grouped overrides the interval-and-rhythm canon, pushing it into the background, and superimposing a process of variation, which is by no means lacking in subtlety, though verbal description inevitably makes it seem rather laborious. A diagrammatic presentation (example 47) at least indicates the manner in which different series of dynamics, articulations, rhythmic and pitch motives all interact in ways that are anything but mechanical. The 31 motivic segments of the movement use three different but closely related rhythmic motives: (1) two quavers, (2) two quavers with grace notes, and (3) two crotchets that overlap by one quaver. There are three different dynamic levels – *p, f* and *ff*. There are five types of articulation (shown on example 47(a)). But there are a larger number of pitch motives: 15 if retrogrades and octave transpositions are discounted, and 10 if the presence or absence of different pairs of grace notes is discounted. It therefore follows that the rate of recurrence for dynamics, rhythm and type of articulation is inevitably greater than it is for pitch.

In example 47(a) the motives are grouped into four broad categories, with each occurrence given once only: category A

Ex.47 (a) Webern: Piano Variations, Op.27/2

Rhythmic patterns	Dynamics	Modes of Articulation

Rhythmic patterns   *Dynamics*   *Modes of Articulation*

(i) ♫   (i) *p*   (i) ⌒
                 (ii) *f*   (ii) · ·
(ii) ♫♪   (iii) *ff*   (iii) – –
                                   (iv) ⌒ ⌒·
(iii) ♪♩ ♩♪   (v) > >

comprises statements built from interval class 2 (with or without
grace notes); category B is the double statement of a single pitch;
category C contains the various statements that employ interval
class 4; and category D includes all the statements in which interval

class 6 is present. (It would obviously be possible to regard statements 9 and 14 as a separate category.) In example 47(b) the contents of all 31 segments of the movement are set out in tabular form, admittedly an abstract and laborious exercise but useful in that it indicates the full extent of the ways in which similarity and

Example 47(b)

type	Segment no.	Rhythmic pattern	Dynamic	Articulation	Pitch/ Interval (types)
a	i	1	2	1	1
b	ii	1	1	2	2 (LH/RH)
c	iii	2	2	3	3
d	iv	3	1	4	4
e	v	1	2	5	5
f	vi	1	1	1	6
a	⌈vii	1	2	1	1 (reversed)
g	⌊viii	1	1	2	7 (RH/LH)
h	ix	3	3	4	8
i	⌈x	2	2	3	9
j	⌊xi	3	1	4	10
k	xii	1	3	5	11
b	xiii	1	1	2	2 (RH/LH)
l	⌈xiv	1	2	1	3
m	⌊xv	1	1	2	9 (reversed)
a	xvi	1	2	1	1
n	⌈xvii	1	2	2	7 (reversed)
g	⌊xviii	1	1	2	7 (LH/RH)
b	xix	1	1	2	2 (LH/RH)
i	⌈xx	2	2	3	9
o	⌊xxi	1	3	5	12
f	⌊xxii	1	1	1	6 (8ve transposition)
p	⌈xxiii	1	2	1	9 (reversed)
q	⌊xxiv	1	1	2	3 (Db = C♯)
r	xxv	3	3	4	13
s	xxvi	3	2	4	14
b	xxvii	1	1	2	2 (RH/LH)
t	⌈xxviii	1	3	5	15
u	⌊xxix	1	1	1	7 (8ve transposition)
h	xxx	3	3	4	8
a	xxxi	1	2	1	1

Segments bracketed together are not separated by rests.

diversity interact in the movement as a whole. The lower-case letters on the extreme left of the table are used to indicate those segments which, even if not literally identical, are so closely related as to be deemed the same. Finally, that column of letters can be presented as a table through which the linear sequence of segments in the movement can be traced by reading each line horizontally in turn:

```
1   a b c d e f
2   a             g h i j k
3     b                     l m
4   a                           n
5             g
6     b           i             o
7           f                     p q r s
8     b                                 t u
9               h
10  a
```

This presentation undoubtedly gives emphasis to the diversities that are present in the music; simply because of that, however, it may well lead the analyst back to a motivic interpretation that sees all the segments as variants of each other rather than as so markedly distinct.

Example 47 does not take account of one basic aspect of the piece, the use of rests. And although, if we exclude the two-quaver 'anacrusis' to bar 1, each half of the movement has a total duration of 44 quavers, the pattern of attacks and rests within each section is quite different. There is certainly no mirror symmetry here, and the simplest way to summarize the difference is to point out that, because the ratio of attacks to rests increases in the second part of the movement, there is room for a relatively long period of silence, the longest in the piece – two crotchet beats – just before the end. The repeat marks may suggest a binary form, but the second half is much more development than recapitulation.

As elsewhere in this part of the book, the purpose of discussing so brief a piece so exhaustively has been to suggest that there should be no short cuts to generalization in the analysis of a twelve-note movement, any more than there can be with tonal or 'free' atonal compositions. Pitch, rhythm, texture, form must all be considered in ways that the music's character and content will indicate. And it is clear that the use of more comprehensive principles of ordering in twelve-note music does not make the result any the less atonal, any the less focused on textural or motivic elements, than in non-twelve-note atonal compositions. Even if these elements may be interpreted as in some sense 'harmonic', that term can never be expected to mean what it means in tonal composition.

17

Coda

Those aspects of the 'atonal revolution' which have been discussed and illustrated here should go some way to demonstrating that the real significance and worth of that revolution was in the balance between logical, and perhaps unique, overall plans (in striking contrast to the fundamental structures which can generate so many different tonal compositions) and the freedom of the ways in which such plans could be 'composed out'. This conjunction of freedom and discipline has ensured that the atonal revolution has tended to have a greater influence on later composers than has the twelve-note technique which appeared, at the time, to supersede it. Nevertheless, much more recent atonal music is even more challenging for the analyst than that of the first generation. In many cases, it may well be neither possible nor desirable to attempt to do more than perceive and describe some kind of overall process: that which is most *fixed* about the piece in question. And that is easier to do when the process involves retention rather than change. For example, in the first movement – 'Anaphora' – of *A mirror on which to dwell* (1975–6), Elliott Carter draws all the pitches from a symmetrically disposed twelve-note collection (example 48). At the most basic level, therefore, the process of the movement involves *not* changing the registers of any of the pitches, and it does not require a very profound study of the score for this 'super-invariance' to become apparent. Beyond that, however, as with all Carter's most characteristic later compositions, the analyst will make very slow progress indeed with any attempt to devise an explanation of what the most significant subsets of this background

Ex.48 Carter: 'Anaphora', *A mirror on which to dwell*

Ex.49 Boulez: *Domaines*, Cahier C

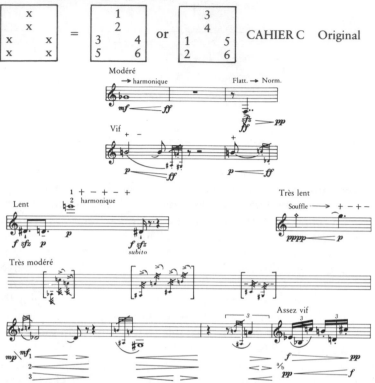

material are – unless (as is the case in Schiff, 1983), the analyst obtains detailed information about compositional techniques from the composer.

The first version of *Domaines*, for solo clarinet (1968), is probably among the least formidable and complex music composed by Pierre Boulez. In the material in *Cahier C* (example 49), for example, it is evident that the 'motive' formed by interval class 1 presented in the first segment is consistently developed in the remaining five segments:

Segment							
1	F Gb						
2		Ab A Bb B C Db					
3				D Eb E			
4	G						
5		Ab A Bb B C Db					
6		Bb B C Db D Eb					

In all cases save the single-note segment 4, complete segments of the total chromatic are involved. Moreover, segments 1–3 gradually assemble, with some repetition, a complete twelve-note statement, with the only remaining gap filled by the single G in segment 4. (It is part of the strategy of *Domaines* that segments need not be performed in numerical order.)

These Carter and Boulez examples are cited simply to indicate that such basic atonal features as mirror symmetry and the completion of chromatic segments may continue to provide the basic elements of process in more recent atonal music than that of Schoenberg and Webern. 'Process', admittedly, means merely process with respect to the selection and placement of pitches. The other dimensions of atonal music must also be brought into any analysis with pretensions to exhaustiveness, not least because they are likely to be an inseparable part of the music's character as well as its process. With Schoenberg's Op. 19 No. 6, for example, the uniformity, with minimal contrast, of the pitch material, is reflected in the dynamics – the most contrasting bar (7) is the loudest – and in the avoidance of a sense of regular pulsation, even very slow pulsation, aspiring to the actual indefiniteness of the final pause.

As far as the interpretation of pitch structures is concerned, it will be evident that the difference between motivic and pitch-class-set approaches to atonal music is very great, and not least because the latter seems to imply that 'free' atonality is more significant for the way it anticipates the twelve-note method than for the way it continues the thematic procedures of tonal music: it is more preface than transition, and because twelve-note compositions are built from successions of set-forms, it is considered plausible to argue that pre-twelve-note music may also be defined through successions of collections – sets – whose interrelations are structurally significant.

As already suggested, the abstractions and classifications of pitch-class-set analysis are likely to be more impressive when a work of the substance of Webern's Op. 6 [Baker, 1982], Stravinsky's *Le Sacre du Printemps* [Forte, 1978b], or Berg's *Wozzeck* [Schmalfeldt, 1983] is under scrutiny. To put it bluntly, the larger the work, the more the analyst may feel the need to establish the minimum number of plausible invariants, and the less practicable an analysis of motivic transformations will be. That such an essentially motivic analysis can itself become formidably elaborate and complex, even with reference to short single-line pieces, has been shown by Jean-Jacques Nattiez, notably in his semiotic study of Varèse's *Density 21.5*

[Nattiez, 1982]. In this case, indeed, it is the pitch-class-set analysis that is likely to be more straightforward and succinct. Whether the composition in question is large or small, it is probable that only those analysts who can see some value in the ends of pitch-class-set analysis will be prepared to accept the necessity for the means. Even for the sceptic, however, exposure to pitch-class-set analytical techniques is salutary: for example, the distinction between an atonal structure controlled, in pitch-class-set terms, by the actual presence of a nexus set or sets, with complements, and a structure where no such controlling entity can be demonstrated, may be of the kind that offers valuable insights to analysts who would never consider working out prime forms and using Forte's tables of set-complex relations. Above all, in the importance it attaches to complementation as a primary 'syntactic' feature of atonal structures, pitch-class-set analysis has focused on a vital principle, even if its actual analytical practices are open to question.

Guidelines for Further Study

It might be useful here to reinforce the objectives of Part III of our study. Since the basic aim of analysing an atonal composition seems to be to establish either a single source of unity, as in Webern's opus 27, or an irreducible field of tension, as in his Op. 7 No. 3, it may appear unnecessary to spend much time on seeking to describe every detail present in small pieces with maximum precision. After all, for much of the time even the most apparently serious commentator on twentieth-century music is content to identify fundamentals – whether of structure or of style – and not seek to relate every possible detail to that framework. Analysis does not usually stand or fall on its statistical comprehensiveness, but on its 'critical' conviction, its relevance to the evolving response to the piece in question of both analyst and reader. Such explorations as are conducted here are, we agree, extremes of 'formalism' which would be ridiculous if regarded either as ends in themselves where atonal miniatures are concerned, or as models to be followed closely for all atonal works however large and complex: they would also be futile if the analyst did not value the music highly and see it, in its historical context, as important enough to warrant such close attention. The journey into the heart of the miniature is the complement to the more detached perspective on the fundamentals, the basic outlines, of larger pieces, to which analysis often aspires. Yet the journey can always provide a model for such perspectives, and even if one's decisions about the 'basics' of the larger piece depend in part on instinct, it will be a more reliable instinct if it has been trained on meticulous observation of the miniature. After all, large-scale atonal works may well share with the smallest the kind of strategic complementation and balancing of contrasts discussed above. And the analyst of even the grandest atonal composition may well start with the kind of simple descriptive tabulation shown for Webern's Op. 7 No. 3 on pp. 184–5 before deciding how much detailed analysis to undertake, and what form to give it. As suggested in the text, the beginning student will probably find it most rewarding to explore in reverse order the topics dealt with chronologically.

Twelve-note Composition

Absolute beginners would do well to study the ways in which composers obtain variety from a single set-form (Webern: *Kinderstück*; Schoenberg: *Piano Piece*, Op. 23 No. 5) before proceeding to movements in which a certain number of transpositions, inversions and retrogrades may be encountered: Webern's Op. 25 No. 1 has the added feature of a text, while Schoenberg's Piano Piece, Op. 33a, (much discussed in the technical literature), is a particularly concise example of an attempt to establish a relationship between serial technique and a traditional form. The comprehensive motivic analysis of the (rather special) Webern movement Op. 27 No. 2 was included not to provide a model for invariable emulation so much as a background against which to measure the suitability of other relatively short Webern instrumental movements for similar treatment: for example, Op. 21 No. 3, Op. 22 No. 1, Op. 24 No. 3, Op. 27 No. 1 and Op. 28 No. 2. We also believe that Webern's Op. 25 No. 1 and Schoenberg's Op. 23 No. 5 and Op. 33a are more useful for exploring set identification, questions of invariance between chosen sets, and general matters of form, than for exhaustive motivic analysis.

Pre-twelve-note Atonality: sets, motives; balance and integration

Here it might seem logical to begin by looking at those shorter items from Schoenberg's opus 19 and Webern's opus 7 and opus 11 not discussed in the text, if only to begin to test the extent to which these collections of pieces are linked by common factors. Other exercises would be to complete the identification of pitch-class sets in Webern's Op. 11 No. 3 begun in the text, and to explore the question of similarity relations and set-complex relations on the basis of Forte's analysis of Op. 19 No. 6 (paying special attention to his criteria for the establishment of nexus sets). Webern's early miniatures provide the principal source for other suitable material: for example, Op. 9 No. 5 and Op. 16 No. 2.

We suggest that pitch-class-set analysis after the Forte model should be complemented by a motivic analysis. Here rhythm and duration are integral, even though it can be instructive to consider the question of an independent structural framework based on purely rhythmic factors. (See the discussion of Schoenberg's Op. 19 No. 2, p. 166.) Moreover, only by attempting a motivic analysis is it possible to decide whether you believe it is necessary to try to include every possible aspect of the music in that analysis or not. In surveying the repertory it will soon become clear that the simplest kind of motivic analysis is that possible when pieces (like Op. 19 No. 6 and Webern's Op. 11 No. 3) are segmental 'monodies'. More commonly, the motivic segments will need to reflect textural complexities by allowing for superimposition.

Extended and Implicit Tonality

Here the repertory of miniatures covers a wide range, from piano pieces by Debussy, Skryabin and Bartók to songs by Stravinsky and Schoenberg. We suggest that the student selects works both with and without explicit 'tonic' harmonies, in order to test the competing claims of voice-leading and chordal analysis, and to establish the extent to which they interact with pitch-class-set analysis, as demonstrated in Forte, 1978a, and Baker, 1983.

From Means to Meaning:
Analysis and the Theory of Signs

Throughout our investigation of the theory and practice of analysis, we have been concerned principally with means of analytical explanation, the object of that explanation being 'meaningful' music. It is the purpose of Part IV to discuss how far we are justified in assuming that music has meaning and, if we are justified, how far such meaning or 'signification' can be considered to be inherent in a score or performance – and therefore something on which different analysts using similar analytical means are likely to be able to agree, and how far analysis may in fact be bringing meaning to music, rather than simply exposing it. If analysis does actually bring meaning to music, we may conclude that theory and the application of theory are unwelcome impositions, substituting for honest intuitive response a preconceived and fundamentally anti-musical approach. The suspicion that such is indeed the case is widespread. Part of our intention in discussing the means of analysis has been to dispel this prejudice to the extent that it may often be based on a lack of understanding of the nature and purpose of specialized analytical theory. But we do not wish to evade a consideration of that most elusive question, what kind of meaning it is that analytical techniques propose to uncover, explain and even enrich. Because it provides a firm point of reference with its categorical stand on these issues, and because it is often, in our experience, a stimulating area of study for students who are, understandably, somewhat impatient with the diffuse and ungainly tradition of informal music aesthetics, we shall discuss musical meaning drawing on some aspects of the study of 'signs': such study may be called either 'semiotics' (the discipline associated with twentieth-century trends in American philosophy and communications theory) or 'semiology' (the discipline associated with French linguistics and literary criticism), the historical distinction having played no great part in musical adaptations of these ideas.

Semiotics rests on an interdisciplinary theory of 'relativism'. It claims that in perception and communication we know what things mean because of the way they relate to other things, rather than solely because of any intrinsic properties they may have. Music analysts, like all those who examine the nature of a human activity and its products, have recourse to a great number of assumptions about what enables us to communicate. Typically, these assumptions are implicit, and indeed most theorists and analysts would be unable to describe the correspondence between their way of thinking or communicating and the general history of thought in these areas – analysts are rarely philosophers, nor are they necessarily educated in the human sciences. The fact that analytical theories rest on difficult philosophical assumptions may not concern the practising musician (though it is unfortunate that such a great art as music has therefore had so little to offer in recent centuries to the humanities and social sciences in general). Yet many analytical theories do not themselves bear serious *analytical* scrutiny, as some of our critical discussion in Parts II and III has indicated. This suggests that a measure of intellectual complacency is endemic in the discipline to its own disadvantage; yet the risk of adopting some non-musical, semiotic concepts partially and superficially is worth taking if they can help the student to think clearly about analytical issues in general.

The exposition and discussion of those analytical theories and practices covered so far has revolved around the question of what music is supposed to mean, or to convey, or at least to have as its effect: it is this, after all, that indicates what analysis is supposed to look for. The question of meaning may now be broached again in a rather different light. Much of our discussion has been based on the assumption that, to explain music, it is necessary to consider any instance of musical communication as an instance of what we *recognize as* musical communication. Most are inclined to think only about their direct contact with the passages or 'messages' which are understood; but there must be some means or 'mechanism' by which we are able to understand (to decipher, or interpret) messages, and these means are called, in the sciences of language and communication, 'codes'. This is not to challenge the notion of intuitive response to music, but to recognize the value that may lie in being able to describe how musical intuition 'works'. In semiotics, the relationship between message and code is conceived in two ways. Either a message is examined to discover how it is organized, what is its code – and this inductive procedure is considered to be an 'analytical' model; or a code already known is used to interpret the message – a deductive procedure considered to be a 'synthetic' model.

Faced with an unknown language, we have to discover the meaning of messages in that language by analysing them in a language we know. Of course, any native speaker can say whether a message is meaningful by testing it against the native code (and everyone has a remarkable capacity to say 'intuitively' whether a message makes sense or not). Note that, in the case of analysis as described here, everything rests on our ability to have procedures for the discovery of the code. For example, on the assumption that it 'means' something, how is the sequence 23233222 to be interpreted? (This is a deliberately abstract example, which might represent, for instance, the practical case of a piece of post-tonal music, to which our intuitive response as regards 'phrasing' is rather uncertain, barred as $\frac{2}{8}/\frac{3}{8}/\frac{2}{8}$ etc.) A discovery procedure will have to consider the possibility that there are, say, four units here, 23, 23, 32, and 22; and it may indeed be the case that a meaningful unit is determined by the presence of an initial 2, so that there are only three units, 23, 233 and 222. Unless it is known what criteria of organization are pertinent, analysis has recourse to nothing other than explicit discovery procedures, showing the many possible meanings. The larger the corpus of information analysed, the more likely it is that we shall come to a view of some determinate meaning – from a few sentences, the meaning of a language can barely be discovered, but from several dozen books, there is some chance that it could. The only chance, however, lies in explication of the discovery procedure. If different analytical criteria are applied to different books in the unknown language, the 'code', the key to the meaning of the language, will never be discovered.

To consider this mode of thought in directly musical terms, it seems possible to imagine good analogies. The analyst may be faced with a tune – for convenience, suppose this to be in modern Western notation – the like of which has not been heard before, from some previously unknown culture (in reality, of course, it is more likely to be a tune, probably a folk song, to which we have only a little 'acculturalized' response). The discovery procedure to analyse this can be enormously elaborate, considering many different segmentations (how many 'phrases' are there if a phrase is defined, for instance, as having between 8 and 12 notes? – do certain pitches always have the same rhythmic value, or perhaps always a different rhythmic value?) of which an exhaustive list is inconceivable, so rich is the capacity of the mind to perceive organization, and it would be elaborate to no special purpose, in the sense of one being able to discover the 'meaning' of the tune 'intended' by its composer, assuming it had a single composer. However, given several tunes of similar provenance, and given the *same* analytical procedures in each case, we could quickly construct a theory about the most likely or the most interesting code (and any further tune could be used to modify that code if necessary, that is, if it showed up inadequacies in the code): the chances of one derived code, our understanding of this music, being the same as that originally ascribed to it in the alien culture are minimal.

A synthetic model is also easy to describe superficially. For instance, by means of the analytical inquiry just described we would indeed be in possession of a synthetic code against which new messages could be compared. But there are even more obvious examples familiar to all musicians, and perhaps the most familiar is harmonic analysis. Any music student can describe – or be expected to! – the harmonic pattern of a previously unknown Bach chorale setting and rules to which it conforms or to which it poses exceptions (it will end with a I_3^5, the majority of chords at pauses will be preceded by a chord with a root a fourth or fifth distant, and so on). In this case, a known code is used (which is, in truth, a pretty vague one) to interpret the message.

These analogies may well have demanded some patience in reading and accepting, since they are not as good as may first appear. Musical meaning is not really like meaning in language. Whereas it is possible to say that 'Jack and Jill' means something but 'Jack Jill and' does not (though the latter could always be made meaningful in context, or 'poetically'), there seems to be no similar experience in music. The passage quoted in example 50 is certainly

Ex.50

not from a Bach chorale. According to almost any conventional 'code' of music theory it may be bad, funny, even unpleasant, but when it appears in Berg's Violin Concerto it would not even occur to us to ask whether it is somehow the equivalent of 'Jack Jill and'. What is the musician to make, then, of this apparently different kind of concept of what a 'language' might be? Perhaps that, in music, messages are made meaningful *only* poetically. Viewed in this light, the distinction between language and music turns out to be quite helpful. Consider a classic English sentence devised to exemplify meaninglessness: 'colourless green ideas sleep furiously'. This sentence, while apparently acceptable grammatically, breaks the code of meaningful English in various ways. On the other hand, as Philip Pettit points out [Pettit, 1975: 102], such metaphors, or poetic images, can be entirely comprehensible, indeed rather enticing: imagine that sentence in a poem about seeds underground in the winter, waiting for the spring. For the musician, it is attractive to think of meaning as strictly 'poetic' in this sense, as never right or wrong, as always 'virtual'. There is no musical message for which the musician cannot find a meaning.

Finally, it has to be said that the argument so far simply defines another set of questions rather than providing an answer to what analytical and synthetic meaning might be in music. If musical meaning is indeed 'poetic' as just described, a further world of unreality has emerged where music can mean and can only mean just what you want it to mean. The musical imagination does have the potential to make music mean just what it wants, but it usually does not want to do this: it wants to focus instead on 'what is meant' in a piece of music. We can, if we choose, hear in a Beethoven symphony by means of intuitive understanding music that no other person, presumably, could ever hear, including Beethoven. This is to assume, along with Schenker, that the structural 'transformations' that may be technically described in a master-piece reach us 'as a power of imagination' over which we do have some active control [Schenker, 1979: 6]. But what we really choose most often is to hear what there is to be heard, believing, to return to the starting point of this discussion, that there is indeed something 'inherently' meaningful in the piece. This belief is fed by the question: how else could works of music have any identity? If there is, by common consent, such a piece of music as 'Beethoven's Ninth Symphony', one musician must be hearing, or must believe she or he is hearing, something more like what another musician is hearing than it is like any other conceivable piece of music. Once again, then, as arose in the discussion of Tovey (see above, pp. 62–73), it appears that underlying the experience of musical meaning, which makes analysis possible, there is relativism at play. We have no determinate idea of what Beethoven's Ninth Symphony is, but we do have the determinate idea that, whatever it is, it is absolutely distinct from any other piece of music for all musicians.

In describing the semiotician's analytical and synthetic models, it has become clear that their direct application to music is problematic. However, some believe that the problems at the heart of traditional music analysis are even more unsatisfactory, and that the clarity and perspective provided by semiotics is worth the trouble it brings – trouble in defining just what kind of meaning is being considered. One of the earliest statements of this turn in musical thinking was in Nicolas Ruwet's *Langage, musique, poésie*. His chapter 'Analytical Methods in Musicology' threw down a strong challenge, along with a wholesale condemnation of the roots of analytical theory as he saw it. It must be remembered that Ruwet is stepping back so far from analytical practice that the kind of theory he addresses may well seem irrelevant to any but the most idealistic ends. He is concerned above all with the infuriating banality of studies of early chant, the kind of research that is so primitive as to be excluded, as here, from what is normally considered analysis. To the student of analytical method from Schenkerian reduction to pitch-class set structure, it may be all too clear that the typical chant study based on non-specific classification and wilful interpretations of 'expression' is not to be taken seriously, or must be taken as part of a different discipline. Yet Ruwet has shown that there are lessons to be learned from the inadequacy of the chant-study tradition, points that may be extrapolated into more sophisticated areas of inquiry:

Let us now consider the present state of musicology from the point of view of the distinction between the two models. It can be said that: (a) the theoretical problem this distinction represents has never been raised; (b) an analytical model has never been explicitly worked out; (c) music analyses . . . do not formulate the discovery procedures on which they are based . . . it seems plain to everyone that a piece of music with a minimum of complexity is subject to hierarchic organization, divides into parts on different levels. Thus, according to Ferretti, Gregorian melodies are divided into *periods*, these in turn into *phrases*, the phrases into *half-phrases* and these into *incises* . . . the crucial question, preliminary to all others, is the following: *what are the criteria which, in any particular case, have governed the segmentation?* Now, no one takes the trouble to answer this question, as if evidence for the criteria leapt from the page . . . the application of explicit discovery procedures to more familiar musical systems may well result only in banal conclusions, already recognized intuitively. But even that is far from being negligible. In fact, it is very useful to be able to verify, step by step, with reference to intuition, the working-out of a procedure . . . [and] well-defined segmentation procedures will result in the revision of traditional analyses. [Ruwet, 1972: 104–7, our translation]

Thus far, we have outlined just one element of semiotic analysis, that it uses *explicit discovery procedures* (and the procedures of most analysis cannot be considered explicit, but implicitly assume the reader's acceptance of a set of assumptions about what constitutes valid musical organization in the first place). This first element must exclude from our consideration various avowedly semiotic musical inquiries that do not take as a premiss explicit discovery procedures (see, for example, Coker, 1972, and Noske, 1977).

A second element is rather simpler to express, and is essential in forming a serviceable conception of what a discovery procedure is – as opposed to a synthetic deduction like a traditional harmonic or formal analysis. Jean-Jacques Nattiez has elaborated on the actual status of analysis with a 'tripartitional' model [Nattiez, 1975] which involves three levels. First, according to this model, the factors involved in the composition of a piece of music leave traces that can often be identified. A good illustration is in the finale of Beethoven's opus 135 String Quartet, where mottos link verbal concepts notated by Beethoven (*muss es sein? es muss sein*) with musical motives, and the intention of the composer is reasonably straightforward and is acceptable for all musicians. This is called the 'poietic' dimension of the tripartition. Conversely, the perception of music that any listener brings to it, the 'esthesic' dimension, is infinitely variable: yet there must be traces in this esthesic dimension of the music in question – as discussed already, the listener's response must be partly determined by the music if there is to be any awareness that the music has an identity (that it exists, in fact). Between these dimensions is a neutral level, the autonomous organization that exists in the work and of which we can never be sure to have made an exhaustive description. This is the dimension that has nothing to do with the conditions of the creation of the music and nothing to do with the choices, habits or intuitive understanding in our response to it. This 'neutral level' is the level at which discovery procedures are carried out. And here it emerges how a second element relates to the first, to the idea of 'explicit discovery procedures'. Semiotic analysis not only uses explicit discovery procedures, but it must do so – and indeed can only do so – at the neutral level, without reference to factors of creation or reception, or with explicit awareness of what is *not* neutral in its application. Nattiez admits that what is regarded as neutral, as systematic, as verifiable, is not, literally, entirely neutral, since it concerns intellectual categories that have no absolute claim to reality. The whole theory is provisional to a degree, but seems more coherent and explicable, if as yet less developed in practice, than what is to be found elsewhere, speaking generally, in music analysis; while the musician may often prize the impressionistic and the inscrutable in many areas of activity, techniques of analysis are surely best conducted, at least initially, with a firm grasp of their foundations.

Much of the research in this area has been carried out with no concession to pedagogical needs. The ground-breaking article by Ruwet analysing a *Geisslerlied* has yet to be translated into English [Ruwet, 1972], and the most extensive analysis in English [Nattiez, 1982] demands the closest specialist study. Introductions to the field have tended towards theory, towards the most general aspects [Dunsby, 1983; Lidov, 1977], while collected sources provide little focus of use to the student [Steiner, 1981; Stefani, 1975]. While these studies and associated literature (for bibliographic information see Nattiez, 1976; 1982) provide good documentation of a new generation of research, the present context demands simple but telling examples that may act as models for analysis. They can do so only by extension and should be studied for method rather than results, which are hardly important as far as the music is concerned, though of some interest in their theoretical ramifications.

Brahms's Intermezzo in B minor, Op. 119 No. 1 (example 51), has been analysed in various ways;* for instance, with a voice-leading graph in Salzer's *Structural Hearing*; and also from a historical point of view in an article where Brahms's reliance on harmonic progression through cycles of descending, diatonic fifths is considered to be the sign of a chaconne-type compositional

---

*The following discussion of Brahms is substantially derived from a section of Dunsby, 1982, and is used here by kind permission of *Music Analysis* (Basil Blackwell Ltd.).

Ex.51 Brahms: Intermezzo in B minor, Op.119/1

procedure [Newbould, 1977]. It is not difficult to imagine that the
smallest unit in such music is the note, more exactly the pitch-class
attack. This in itself implies two analytical operations, the elimination
of the variables duration and register. These operations do not
necessarily have an equal status from an interpretative point of
view: in other words, we do not have to suppose that duration and
register are of precisely equal significance in the articulation of
pitch-structure. From the point of view of method, however, eliminating these variables is an explicit step, where there is no place for
interpretation – a form of analysis where it is not possible to make a
mistake (except trivially). The pitch-class attacks may also be
counted without error and the results arranged arithmetically (see

line (a) in Table A below). If these units are signs in any sense, perhaps they signify more if there are relatively more of them, and less if there are relatively fewer.

Table A

(a) pitch classes:	F♯	C♯	A	D	B	E	G	A♯	G♯	E♯	C	D♯
number of attacks												
(= 163):	28	24	20	19	19	16	15	7	6	4	3	2

(b) degree status:												
B minor:	D	St	(L)	M	T	Sd	Sm	L	(Sm)	?	?	?
D major:	M	L	D	T	Sm	St	Sd	?	?	?	?	?
F sharp minor:	T	D	M	Sm	Sd	(L)	?	?	St	L	?	(Sm)

| (c) B flat major: | ? | ? | L | M | ? | ? | Sm | T | ? | D | St | Sd |

(T = tonic, St = supertonic, M = mediant, Sd = subdominant,
D = dominant, Sm = flat submediant in minor or submediant in major,
(Sm) = sharp submediant in minor, L = leading note, (L) = flat seventh
degree in minor)

Table B

Distribution of pitch-class attacks	F♯	C♯	A	D	B	E	G	A♯	G♯	E♯	C	D♯
(a) in melody (= 38):	8	7	5	4	5	2	4		1	2		
(b) first beats:	3	3	1	1	1	2	3		1	2		
(c) first beats of bars 1, 3, 5, etc.:	3	3	1							1		
(d) of bars 1, 5, 9, 13:	3	1										
(e) of bars 1, 9:	2											
(f) of bar 1:	1											

Such comments will in themselves suggest a fool's errand, 'unmusical' and of doubtful potential musical value. Intuitive support, though, is easily found. Table A shows an interpretation of the initial results in terms of traditional harmonic theory. A grid is applied to the count of pitch-class attacks set out in line (a). Below the pitch-class names is a classification of each according to its degree status (which in minor raises less than 'neutral' issues, of course, about the sixth and seventh degrees) in one of three tonal levels, B minor, D major and F sharp minor. It is a large step from the explicit discovery procedure, here a simple arithmetical logic, to the intuitive choice of harmonic classifiers. The results can be

tested, however, by the application of counter-intuitive classification, for instance by applying B flat major – a key that is
decidedly remote from the others chosen – as in line (c). This kind
of classification could be completed by examining the distributional
pattern that would arise if all keys, major and minor, were applied
to line (a), but it suffices to observe the predominance of important
scale-degrees on the left-hand side of Table A, given that the most
pertinent harmonic grids are assumed to be those in the (b) lines.

The analysis suggests there is a special relationship between the
quantity of pitch-class attack and the *quality* of harmonic effect in
the music. This relativity, that is, forms a tonal 'sign', perhaps
specific to the piece, perhaps not. And the analysis so far has moved
from distribution *to* interpretation. The results can best be tested,
therefore, by reversing that procedure. The first step is now interpretative or intuitive: it is to identify a melody (not a controversial
step here, but frequently elsewhere in Brahms itself a challenge for
the analyst). Table B shows the results of this new approach to the
music. The relative quantities of pitch-class attack in the melody
(the top part of the music) are presented in line (a). Even allowing
for the deliberately weighted presentation (taking the order of
pitch-classes from Table A rather than from line (a) of Table B), this
distribution is evidently akin to that of line (a) in Table A. The
distribution in Table B is not independent of that in Table A since
the pitch classes of the melody were counted in with the totals first
examined. However, a new kind of grid will be able to separate this
statistical interaction. In Table A the grid was frankly intuitive,
classification according to traditional harmonic concepts. The grid
applied in Table B is that of periodic emphasis and seems rather less
interpretative and rather more, in Nattiez's sense, neutral. Successively
larger metrical groupings are used to eliminate metrically subsidiary pitch classes, in a self-limiting procedure that ends at line (f)
with the beginning of the 16-bar period, a melodic F sharp. It
appears from the left-hand bunching of Table B, which is akin to
the left-hand bunching of scale degrees in Table A, that the relativities of pitch-class attack operate in two ways. First, the texture
as a whole and the melody as a special structural layer both display
a hierarchy of pitch-class attack that represents something like the
harmonic emphasis any informed listener would predict. But there
is also an equivalence between this hierarchy and the hierarchy of
metrical emphasis. Simply, what appear to be the most important
harmonic notes are also the most important notes metrically in the

melody. While one can assume that the periodic metre of nineteenth-century music must play an important role in the structural synthesis of a tonal piece, one would hardly expect what Table B seems to indicate, that periodic metre enables us to identify units of the melody alone, deprived of registral and of actual durational value, representing harmonic values of the entire music.

It cannot be stressed too much that these observations are not put forward as a new contribution to our enjoyment of Brahms. They are introduced here as an uncomplicated example of the best-known and most easily tested aspects of 'distributional' analysis (which is, as will be considered later, in essence 'paradigmatic'). They concern units segmented in a consistent way, and demand some form of analysis which can be applied quite mechanically, without interpretation, and is self-limiting. They establish a consistent, strictly patterned form of relationality for the units and pass them through 'grids', or 'codes', to investigate their signifying potential. It is that potential which is available to the listener, whose role can be exxamined in terms of the information on offer. For example, we have been tacitly assuming that the modern Western musician will find the 'signs' on the left of Tables A and B to be pertinent compared with those on the right (the question marks and void entries). This need be the case only if a particular code, that of major–minor tonality, is in play. Here we return to the very beginning of the subject, when it was established that it is possible to think of music in terms of message and code, and that the most probing and objective analysis is a matter of proceeding from message to code, not the reverse. It is also shown here how implicit in most analysis is the fusion of neutral and esthesic levels. In most analysis, that is, there would be no question that the Brahms is a tonal piece, no question about what code is in play; this would simply be an esthesic (perceptual) assumption. But if we want to hear the piece 'atonally', it is conceivable (and a listener from another culture may have no choice in the matter). The analysis of degrees provided the basis for an 'atonal' listening; in such listening right-hand signs would be taken as more pertinent than left-hand signs (or, more exactly, the distribution of right-hand in relation to left-hand signs would be considered more pertinent). Poietically, there can be little doubt, of course, about what code Brahms had in mind.

Much has had to be forfeited here in the interests of neutrality and specificity. The analyst is required to suspend intuition in those aspects of the inquiry where descriptive adequacy is the goal. It is as if everything the musician instinctively 'knows' or 'feels' about the music counts for nothing; such pretended ignorance seems to run counter to the musician's basic instincts about understanding works of art, and it would be a futile gesture indeed if the results did not bring some other kind of gain. Pitch-class-set theory throws up similar issues. The more refined the student's intuition about an atonal piece, the more it seems that instinctive response has to be suspended in favour of a descriptive system. A semiotic approach is more readily acceptable, perhaps, in ethnomusicology, where there is no instinct in principle to be suppressed on the part of the culturally external observer. Yet semioticians believe that, in the spirit of a genuinely receptive artistic sensibility, we should be able to treat our own culture as if it were an ethnomusicological experience. The shock of the new is a shock we hope to be able to find in Brahms as much as in Boulez.

Those who already know something of the impact of semiotics on analysis may be surprised to find it represented here at some length without mention of 'oppositionality' and its methodological consequences. This has been postponed in the interests of trying to convey concretely the interplay in the analyst's mind between synthetic and semiotic analysis, between the partiality of taking any code as premiss and the supposed impartiality, the neutrality, of examining the message itself systematically. In practice, music semiotics has been preoccupied with neutral analysis that is, viewed critically, not so much neutral as explicit. The basis of semiotic analysis has been taken to be identity, or similarity relations, so that pattern is defined as either the presence or absence of repetitions. The presence of repetition not only offers a simple theory of pattern, but it makes one simple and crucial assumption about how the mind organizes what it perceives. It also offers the analyst a convenient symbolization, of which example 52(a) provides a rudimentary example. Here, sequences of notes have been grouped according to the explicit discovery procedure: 'Is x a rhythmic and melodic repetition of y with respect to all factors except transposition in the diatonic major scale?' Put more simply, but less exactly, both repetition and melodic sequence are regarded as repetition. The vertical columns (numbered I–VIII) each establish a 'paradigm', that is, a grammar (so that unit 3 is 'grammatically' equivalent to unit 1, 11 to 2, 9 and 7 to 4, etc.). The continuous sequence of the music, the 'syntagm', has thus been segmented into its 'neutral'

Ex.52 'God Save the Queen'

(a)

(b)

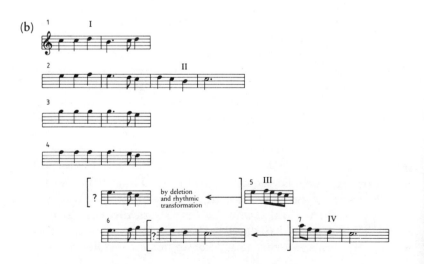

constituents (assuming that the question asked is regarded as neutral). As a result, it is proved that there are eight paradigmatic components. Clearly all depends on the transformational rules in any such analysis. An example of a transformational rule has already been given: transposition is regarded here as equivalent to repetition. Suppose we allow two more transformational rules, that an equivalence class may also entail: (1) variation of one note after two repeated notes, and (2) inversion. Example 52(b) shows the new segmentation. It has thrown up what might be described as a more coherent structure, now with only four paradigms, but it has done so at the expense of a counter-intuitive segmentation, since 5 and 6 are still separated (and, strictly according to the rule that segments must be entirely repetitions of segments, 6 should not be aligned under paradigm I). The annotations in square brackets pose further transformational questions.

If all repetitions, from segments of minimal length (as in Table A of the Brahms example) to maximal length (the longest possible repetitions – excluding any 'remainders' that may arise – of which example 52(b) is an example, with example 52(a) at an intermediate level), can be investigated, producing a variety of paradigmatic analyses, an information base is established with which to evaluate poietic and esthesic factors. One of Nattiez's criteria of neutral method is also satisfied here: that a discovery procedure should be applied until it is exhausted – which does not mean that an analysis is complete, since another procedure can then be applied. Such methods are obviously quite distinct from non-neutral methods. It can never truly be said that a motivic or harmonic analysis is literally exhaustive. On the other hand, the possibilities in any particular case for applying different kinds of distributional analysis are seemingly infinite. The semiotic analysis can always, ideally, reveal some neutral aspect of distribution to justify an esthesic perception, possibly even to modify it (Ruwet's 'revision of traditional analysis'). Yet the value of the result will rest on how interesting are the poietic and esthesic matters to be explained as much as on an exposition of all the potential patterns inherent in the music. And, to underline a point made already, we are making a sweeping assumption about what constitutes a pattern in the first place (see in this connection Culler, 1975, and Pettit, 1975).

As a last concrete illustration, a distributional approach will be applied to the pitch-structure of Webern's Op. 7 No. 3, in an attempt to arrive at a coherent picture – or at least one that displays some essential unity – without the preconceptions of pitch-class-set theory. In discussing Forte's analysis of the piece in Part III (see pp. 140–50), we did not comment in detail on the segmentation beyond noting that the nexus sets are of considerable musical importance – in particular, the hexachords are supersets for what seem, intuitively, the 'sections' of the piece. Table C shows a more neutral approach using paradigmatic analysis. It is assembled on the following basis:

(i)   Pitch-class numbers are assigned with 0 = A (see score, example 53).
(ii) These are taken in sequence regardless of instrumentation. When there is no sequence – that is, when notes sound together – this is indicated by a line joining relevant pitch classes.
(iii) Upper-case letters denote Forte's four sections, and for ease of reference piano notes are given in **bold**:

Such a paradigmatic score is characterized by the degree to which horizontal strings are present. The first horizontal string – 0, 1, 11, 6, 5 – is demarcated by the first pitch-class repetition (the repetition of the piano B flat by the violin in bar 4). The next string (2, 8, 7) is in fact the last one to involve new pitch classes. Since the three-note string in bar 7 (0, 5/9) does not count because of the simultaneity – and this also applies to section D – the only other string is in bar 9 (1, 2, 3). With this segmentation, then, it appears that the order in which the first five pitch classes appear does not make a significant paradigm or 'grammar' for the piece.

Nevertheless, there is a distributional pattern in evidence, as Table D indicates. Here we have introduced a transformation rule, that the 'paradigmatic head', the collection 0, 1, 11, 6, 5, may be regarded as unordered: this has the effect of patterning both the opening 0, 1 units and the repeated violin figures in section B. Since in Table C the violin's repetition of 3, 8, 9, 2 (in section B) necessarily produces a pattern repetition, this has also been turned into a string on its second appearance in Table D. Note that both strings form set 4–9 (0, 5, 6, 11 is, reordered, 11, 0, 5, 6 or 0, 1, 6, 7 = 4–9 and 2, 3, 8, 9 = 0, 1, 6, 7), which Forte identifies as a secondary nexus set, while the all-important paradigmatic string that heads the tables is set 5–7 (0, 1, 11, 6, 5 reordered is 11, 0, 1, 5, 6 = 0, 1, 2, 6, 7), which Forte regards as a significant invariant

Ex.53 Webern: Four Pieces for Violin and Piano, Op.7/3

Table C

A	0	1	11	6	5					
bar 4		1								
	0									
		1								
	0			6						
						4				
bar 5					5					

B						2	8	7		
bar 6							8---			
	0				5					
				6------4						
			11					3		
						8				
			6						9	
bar 7					5-------2					
	0				5----------------9					
			6							
		11								
							3			
					8					
bar 8								9		
					2					

C	0				5					
bar 9			6							
			11							
		1			2		3			
bar 10	0	11								
	0	11								
	0	11								
	0	11								

D	6-----4--------7--3--9---10
	6------------------9

Table D

A	0	1	11	6	5							
	1	0										
	1	0										
				6								
						4						
					5							
B							2	8	7			
								8				
	0		5	6	11	4						
								8				
				6							9	
					5		2				9	
	0		5	6	11							
							2	8		3	9	
C	0		5	6	11							
		1					2			3		
	0		11	(four times)								
D				6		4			7	3	9	10
				6							9	

subset of the complementary hexachords that link the A and B sections. This distributional analysis does not fundamentally confirm Forte's analysis, because it does not reveal hexachordal correspondences. But it does confirm the point that 4–9 represents the 'invariant essence' of the piece, since that set is the only significant grouping to appear distributionally. Interestingly too, it appears only when the transformation of 'dis-order' is used; in other words, the distributional pattern emerges clearly only if we allow correspondences between *unordered* sets. This shows just the beginning of a full approach to the piece, and there is no reason to suppose that such techniques could not shed equally valuable light on aspects of this music other than pitch-class-set relations, such as were discussed in Part III, chapter 15. Yet it is rewarding enough in relation to set-theoretic discoveries alone to suggest an important line of development of the relatively narrow field of view of pitch-class-set analysis.

What are the achievements of paradigmatic analysis and of semiotic music theory, of which some samples have been presented here? In the first place, this approach provides a penetrating assessment of other kinds of analysis. Merely to satisfy oneself of the relationship of, say, a Schenkerian analysis to the tripartitional model is to find many aesthetic aspects of that method clarified – though it is beyond the scope of this book to consider such matters fully in ways that are adequate on their own terms, given our intention here to concentrate on the workings of analytical techniques so that the student can challenge them from within on the basis of knowledge and sympathy. Even if the tripartitional model is taken to be an operative device, not a final truth but a way of ordering perception, it helps efficiently to untangle the confusion of strands typical of analytical narrative – is this about what the composer did? about what the analyst insists is there, without being able to confirm it? about what is claimed to be inherent in the music, patent for all listeners, or only for 'skilled' listeners?

Secondly, as far as its neutrally descriptive power is concerned, semiotics offers some release from the constraints of an organicist approach. In music where the analyst of organic unity becomes convinced that disruptive features are part of the essence of the structure – not the failures of a composer whose intention was to produce a totally unified 'masterpiece', but the successes of one who aims at a 'symbiosis' of disparate elements – mere description of the distribution of musical elements is itself a critical stage of analysis, and the more methodically it can be executed, the more secure the analyst can feel in the intuition that 'unity' is not the point of the piece.

Thirdly, semiotics has brought a measure of reason into ethnomusicology and has, in a sense, brought ethnomusicology within the responsibility of any analyst. Since one can never know what the music of an 'alien' culture is 'supposed' to mean (evidence is always suspect: even the report of a member of that culture may, after all, be a lie, and the very assumption that it is not a lie would be an act of interpretation about the culture), it is a primary responsibility to examine the music's *possible* organization – in cases where there is simply no 'agreed' organization to be demonstrated. Ultimately, as we noted above, this line of thought can be turned inward within a culture – which implies some frustration with the established order of academic thought. John Blacking, for instance, argues that the only realistic analysis of Western music is – and it seems a surprising thought at first, but the genuine consequence of pushing relativistic thinking to its limits – the analysis of the differences between performances [Steiner, 1981: 194]. Nattiez, in his Varèse analysis, does not go so far, but his solution is an admirable one, which pays dividends in return for a laborious investigation: the analysis results in a view of prolonged pitch levels that, unlike any other middleground analysis of a post-tonal piece, can certainly be verified with reference to paradigmatic segmentation; it results too in the possibility of examining whether what Varèse said about composing (the poietic level) is confirmed in what he composed, and it results in the ability to compare recorded performances with reference to a consistent information base.

It would be unthinking and injudicious to deny the many questionable aspects of semiotic analysis and of any particular analysis conducted in its name, aspects that have not been concealed in this brief treatment. Yet the field may be considered central to the student's development of an intellectual sensitivity that is directly relevant to any analytical work. We have argued that it is important to distinguish between the activity of analysis and its product. Part II concentrated much more on the product than on the activity, and in Part III there was a necessary emphasis on the activity. Semiotic thinking of the kind outlined here cuts through this distinction and, in a way which may seem rather welcome in this paradoxical discipline, offers viable terms of reference. In discussing Schenker or Schoenberg, pitch-class-set analysis or post-tonal voice-leading, there is an inescapable stage at which we have taken on the responsibility of considering their claims to be true, to be valid, or to be more convincing than any alternative. Semiotics offers something beyond this, a programme for assessing relativities. It does not claim to be able to argue for what is true, but to argue one case against another on the same ground. In a discipline that has often been plagued by the apparent mutual incomprehension of analysts who differ in their views, or of musicians who believe they differ in their aims from analysts, that is an end worth pursuing.

BIBLIOGRAPHY

Abbreviations:
JASI   Journal of the Arnold Schoenberg Institute
JMT   Journal of Music Theory
MA   Music Analysis
MQ   The Musical Quarterly
MR   The Music Review
MT   The Musical Times
MTS   Music Theory Spectrum
PNM   Perspectives of New Music

ADORNO, T. W., 1959: 'Zu den Georgeliedern'. Afterword to Arnold
    Schoenberg: Fünfzehn Gedichte . . . (Wiesbaden: Insel-Verlag)
——, 1982: 'On the Problem of Musical Analysis', MA 1/2
ALDWELL, Edward and SCHACHTER, Carl, 1979: Harmony and Voice
    Leading (New York: Harcourt, Brace, Jovanovich)
BABBITT, Milton, 1955: 'Some Aspects of Twelve-Tone Composition', The
    Score June
BACH, C. P. E., 1974: Essay on the True Art of Playing Keyboard
    Instruments, trans. W. J. Mitchell (London: Eulenburg)
BAKER, James, 1982: 'Coherence in Webern's Six Pieces for Orchestra,
    Op. 6', MTS 4
——, 1983: 'Schenkerian Analysis and Post-Tonal Music' in BEACH, 1983
BAKER, N. K., 1983: H. C. Koch. Introductory Essay on Composition. The
    Mechanical Rules of Melody, Sections 3 and 4. A Translation with an
    Introduction (New Haven: Yale UP)
BATSTONE, Philip, 1979: 'Musical Analysis as Phenomenology', PNM 7/2
BEACH, David, 1969: 'A Schenker Bibliography' in YESTON, 1977
——, 1974: 'On the Origins of Harmonic Analysis', JMT 18/2
——, 1979: 'A Schenker Bibliography: 1969–79', JMT 23/2
——, ed., 1983: Aspects of Schenkerian Theory (New Haven: Yale UP)
BEACH, David and THYM, Jurgen, 1979: 'The True Principles for the
    Practice of Harmony by Johann Philipp Kirnberger: a Translation',
    JMT 23/2
BECKETT, Lucy, ed., 1981: Richard Wagner: Parsifal (Cambridge: CUP)
BELLERMAN, Heinrich, 1862: Der Kontrapunkt (Berlin)

BENJAMIN, William E., 1979: 'Ideas of Order in Motivic Music', *MTS* 1

BENT, Ian, 1980: 'Analytical Thinking in the First Half of the Nineteenth Century', in OLLESON, 1980

——, 1984: 'The "Compositional Process" in Music Theory, 1713–1850', *MA* 3/1

BERGER, Arthur, 1963: 'Problems of Pitch Organisation in Stravinsky' in BORETZ, 1968

BERRY,Wallace, 1976: *Structural Functions of Music* (Englewood Cliffs: Prentice-Hall)

BORETZ, Benjamin, 1972 and 1973: 'Meta-Variations, Part IV: Analytic Fallout', *PNM* 11/1 and 11/2

BORETZ, Benjamin and CONE, Edward T., eds, 1968: *Perspectives on Schoenberg and Stravinsky* (Princeton: Princeton UP; 1972/New York: Norton)

BOULEZ, Pierre, 1975: *Boulez on Music Today*, trans. Susan Bradshaw and Richard Rodney Bennett (London: Faber)

——, 1976: *Conversations with Célestin Deliège* (London: Eulenburg)

BRINKMANN, Reinhold, ed., 1975: *Arnold Schönberg, Sämtliche Werke, Abteilung II: Klavier- und Orgelmusik, Reihe B, Band 4 (Werke für Klavier zu zwei Händen); Kritischer Bericht, Skizzen, Fragmente* (Vienna: B. Schotts Söhne)

BURKHART, Charles, 1980: 'The Symmetrical Source of Webern's Opus 5, No. 4', *The Music Forum* Vol. 5

CARPENTER, Patricia, 1983: 'Grundgestalt and Tonal Function', *MTS* 5

CHRISTENSEN, Tom, 1982: 'The Schichtenlehre of Hugo Riemann', *In Theory Only* 6/4

COKER, Wilson, 1972: *Music and Meaning: A Theoretical Introduction to Musical Aesthetics* (New York: The Free Press)

CONE, Edward T., 1968: *Musical Form and Musical Performance* (New York: Norton)

——, 1971: *Berlioz. Fantastic Symphony*. Norton Critical Score (New York: Norton)

CULLER, Jonathan, 1975: *Structuralist Poetics: Structuralism, Linguistics and the Study of Literature* (Ithaca: Cornell UP)

DAHLHAUS, Carl, 1974: 'Schoenberg and Schenker', *Proceedings of the Royal Musical Association* 100

——, 1979: *Richard Wagner's Music Dramas*, trans. Mary Whittall (Cambridge: CUP)

——, 1980: *Between Romanticism and Modernism: Four Studies in the Music of the Later Nineteenth Century*, trans. Mary Whittall (Berkeley: UC Press)

DIEPERT, Randall, 1983: 'Meyer's *Emotion and Meaning in Music*: A sympathetic Critique of its Central Claims', *In Theory Only* 6/8

DÖHL, Friedheim, 1976: *Webern: Weberns Beitrag zur Stilwende der neuen Musik; Studien über Voraussetzungen, Technik, und Ästhetik der*

'*Komposition mit 12 nur aufeinander bezogenen Tönen*' (Munich: Katzbichler)

DUNSBY, Esther, 1983: 'Explaining Meyer', *MA* 2/2

DUNSBY, Jonathan, 1977a: 'Schoenberg's *Premonition*, Op. 22, No. 4, in Retrospect', *JASI* 1/3

——, 1977b: 'Schoenberg and the Writings of Heinrich Schenker', *JASI* 2/1

——, 1979: Review of EPSTEIN, 1979, *JASI* 3/2

——, 1980: 'Heinrich Schenker and the Free Counterpoint of Strict Composition', *R.M.A. Research Chronicle* 16

——, 1982: 'A Hitch Hiker's Guide to Semiotic Music Analysis', *MA* 1/3

——, 1983: 'Music and Semiotics: The Nattiez Phase', *MQ* 69/1

EPSTEIN, David, 1979: *Beyond Orpheus: Studies in Musical Structure* (Cambridge, Mass.: MIT Press)

EVANS, Edwin, Snr, 1935: *Handbook to the Chamber and Orchestral Music of Johannes Brahms. 2nd Series* (London: Reeves)

[EVANS], 1936: Initialled review of EVANS, 1935, *MT* 1123 (Vol. 77)

FEDERHOFER, Hellmut, 1981: *Akkord und Stimmführung in den Musiktheoretischen Systemen von Hugo Riemann, Ernst Kurth und Heinrich Schenker* (Vienna: Verlag der Österreichischen Akademie der Wissenschaften)

FORTE, Allen, 1973: *The Structure of Atonal Music* (New Haven: Yale UP)

——, 1974: 'Theory' in VINTON, 1974

——, 1977: 'Schenker's Conception of Musical Structure' in YESTON, 1977

——, 1978a: 'Schoenberg's Creative Evolution: The Path to Atonality', *MQ* 64/2

——, 1978b: *The Harmonic Organization of 'The Rite of Spring'* (New Haven: Yale UP)

——, 1980: 'Aspects of Rhythm in Webern's Atonal Music', *MTS* 2

——, 1981: 'The Magical Kaleidoscope: Schoenberg's First Atonal Masterwork, Opus 11, No. 1', *JASI* 5/2

——, 1983: 'Foreground Rhythm in Early Twentieth-Century Music', *MA* 2/3

FORTE, Allen and GILBERT, Stephen, 1982: *Introduction to Schenkerian Analysis* (New York: Norton)

FRISCH, Walter, 1984: *Brahms and the Principle of Developing Variation* (Berkeley: UC Press)

FUX, Johann, 1967: *Gradus ad Parnassum*, ed. A. Mann (Kassel: Bärenreiter); facsimile of the edition first published in Vienna, 1725

GOEHR, Alexander, 1977: 'Schoenberg's *Gedanke* Manuscript', *JASI* 2/1

GOODE, Daniel, 1967: Correspondence about TRAVIS 1966, *PNM* 6/1

GRIFFITHS, Paul, 1982: *Peter Maxwell Davies* (London: Robson)

[GROVE], 1906: *Grove's Dictionary of Music and Musicians*, 2nd ed., ed. J. A. Fuller Maitland (London: Macmillan)

HARRISON, Frank, HOOD, Mantle and PALISCA, Claude, 1963: *Musicology* (Englewood Cliffs: Prentice-Hall)

HARVEY, Jonathan, 1982: 'Reflections After Composition', *Tempo* 140
——, 1983: 'New Directions: A Manifesto', *Soundings* 11 (Winter 1983–84)
HASTY, Christopher, 1981: 'Segmentation and Process in Post-Tonal Music', *MTS* 3
HEARTZ, Daniel and MANN, Alfred, eds., 1965: *Mozart, Neue Ausgabe: Sämtliche Werke, Series X*, Supplement (Kassel: Bärenreiter)
HINDEMITH, Paul, 1945: *The Craft of Musical Composition*, trans. A. Mendel and O. Ortman (London: Schott; revised ed.)
JONAS, Oswald, 1982: *Introduction to the Theory of Heinrich Schenker: The Nature of the Musical Work of Art*, trans. and ed. J. Rothgeb (New York: Longman)
KALIB, Sylvan, 1973: 'Thirteen Essays from the Three Yearbooks *Das Meisterwerk in der Musik* by Heinrich Schenker: An Annotated Translation', PhD Dissertation (UMI)
KATZ, Adele, 1945: *Challenge to Musical Tradition: A New Concept of Tonality* (London: Putnam & Co.)
KEILER, Allan, 1978: 'The Empiricist Illusion: Narmour's *Beyond Schenkerism*', *PNM* 17/1
KELLER, Hans, 1956: 'K. 503: The Unity of Contrasting Themes and Movements', *MR* 17/1
——, 1965: 'The Chamber Music' in ROBBINS LANDON, 1965
KERMAN, Joseph, 1977: 'Tovey's Beethoven' in TYSON, 1977
——, 1980 and 1981: 'How We Got into Analysis, and How to Get Out', *Critical Inquiry* 7, and in PRICE, 1981
KOLNEDER, Walter, 1968: *Anton Webern: An Introduction to His Works*, trans. H. Searle (London: Faber)
KOMAR, Arthur, 1971: 'The Music of *Dichterliebe*: The Whole and Its Parts' in KOMAR, 1971
——, 1971: *Robert Schumann 'Dichterliebe'* (London: Chappell. Norton Critical Score)
LAUFER, Edward, 1981: Review of SCHENKER, 1979, *MTS* 3
LEIBOWITZ, René, 1975: *Schoenberg and His School: The Contemporary Stage of the Language of Music*, trans. D. Newlin (New York: Da Capo. 1st paperback ed.)
LEICHTENTRITT, Hugo, 1951: *Musical Form* (Cambridge, Mass.: Harvard UP)
LEHRDAHL, Fred and JACKENDOFF, Ray, 1983: *A Generative Theory of Tonal Music* (Cambridge, Mass.: MIT Press)
LENDVAI, Ernö, 1971: *Béla Bartók: An Analysis of His Music* (London: Kahn and Averill)
LEWIS, Christopher, 1981: 'Tonal Forms in Atonal Music: Berg's op. 5/3', *MTS* 3
LIDOV, David, 1977: 'Nattiez's Semiotics of Music', *The Canadian Journal of Research in Semiotics* 5/2

LORENZ, Alfred, 1966: *Das Geheimnis der Form bei Richard Wagner* (Tützing: Schneider; 2nd ed., 4 vols)

MACPHERSON, Stewart, 1930: *Form in Music, with Special Reference to the Designs of Instrumental Music* (London: Joseph Williams)

MCFARLANE, J., 1976: 'The Mind of Modernism' in MCFARLANE, J. and BRADBURY, M. 1976

MCFARLANE, J. and BRADBURY, M., 1976: *Modernism 1890–1930* (Harmondsworth: Penguin)

MEYER, Leonard B., 1956: *Emotion and Meaning in Music* (Chicago: University of Chicago Press)

——, 1973: *Explaining Music: Essays and Explorations* (Chicago: University of Chicago Press)

MOLDENHAUER, Hans, 1978: *Anton von Webern: A Chronicle of His Life and Work* (London: Gollancz)

MORGAN, Robert P., 1976: 'Dissonant Prolongations: Theoretical and Compositional Precedents', *JMT* 20/1

NARMOUR, Eugene, 1977: *Beyond Schenkerism: The Need for Alternatives in Music Analysis* (Chicago: University of Chicago Press)

NATTIEZ, Jean-Jacques, 1975: *Fondements d'une sémiologie de la musique* (Paris: 10/18)

——, 1976: 'Sémiologie musicale. Essai de bibliographie systématique', *Versus: Quaderni di studi semiotici* 13

——, 1982: 'Varèse's "Density 21.5": A Study in Semiological Analysis', *MA* 1/3

NEWBOULD, Brian, 1977: 'A New Analysis of Brahms's Intermezzo in B minor, op. 119, no. 1', *MR* 38/1

[NEW GROVE]: *The New Grove Dictionary of Music and Musicians*, ed. Stanley Sadie (London: Macmillan, 1980)

NOSKE, Frits, 1977: *The Signifier and the Signified: Studies in the Operas of Mozart and Verdi* (The Hague: Nijhoff)

OLLESON, Edward, ed., 1980: *Modern Musical Scholarship* (Stocksfield: Oriel)

OSTER, Ernst, 1977: 'Register and the Large-Scale Connection' in YESTON, 1977

PERLE, George, 1977: *Serial Composition and Atonality: An Introduction to the Music of Schoenberg, Berg and Webern* (Berkeley: UC Press, 4th revised ed.)

PETTIT, Philip, 1975: *The Concept of Structuralism: A Critical Analysis* (Dublin: Gill and Macmillan)

PHIPPS, Graham, 1983: 'A Response to Schenker's Analysis of Chopin's Etude, Op. 10, No. 12, Using Schoenberg's *Grundgestalt* Concept', *MQ* 69/4

——, 1984: 'Tonality in Webern's Cantata I', *MA* 3/1

PISK, Paul, 1976: 'Memories of Arnold Schoenberg', *JASI* 1/1

PLUM, Karl-Otto, 1979: *Untersuchungen zu Heinrich Schenkers Stimm-*

führungsanalyse (Regensburg: Gustav Bosse Verlag: *Kölner Beiträge zur Musikforschung* 102)

PRICE, Kingsley, ed., 1981: *On Criticising Music: Five Philosophical Perspectives* (Baltimore: Johns Hopkins University Press)

RAHN, John, 1980: *Basic Atonal Theory* (New York: Longman)

REGENER, Eric, 1974: 'On Allen Forte's Theory of Chords', *PNM* 13/1

RÉTI, Rudolph, 1962: *The Thematic Process in Music* (New York: Macmillan)

——, 1967: *Thematic Patterns in the Sonatas of Beethoven*, ed. D. Cooke (London: Faber)

RIEMANN, Hugo, 1977: *History of Music Theory, Book 3*, trans. and ed. W. C. Mickelson (Lincoln: University of Nebraska Press)

ROBBINS LANDON, H. C. and MITCHELL, Donald, eds, 1965: *The Mozart Companion* (London: Faber)

ROSEN, Charles, 1972: *The Classical Style: Haydn, Mozart, Beethoven* (London: Faber)

ROTHGEB, John, 1981: 'Schenkerian Theory: Its Implications for the Undergraduate Curriculum', *MTS* 3

RUFER, Josef, 1961: *Composition with Twelve Notes* (London: Barrie & Rockliff)

RUWET, Nicholas, 1972: *Langage, musique, poésie* (Paris: Le Seuil)

SALZER, Felix, 1962: *Structural Hearing: Tonal Coherence in Music* (New York: Dover)

SCHACHTER, Carl, 1981: 'A Commentary on Schenker's *Free Composition*', *JMT* 25/1

——, 1983: 'The First Movement of Brahms's Second Symphony: The First Theme and its Consequences', *MA* 2/1

SCHENKER, Heinrich, 1910 and 1922: *Kontrapunkt (Neue Musikalische Theorien und Phantasien 2)*, Part I and Part II (Vienna: Universal Edition)

——, 1912: *Beethovens Neunte Sinfonie* (Vienna: Universal Edition)

——, 1921–4: *Der Tonwille*, 10 vols (Vienna: A. Gutmann Verlag)

——, 1924: 'Brahms: Variationen und Fuge über ein Thema von Händel, opus 24' in SCHENKER, 1921–4, vol. 4, Books 2/3 (Books 8/9 in series)

——, 1969: *Five Graphic Music Analyses*, ed. Felix Salzer (New York: Dover)

——, 1973: *Harmony (Neue Musikalische Theorien und Phantasien 1)*, ed. Oswald Jonas, trans. Elisabeth Mann Borgese (Cambridge, Mass.: MIT Press. Paperback ed.)

——, 1974: *Das Meisterwerk in der Musik*. 3 Yearbooks (Hildesheim: Georg Olms Verlag)

——, 1979: *Free Composition (Der freie Satz): Volume III of New Musical Theories and Fantasies*, trans. and ed. Ernst Oster (New York: Longman)

SCHIFF, David, 1983: *The Music of Elliott Carter* (London: Eulenburg)

SCHMALFELDT, Janet, 1983: *Berg's Wozzeck: Harmonic Language and*

Dramatic Design (New Haven: Yale UP)

SCHOENBERG, Arnold, 1963: *Letters*, ed. Erwin Stein, trans. Eithne Wilkins and Ernst Kaiser (London: Faber)

——, 1968: 'Analysis of the Four Orchestral Songs Opus 22' in BORETZ and CONE, 1968

——, 1969: *Structural Functions of Harmony* (London: Faber)

——, 1970a: *Preliminary Exercises in Counterpoint* (London: Faber)

——, 1970b: *Fundamentals of Musical Composition* (London: Faber)

——, 1972: *Models for Beginners in Composition*, rev. Leonard Stein (New York: Schirmer)

——, 1975: *Style and Idea*, ed. Leonard Stein (London: Faber)

——, 1978: *Theory of Harmony*, trans. Roy Carter (London: Faber)

SECHTER, Simon, 1853: *Die Grundsätze der musikalischen Komposition* (Leipzig)

SIMMS, Bryan, 1975: 'Choron, Fétis, and the Theory of Tonality', *JMT* 19/1

——, 1977: 'New Documents in the Schoenberg–Schenker Polemic', *PNM* 16/1

STEFANI, Gino, ed., 1975: *Actes du 1er congrès internationale de sémiotique musicale, Beograd 17–21 Oct. 1973* (Pesaro: Centro di Iniziativa Culturale)

STEINER, Wendy, ed., 1981: *The Sign in Music and Literature* (Austin: University of Texas Press)

STOPFORD, John, 1983: 'Structuralism, Semiotics and Musicology', *Journal of the British Society of Aesthetics* 24/1

STRAVINSKY, Igor, 1947: *Poetics of Music, in the Form of Six Lessons*, trans. Arthur Knodel and Ingolf Dahl (London: OUP)

TOVEY, Donald, 1931: *A Companion to 'The Art of Fugue' (Die Kunst der Fuge) by J. S. Bach* (London: OUP)

——, 1935–9: *Essays in Musical Analysis*, 6 vols (London: OUP)

——, 1944: *Essays in Musical Analysis: Chamber Music* (London: OUP)

——, 1948: *Companion to Beethoven's Pianoforte Sonatas* (London: OUP)

——, 1949: *Essays and Lectures on Music*, with an introduction by Hubert Foss (London: OUP)

TRAVIS, Roy, 1966: 'Directed Motion in Schoenberg and Webern', *PNM* 4/2

——, 1967: Reply to D. Goode, *PNM* 6/1

——, 1974: 'Analysis Symposium: Webern Orchestral Pieces (1913), Movement 1 ("Bewegt")', *JMT* 18/1

TYSON, Alan, ed., 1977: *Beethoven Studies 2* (London: OUP)

VINTON, John, ed. 1974: *Dictionary of Twentieth-Century Music* (London: Thames and Hudson)

WASON, Robert, 1984: *Viennese Harmonic Theory from Albrechtsberger to Schenker and Schoenberg* (Ann Arbor: UMI Research Press)

WEBER, Gottfried, 1846: *Theory of Musical Composition*, trans. James Warner (Boston: O. Ditson)

WEBERN, Anton, 1963: *The Path to the New Music*, trans. Leo Black (Bryn Mawr: T. Presser)

WESTERGAARD, Peter, 1963: 'Webern and "Total Organization": An Analysis of the Second Movement of the Piano Variations, Op. 27', *PNM* 1/2

WHITTALL, Arnold, 1977: *Music Since the First World War* (London: Dent)

——, 1981a: Review of EPSTEIN, 1979, *JMT* 25/2

——, 1981b: 'The Music' [*Parsifal*] in BECKETT, 1981

——, 1982: 'Music Analysis as Human Science? *Le Sacre du Printemps* in Theory and Practice', *MA* 1/1

——, 1983: 'Webern and Atonality: The Path from the Old Aesthetic', *MT* 1690 (Vol. 124)

WILDGANS, Friedrich, 1966: *Anton Webern*, trans. E. T. Roberts and H. Searle (London: Calder)

WILLIAMS, C. F. Abdy, 1909: *The Rhythm of Modern Music* (London: Macmillan)

——, 1925: *The Rhythm of Song* (London: Methuen)

WINTLE, Christopher, 1975: 'An early version of derivation. Webern's Op. 11/3', *PNM* 13/2

——, 1982: 'Analysis and Performance: Webern's Concerto, Op. 24/ii', *MA* 1/1

WUORINEN, Charles, 1967: Reply to D. Goode, *PNM* 6/1

YESTON, Maury, ed., 1977: *Readings in Schenker Analysis and Other Approaches* (New Haven: Yale UP)

ZIEHN, Bernhard, 1976: *Canonic Studies* (London: Kahn & Averill)

INDEX

accuracy, in analysis, 71
Adorno, T.W., 18–19, 113–14
America, analysis in, 29
analysis, 3–10; of atonal music,
201–5; and criticism, 102; history
of, 14–19, 62–5; and musical
meaning, 94, 211–18, 230–1; and
organicism, 17–18; study of, 6–12,
29, 100–2, 205–7; and theory,
13–14, 41, 71–3; of twelve-note
compositions, 187
analyst: qualifications for, 3–4; and
study of composition, 12
analytical techniques, 4–5, 6, 8, 93;
assumptions underlying, 212, 230;
choice of, for free atonality, 203–4;
choice of, for transitional works,
113–20, 203–4, 207
antecedent and consequent, 84
Aristoxenus, 7, 13, 14
articulation, types of, 196–8
ascent, to fundamental line, 43, 50
atonality: concept of, 105–6; and
dissociation, 19; and formal
organization, 163–5, 206; free,
compared to twelve-note
composition, 186–7, 201–3;
motivic analysis of, 131, 154–61,
203–4; neo-Schenkerian analysis of,
54–61, 108–19; process in, 201–3;
study of, 6–8, 201–7; structure of,
150–2; transition to, 113–18. *See
also* harmony; pitch-class sets;
symmetrical pitch constructs
atonal voice-leading, 115. *See also*
voice leading
attack points, and rhythmic profile,
168n, 171, 199. *See also* pitch-class
attacks
Attwood, Thomas, 29
augmentation, 68–70
Austro-German musical tradition: and
Schenker, 24, 25–6; and
Schoenberg, 62–3

autograph study, 29, 30
axis of symmetry: testing for, 126–9,
175n, 195–6; 'tonic', 118–19

Babbitt, Milton, 63, 186
Bach, C.P.E., 16, 31, 46, 55; in history
of analysis, 15, 24, 25, 28
Bach, J.S., 24, 27–8, 55; chorales,
analysed, 47–9, 214; *Generalbassbüchlein*, 24–5; *St Matthew
Passion* No. 16, 33–8; *Well-
Tempered Clavier*, 16; mentioned,
7, 31
background(s): chromatic scale as,
134; definition of, 35, 50; and form,
38, 39; modification of Schenkerian
concept, for post-tonal analysis, 55,
59–61, 109–13, 115–16, 118–19,
120; pitch-class sets as, 135, 171.
See also fundamental structure
Baker, James, 111–13, 114–15, 153,
174, 207
Baker, N.K., 16
Bartók, Béla: *Mikrokosmos* Book 4,
Bourrée, 112; Piano Concerto No.
3, 60; Schenkerian analysis of, 108;
mentioned, 91, 121, 207
basic shape, concept of, 75, 84, 85,
156–7, 158
bass arpeggiation, 41–7, 50;
substitution in, 110
bass 'couplings', and phrase structure,
38
bass line: and diatonic functions, 116,
120; and tonal symmetry, 123–4
Beach, David, 100; mentioned, 16, 17,
33
Beethoven, Ludwig van, 15, 16, 24;
Piano Sonata Op. 13 (*Pathétique*),
49, 92, 93; Piano Sonata Op. 57
(*Appassionata*), 93; Piano Sonata
Op. 81a (*Les Adieux*), 96, 98;
String Quartet Op. 135, 217; and
Schoenberg, 85; and sonata form,